GOVERNMENTS AND SMALL BUSINESS

GOVERNMENTS AND SMALL BUSINESS

Graham Bannock
and Alan Peacock

Paul Chapman Publishing Ltd.
for
The David Hume Institute

Published by
Paul Chapman Publishing Ltd
144 Liverpool Road
London N1 1LA

British Library Cataloguing in Publication Data

Bannock, Graham, 1932–
Governments and small business.
1. Great Britain. Small firms
I. Title II. Peacock, Alan, 1922–
338.6'42'0941

ISBN 1-8596-035-7

The following are thanked for their permission to reproduce material:

Chapter 3: Department of Trade and Industry
Chapter 5: Investors in Industry — 3i PLC
Chapter 7: Canadian Federation of Independent Business and National Federation of Independent Business
Chapter 8: Anglo-German Foundation
Chapter 9: Commission of the European Communities and the Minister of State, Turkey
Chapter 10: Organisation for Economic Co-operation and Development

Typeset by Burns & Smith, Derby
Printed and Bound in Great Britain by
St Edmundsbury Press Ltd, Bury St Edmunds, Suffolk

ABCDEFG 432109

TABLE OF CONTENTS

PREFACE

Despite the now universal commitment of governments (including in a more limited way those in communist countries) to the promotion of small business in one form or another, much more remains to be done. In particular there is a need for greater understanding of the unfavourable though unintended consequences for small firms of the growth of government itself.

This book collects together six recent research studies on small firms directed by myself and financed by various organizations, three other papers of my own and an introduction by Professor Sir Alan Peacock. With three exceptions, none of this material, most of which is international in focus, has previously been published. Except for an occasional updating footnote and some deletions to avoid repetition they remain in the form in which they were originally written (over the period 1985–8).

Alan Peacock has provided me with continuous inspiration and support since I first attended his lectures at the London School of Economics in 1955. I am grateful to Sir Alan and the David Hume Institute for their assistance and encouragement as well as to our publisher for making this volume possible and to my colleagues in Graham Bannock & Partners Ltd, who assisted me in much of the research and produced the final text.

The choice of studies included in this book has been largely determined by the interests of clients who have paid Graham Bannock & Partners Ltd the compliment of selecting us to do the work and then freely allowed us to reproduce it here. A few important aspects of the relationship between governments and small business are not covered (notably public purchasing) and others deserve treatment in greater detail. However, the scope of our work is broadening all the time in these and other aspects of small firms studies (notably in statistical measurement). If the reception of this volume justifies it, therefore, others may follow.

Eight organizations financed and provided other assistance in the research studies and have given permission for the reports to be reproduced here. This permission is acknowledged both on the reverse of the title page and in a footnote at the appropriate point in the text, but their names bear repetition: the Anglo-German Foundation, the Department of Trade and Industry, the Canadian Federation of Independent Business, the Commission of the European Communities, the Ministry of State of Turkey, the National Federation of Independent Business, the Organisation for Economic Co-operation and Development and Investors in Industry (3i). The views expressed in this book should not be ascribed to any of these organizations and are the responsibility of the authors alone.

Finally, acknowledgements in the original research reports of the various studies have been omitted but I particularly want to record the contributions of Atila Alpoge, Yvonne Bernhardt, Evan Davis, William Dennis Junior, Axel

Dahremoller, Dr Gunter Kayser, Alan Doran, Stephen Bond, Peter Hart, Stan Mendham, David Rushforth, Cedric Sandford, Elaine Wagner and the late Richard Wietfeldt.

Graham Bannock
July 1988

Part I
The Role of Small Business

Chapter 1

INTRODUCTION

Alan Peacock

PRELIMINARIES

I welcome this opportunity to introduce these contributions to the study of small firms and policies towards them which have been written by Graham Bannock, an internationally known authority. My own credentials for doing so are rather mixed. I have written relatively little, until fairly recently, on industrial economics, though I was Chief Economic Adviser to the Department of Trade and Industry from 1973 to 1976. Then, as now, I took a manifestly sceptical view of both Tory and Labour industrial policies, which presumed that the carrot of large selective subsidies and the stick of incomes and prices policies would dynamize the British economy (Peacock, 1979). I remember very well when the Bolton Committee on Small Firms first appeared and how sceptically it was regarded by powerful politicians and civil servants who had all too readily accepted the Galbraithian thesis that the small person in business was a tedious anachronism.

If I have some claim to an understanding of small firms from experience in government, I have perhaps a better claim in having been part of this book's subject matter. Over 20 years ago Professor Victor Morgan founded the Economist Advisory Group (EAG) in which I became a partner along with Professors John Dunning, Dennis Lees and Jack Wiseman. It cannot be denied that we started up in the expectation that we would supplement our academic incomes, which were becoming severely eroded, but we shared the belief that practical experience in consulting work and the discipline of meeting strict deadlines would increase our credibility as teachers and sharpen our own perceptions of how economics could be sensibly applied in the real world. It was hard to get established and my own participation was limited by lack of experience in the kind of work which came our way, but I do not regret for one moment having spent several years as a partner, particularly when EAG recruited Graham Bannock as its managing director! EAG burgeoned during a period when long-established economic consultancies ceased to trade, and became a private company. Today it flourishes still, though I believe only one of the original partners remains connected with it, as so often happens in the course of the rapid evolution of small companies.

My second experience in administering a small firm is more unusual. In 1978 I joined and in 1980 took over as Principal of the (then) University College of

Buckingham, which was set up without any government support. Although a company limited by guarantee, and therefore non profit-making, it had to aim to cover all its current academic costs by fees paid by students. My job was to see that the 'product', the Buckingham 'licence', was a credible alternative to a degree offered by state universities and with students willing to pay the full cost of their higher education, instead of only a small part of it. I have described the experience in detail elsewhere (Peacock, 1986). It is sufficient to say that competing in a market against highly subsidized and well-established competitors was an exhilarating if exhausting experience. At least as an economist who is a strong supporter of competition, I had put myself in the position of experiencing its rigours!

The political and therefore the economic climate for small firms appears to have changed for the better in recent years and, to quote the subtitle of Graham Bannock's well-known book *the Economics of Small Firms*, there has been a 'return from the wilderness'. However, even if governments are disposed to accept the proposition, at least in part, that efficient allocation of resources depends on the promotion of competition and therefore that freedom of entry into an industry or service is essential, there are many problems still remaining in developing a consistent policy towards small firms as a potent source of new entry. This introductory chapter offers a survey of those problems as a prelude to their more extensive discussion in the rest of the book. The survey begins by reviewing the case for competition and why its amelioration by government action may be counter-productive. It then demonstrates that an effective competition policy, mindful of small firms' role in the competitive process, is vitiated by the fact that the public sector in EC countries is itself so large that it creates market imperfections which are impossible to eradicate. If there is little prospect of the relative size of the public sector diminishing, then many further difficulties remain in developing a consistent and equitable policy towards small firms, as later chapters make abundantly clear.

THE CASE FOR COMPETITION

Introduction

The market and competition are inseparable. The main characteristic of the market which confers its benefits is the existence of alternatives; in other words, buyers have a choice. The availability of choices means that producers have to compete in order to meet their objective of making a living, however 'making a living' is to be defined. Those who offer the best alternatives are suitably rewarded, and these rewards are normally a positive function of quality and a negative function of price.

However, it is not surprising that most of us may have either a hostile attitude to the market, or an ambivalent one, as we are all producers of goods and services. If you are a manager, competition is hard work. Keeping ahead of your competitors imposes psychological costs, unless you are imbued with what Joan

Robinson called 'animal spirits', which give you a kick out of competing in business as well as on the golf course. Why not combine with rivals and share the gains? If you are on the shop floor, it may appear that competition with your fellow workers weakens workers' bargaining positions and that elusive spirit of 'solidarity'. Perhaps only academic economists in safe jobs can afford to be unequivocal supporters of the market and competition — they obtain all the benefits of it as consumers but are immune from its immediate pressures as producers.

If the market and competition are subject to such widespread suspicion and hostility, how can one defend them? The simple general answer is obtained by adapting Churchill's famous defence of democracy: 'the market may be poor way of organising the economy, but it is better than any other'.

I begin by stressing that the market and competition are means and not ends. They are instruments to be used in achieving objectives. Judgement of their efficiency depends on the choice of objectives and trade-offs, the view taken of how the economy functions and how improving the operation of market forces compares with other methods of intervention in the economy. Reasonable people can disagree about values, but one lives in the hope that they will broadly agree on questions of logic and fact, though unfortunately their views of logic and facts may be coloured by their values.

Identifying Objectives

Take values first. We would all agree that the organization of the economy is to be directed towards improving human welfare, which is like saying that we are all against sin. It is better to look at specific *intermediate* objectives or tasks of the economy which command consensus. We probably all agree that resources should be allocated efficiently between competing uses both at a point in time and through time, allocation through time being associated with growth objectives. We probably all agree that resources should be equitably distributed, and that our definition of equity would at the very least imply that no persons should fall below some poverty line. Where we would reasonably disagree with one another is over the trade-offs between these objectives and the 'boundary conditions' which should apply in maximizing them. An extreme example will help to underline this point. If one believes in complete economic equality to the exclusion of all other objectives, then the market is not only a totally inefficient instrument to achieve it but markets must also be destroyed in vital instances. Thus, if inequality is a function of differential saving rates among individuals, differential skills and differential health risks, then complete economic equality implies that there must be no market in savings, and strict rationing of educational and health investments. An important boundary condition in seeking to achieve the objective is already apparent — the restriction of individual freedom over a whole range of decisions. The central government would have to collectivize major items of consumption and investment and control international movements of capital and labour. However, if it is once agreed that equity objectives must be traded off against others, the destruction of the market means destroying one of the principal instruments for improving social welfare.

Allocation of Resources and Public 'Intervention'

Concentrating on the efficient allocation of resources assumes that the aim is to maximize the welfare of consumers — consumption is the sole end of production, as Adam Smith reminds us. Competition through the market is essential to achieve this aim. The existence of alternatives to consumers keeps producers on their toes and rewards those who keep their costs down or offer a superior product. Just as important is the function of the market and competition as the most effective device for registering *changes* in consumer tastes and preferences. What is often described in emotive terms as the 'chaos' of the market is a highly sensitive process of adaptation of prices, new processes of production and new and improved products to accord with consumer demand. While the process of adaptation to rapid changes in demand is painful, if the market and competition are in operation internationally, the alternative of a siege-type economy with strict control over international trade and payments, whether at national or EC level, is neither desirable, given the objective of efficient allocation, nor in the end feasible.

Of course, there are instances of importance where the market and competition do not by themselves promote the desired end. There is no efficient means of providing defence and law and order through the market, as those not prepared to pay for these services cannot be excluded from enjoying them. It is rightly claimed that consumers can benefit (as with better education and better health) or suffer (as with pollution) from each other's consumption and that such uncovenanted benefits and costs are not taken account of in the market adjustment process. Neither of these two closely related arguments makes a case for destroying the market. Too often it is assumed that a case for public *production* under monopoly conditions is the sole answer to so-called 'market failure' of this kind, instead of a case for using *public finance* as a device for influencing consumer and producer decisions in the required direction. And where nationalization of production is demanded — as is frequently the case with a whole range of environmental and social services as well as defence and law and order — we have to balance 'market failure' against 'collective failure'. When consumers have only an indirect control over what is produced and how it is produced, i.e. as voters in a representative democracy with a large public sector, the checks operating on bureaucratic efficiency are weak.

There are also important instances where consumers may prefer others to choose for them because they cannot readily acquire the experience which would make them efficient promoters of their own interest. The risks of choice to the consumer are clearly less in the case of repeated choices than in once-and-for-all choices such as buying a new house or undergoing surgery. However, this is hardly an argument for single sources of supply and collectivization of production.

Consider now the allocation of resources through time — the choice between 'jam today' and 'jam tomorrow'. If we measure the success of policy in terms of a crude measure such as the growth in the national product, so far as I am aware there is nothing to suggest that this rate of growth is unambiguously correlated with the size of the public sector *vis-à-vis* the private sector. The dispersion in growth rates within collectivized and 'market-type' economies may be much the same (though this is difficult to check). What is different is that in collectivized economies the pattern of resource use through time bears little relation to the consumption and saving plans of *individual* members of the community and is therefore dictated.

A more relevant consideration is how far in mixed economies, in which competition in internationally traded goods is the order of the day, the economic planning authorities can improve economic prospects by supply-oriented policies which entail large-scale intervention in the market. This is not simply a question of using policy measures to increase investment at the expense of consumption in order to promote growth, but of improving the efficiency in factor use, including the promotion of new technology. These policies are still very popular with politicians, though some of them only pay lip-service to the ultimate objective.

I have had the opportunity of taking part in government programmes designed to promote supply-oriented policies on a large scale, and these turned me into a complete sceptic. I can only give the reasons in brief.

1 It is considered necessary to obtain a 'consensus' view of managers, trade unionists and government on specific aims of economic policy. As this is impossible, the aims are deliberately obfuscated to keep everyone happy. This suits bureaucrats and politicians particularly as, if aims are unclear, then the risks to them of policy failure can be reduced by redefining the aims when the results of programmes are known.

2 There is bound to be lack of technical agreement on the effects of selective aid policies promoting efficiency and growth in individual sectors, because appraisal is so difficult. Such cautious and considered advice (as economists must give) is not very helpful to ambitious politicians and bureaucrats who have a vested interest in selective aid policies which dramatize their own actions. They prefer to listen to apologists for their pet schemes, safe in the knowledge that they suffer no financial penalties if things go wrong and with the possibility, already mentioned, that the aims of policies can be 'adjusted' after their results are known.

3 The proliferation of selective aid schemes fosters a 'pork barrel' mentality among those who might qualify for support. On top of the growing cost of government regulation and taxation of business there is placed an inducement to incur the cost of 'liaison' with government departments who might be induced to part with money. The link between profitability and efficiency is broken, if profitability depends on bargaining skill in the interface with government officials instead of satisfying domestic and international consumers. A feather bed is to be preferred to a bed of nails.

4 The costs, in terms of the alternative policies foregone to achieve the same ends, are often deliberately ignored. It is administratively easier to deal with a few established large firms in conducting such policies than with scores of small fry trying to edge into the established firms' markets. More political kudos will be gained from dramatic schemes of industrial revival and development than from reducing government expenditure and therefore taxation in order to promote general economic incentives.

COMPETITION POLICY AND THE SMALL FIRM

The conclusion concerning the allocation of resources is that the main thrust of industrial policy must be found in the preservation of both domestic and international free trade. The case for free trade is too well known to need delineation, but there are some features of its pursuit which are highly relevant to the position of small firms.

1 While most economists would accept that competition in internationally and domestically traded goods promotes the efficient allocation of resources, they differ as to the extent to which this requires state intervention in order to promote competition. 'Austrian-type' economists argue that attempts by the state to 'create' competitive markets are both undesirable and ineffective; undesirable because regulation of the structure of the market leads too readily to the growth of bureaucracy and loss of freedom, and ineffective because bureaucrats cannot foresee changes in the structure of markets and in the process of invention. The best defence against monopoly, they argue, is to remove all tariff barriers and 'hidden' subsidies to business in the form of selective aid and tax reliefs. Others, equally concerned with the need for competition, such as the influential 'social market' economists in West Germany, believe that a vigorous anti-cartel and anti-merger policy is essential to achieve the common end. Furthermore, these economists have been closely concerned with the need to ensure that small firms are not disadvantaged by the ability of large firms to create 'artificial' barriers to entry.

2 Even if governments are committed to positive action to control market power, they are strongly influenced by arguments that industrial concentration is also necessary in particular sectors in order to promote economies of scale. As Professor Morgan has shown, the British Monopolies and Mergers Commission has been particularly sympathetic to this argument (Morgan, 1987). The greater the hold of this argument on the public authorities, the more difficult it becomes to ensure that the small and growing firm can enter the market. The result has been that governments, simultaneously concerned about the 'small firm' problem, if only because it may represent an important source of employment, have had to seek ways to support small firms through methods which would otherwise not require to be introduced and which may be self-defeating. The use of cheap loans and grants to protect small firms entering the market from the rigours of the

market may be a much less effective way to ensure their ultimate success than ensuring that competition law does not discriminate against them.

3 The extent to which government can run a fully effective competition and anti-monopoly policy is severely constrained by the relatively large size of the public sector itself. Government monopoly 'production' of welfare services, transport services and roads, defence, and a whole range of public corporations must mean that private suppliers of raw materials, capital goods and labour, faced with a monopoly or quasi-monopoly buyer, will seek to organize themselves through trade associations and trade unions to exercise countervailing power. The creation of bi-lateral or oligopolistic markets in transactions with government is not exactly a congenial atmosphere for small firms. There is clear evidence that it suits government officials, as purchasers, to treat with a few major suppliers instead of with a wide dispersion of firms according to size. At the local government level, where small firms might compete effectively in providing cleaning and catering services on contract, opportunities are limited by the intense opposition of Labour-controlled councils and unions to the perceived threat of outside contracting to the employment prospects of their own employees already undertaking such work. Likely as not, even with a government in power which is particularly sympathetic to outside contracting, small firms will be 'upstream' suppliers to large firms awarded government contracts and therefore often in a vulnerable competitive position.

4 Much has been made of the present moves, notably but by no means exclusively in the UK, to privatize public corporations, and the effect that this could have in extending the influence of competition. It is of course true that when a public corporation becomes a fully-fledged private concern with shares quoted on the Stock Exchange, at the very least it has to satisfy shareholders with alternative uses of their capital. However, privatization may do nothing by itself to force a privatized public corporation to be more competitive in the product market unless it was previously subsidized and will no longer be so. Furthermore, the market form will not be altered unless simultaneously freedom of entry into the market is guaranteed. The privatization of British Airways only makes sense, if improving efficiency in passenger and freight air transport is to be taken as the aim, if simultaneously it loses privileges in the allocation of air routes so that small air lines have a proper opportunity to compete. An example more close to my interests concerns proposals to privatize universities or certain branches of university teaching and research. The small and growing University of Buckingham in the UK has had to finance a considerable proportion of its capital stock by term loans. Having bravely set up as a private institution, and often held up as an example of a private initiative which has overcome considerable obstacles in entering the higher education market, it would be paradoxical if university departments or even whole universities 'going it alone' were given their present capital stock as a gift.

5 Whether or not privatization continues apace, it has no marked effect on the burden of taxation for only a small proportion of government revenue is

raised in order to provide selective aid to public corporations. Even if social services were privatized to a major extent, so that health services and education were provided by private (not necessarily profit-making) concerns, what would happen is that direct expenditure on goods and services would decrease. However, the government would be bound to substitute transfers in order to ensure that access to these services would be available to those who could not be reasonably expected to pay the full economic price. In short, there would be a major change in the composition but not necessarily in the magnitude of public expenditure, and therefore the continuation of a situation where taxation would form a large part of the current outlays of individuals and business. Correspondingly, there is unlikely to be any reduction in the extent to which Western governments will retain regulation designed to induce or indeed force firms to comply with measures designed to implement social and environmental policy.

Important features of later chapters of this work (notably Chapters 8 and 9) are the original research and collation of available research findings from a wide variety of sources on the relative impact of social legislation and taxation on small firms. It is conclusively shown that small firms have been faced with relatively greater direct and indirect costs in complying with government regulations and with the laws of taxation; in consequence this has been inconsistent with measures designed to make competition more effective. If there are signs that this important point has struck home with governments, this in itself is a tribute to those, of whom Graham Bannock is an important figure, who have hammered away at it over at least two decades. It cannot be denied that the recognition of the problem does not suggest automatic and easy solution, but Chapter 10 does give a clear indication of the steps and procedures that governments should follow if they are to match sympathy with effective action

CONCLUDING REMARKS

While this book examines in detail the impact of government policies on small firms and how those policies might be improved, one has to recognize that even a government completely committed to helping small firms to help themselves cannot devise measures which will produce optimum conditions. In particular neither Graham Bannock nor myself would want to recommend that positive discrimination in favour of small firms should entail penalizing large firms by regulatory devices which would increase their costs of compliance so that they became unduly onerous. To produce optimum conditions would require that the government laid down and enforced some code of practice which regulated all aspects of business ethics in the transactions between large and small firms.

There is no doubt something in the argument that large firms may be tempted to indulge in business practices which exploit their market power to the disadvantage of small firms. I can recall a case when John Dunning and I were invited to prepare a detailed, costly memorandum on how a particular statistical and economic investigation for a large conglomerate might be carried out, and on the sole understanding that if it were approved, our small consultancy would undertake the work. After submission there was a long silence, and then we heard that our memorandum was being used by the large firm's economic section in order to carry out the investigation 'in-house'! I also recall that the 'knocking copy' issued by academic institutions of considerable influence against the (now) University of Buckingham was of a kind which in commercial life might have been the subject of a court action. It would be foolish to generalize from this and several other examples one might give from personal experience. For one thing, such practices may be used in dealings between firms of any size. For another, it would be hazardous to argue that small firms profess ethical standards which transcend those of a large firms. It would be a brave person who entered into debate about whether the criminal or civil law should be changed in order to control business ethics any more than it is at present. We are content to assume that the policy recommendations considered in this volume will not work in such a way as to affect the standards of behaviour normally expected to prevail in firms of any size

REFERENCES

Peacock, Sir Alan (1979), *Giving Economic Advice in Difficult Times*, in *The Economic Analysis of Government*, Martin Robertson, London, Ch 16.

Peacock, Sir Alan (1976), *Buckingham's Fight for Independence*, *Economic Affairs*, February to March 1986.

Morgan, E V (1987), *Monopolies, Mergers and Restrictive Practices: UK Competition Policy 1948–87*, The David Hume Institute, Edinburgh.

Chapter 2
CHANGING VIEWPOINTS*

INTRODUCTION

There is more than one way of looking at small firms, even from the limited point of view of this conference. Here are five viewpoints from which small firms can be regarded:

1 as an anachronism;
2 as a proper subject for academic and professional inquiry;
3 as a source of jobs and votes;
4 as a market for goods and services;
5 as an essential (and inevitable) part of the market economy;

I shall talk about each in turn, but first, let us dispose of the question of definition. This is undoubtedly the most boring aspect of what is, on the whole, a fascinating and important subject. The simplest definition of the small business sector is that it comprises all unquoted business enterprises. You will object that this is a very wide definition and wonder what problems say, Ernst and Whinney (an unincorporated enterprise with a turnover in excess of £100 million) and our self-employed matchseller have in common, apart from an inability to raise capital on the Stock Exchange. You are right, there isn't much, but business is a continuum from the smallest to the largest with no more obvious breakpoint than public quotation. The reason is that this is the point at which the last of the size-related problems which firms face more or less disappears. Ernst and Whinney themselves tell me that their working definition is a business in which the working proprietors control more than 50 per cent of the equity, which is also true of their own business. Some of you will know that in the Bolton Report (1971) we included owner-managed businesses with a small share of the market and it is this last criterion, market share, that is essential in any comprehensive definition. I hope to convince you later, however, that precise, watertight definitions, except for specific, practical purposes such as legislation (when philosophic rigour has to be sacrificed anyway), are not necessary. The attempt to find them is a black hole down which many precise minds have disappeared. I should like to tell you a story to make my point more concretely.

---

* An address given at a conference entitled *Small Business Policy: The Future* and held at The Savoy, London, on 18 June 1987. The conference was organized by Graham Bannock & Partners Ltd and sponsored by the Anglo-German Foundation, the David Hume Institute and Ernst and Whinney.

I have had the privilege, these past six months, of sitting on a Section of the Economic and Social Committee in Brussels charged with the job of writing an Opinion on the Action Programme of the SME Task Force, a body set up within the European Commission that you will hear more about this afternoon. Predictably, the Committee got bogged down on this question of definition at its very first meeting. So much so that it clearly had to be left on one side if any progress was going to be made at all. That done, work proceeded apace, though not always smoothly because small business touches on all the raw spots of our society. A few weeks ago at the final meeting to approve the 17-page draft Opinion, the Committee was again confronted with the question of inconclusive discussion. Finally, Alan Mayhew, Director of the Task Force, said (or words to this effect): 'Gentlemen, I think we can safely leave a definition of SMEs, you have produced a 17-page paper on the subject without defining it and we all clearly know what we are talking about'. I hope, Ladies and Gentlemen, that you here today will agree that we can also leave the question of definition to one side.

AN ANACHRONISM

In the post-war boom of the 1950s and the 1960s, when the number of small firms and their share of output and employment were declining in most countries, it became the accepted wisdom that this was a good and indeed an inevitable thing. I never tire of quoting J.K. Galbraith: 'By all but the pathologically romantic, it is now recognised that this is not the age of the small man'. He went on to write 'But there is still a lingering presumption among economists that his retreat is not before the efficiency of the great corporation, or even its technological proficiency, but before its monopoly power' (Galbraith, 1967). In other words small firms were a vestige of the cottage industries of the past and largely irrelevant at that time.

But now, when the numbers of small firms have been increasing in most countries since the early 1970s or before, and when the sole entrepreneur is once again becoming a folk hero, the view that small firms do not matter has itself become anachronistic. The rise of Mr Alan Sugar from selling car aerials from the back of a van at about the time Galbraith wrote, to his present position at the head of Amstrad, shows how little has changed from the 1900s when W.R. Morris began with his bicycle shop in Oxford and developed it into a great car manufacturing enterprise. Small beginnings can still lead to great things.

A SUBJECT FOR SERIOUS RESEARCH

The publication of the report of the Committee of Inquiry on Small Firms in 1971 (Bolton Committee, 1971), the ensuing resurgence of small business in the face of rising unemployment and shifts in cultural values that accompanied the sea change in world economic fortunes, have led since to an exponential growth in academic research on small firms. In the 1960s, few academics had even a partial interest in the subject in Britain. Today there are hundreds of researchers and teachers on small business and most centres of higher learning also now have practical courses on business. It is interesting that most of this work is going on in the newer centres; the great traditional sources of distinction in economics, Oxford, Cambridge, Bristol and, for example, the London School of Economics, show little interest in the economics or other aspects of small firms.

I shall not attempt to summarize what has been learned since Bolton, that would take too long and has been very well done already by James Curran for the Small Business Research Trust (Curran, 1986). Much of the work has focused on the role of small business in employment change, on the characteristics of entrepreneurs and their place in the firm and in society, on training needs and on the efficacy of small business policy measures. Much of the research, too much in my view, has been with normative purposes in mind; in other words, how small firms can be an instrument of policy, rather than on how small firms actually function in the economy. We still know very little about how business proprietors spend their time, how management changes as firms grow, how small firms are financed and what returns they earn. We do not know enough about how many small firms there are and what sectors they are in, where they are expanding and where contracting. We have not begun to establish the contribution which start-ups make to economic growth and so on (see Bannock, 1985).

A SOURCE OF JOBS

Small firms and their proprietors account for perhaps 30 per cent or more of the employed labour force in Britain and considerably more than that in other countries. It is now well established that small firms have accounted for a disproportionate share of net employment creation during the past decade or so. It is important to be careful about terminology here because new and very small firms have a high mortality rate and lots of jobs are lost as well as gained in the small firm sector every year. As a group, large firms have shed employees since 1980 while job gains in new and existing small firms have not been great enough to prevent unemployment from rising. None of the people working in this field would, I think, disagree with that bald summary. The argument, for there has been a great deal of argument, has been about the significance of these findings for policy. There is a higher proportion of part-time jobs in small firms than in large ones, and average earnings are lower so that it is possible to argue that the quality of jobs is lower. It is also argued that only a few surviving small firms grow to become major employers. In fact, in Britain this proportion may be lower than in other countries and it is true that fewer firms in Britain seem to expand beyond 20 employees than in some other countries. The general consensus is that no more than 10 per cent of total employment today is accounted for by firms that were started up in the past 10 years.

While undoubtedly true (though some of the claims made by the opponents of small business promotion are untrue or at best unproven), these objections seem to me to be mere cavils and assume that the devotion of resources to alternative policies would reverse the trend for large firms to become less labour intensive, or eliminate the need for large firms in declining industries to contract. We are simply saying that small firms alone cannot, in the short-term, solve the unemployment problem. I agree with that but point out that 10 per cent of the employed labour force represents 2.5 million people. That is the contribution of new start ups, we guess, in the past 10 years. Without that contribution, unemployment now might be nearly twice as great. This is an argument for having started active small business promotion earlier, not for abandoning it now. Though it is not, I agree, an argument for relying on small firms alone to solve the unemployment problem. There are votes in jobs and votes in small firms. There may be about 3.5 million self-employed and small business proprietors and if you count non-working spouses, as the Forum of Private Business does, the number would be greater.

A MARKET FOR GOODS AND SERVICES

There is increasing interest in small business as a market for big firms, though small firms also sell a lot to each other. This growing interest follows both the growth of the sector and a realization that its customer potential has been neglected in the past in favour of other markets where, for competitive or other reasons, scope for increased sales and profitability is more limited.

Some big firms have, of course, long been heavily dependent on small firms for custom. Tobacco and newspaper manufacturers and wholesalers and other traders who sell a large proportion of their output through thousands of small retail outlets are obvious examples. Others are the oil companies, the brewers, confectionery, publishing, agricultural supplies and insurance companies.

Some sectors which have long dealt with small firms have in recent years been increasingly interested in their potential. Prominent among these are the clearing banks and the bigger accounting firms, witness their good representation here today. Their motives are similar. For the 'Big Eight' accountants, auditing for big clients has gone 'ex-growth', but this is not true of the upper end of the small business market. Great rewards await those who can overcome the obstacles presented by their high fee and overhead structure to push still further down the size scale.

The banks too have found that big business is not as profitable as it was. Big business can easily bypass them altogether by securitizing loans and developing its own foreign exchange and money transmission facilities. Lending to small firms at several points over base rate, despite greater risk and administrative hassle, can be more profitable than lending to ICI at a decimal of 1 per cent, even if you can get the business. Small firms also tend to keep relatively larger idle balances with the banks and offer more scope for other services than self-sufficient large firms.

Even though the banks have advanced enormously in their attitudes to the small business market, however, there is lots of scope yet. Virtually every small business has a bank account and this offers enormous scope for tailored services. For example, I am still waiting for a bank to design a credit card service that would help small firms compile their VAT records, or a means that would help small retailers to bank cash at the end of the day, or a means of getting down the costs of cashing foreign cheques and issuing small payments in foreign currencies.

Think of the scope that British Telecom has! Almost all small firms have a telephone line which one day is going to be a wonderful conduit for value-added services, perhaps in solving some of the small business banking problems I have just mentioned. Fax services are already growing fast among small firms and about 70 per cent of car telephones are for people working in firms with fewer than 50 people.

British Telecom and the banks know all this. But has the computer and software industry fully woken up to the opportunities of the small business market? Apparently it has not. Incomprehensible user manuals, inadequate and user unfriendly software, primitive dealership, training and customer back-up services are all holding up the spread of computerization in small firms, despite rapidly falling product prices. According to a recent survey (Small Business Research Trust, 1985), no more than 25 per cent of small firms have a computer and many of these use their equipment at a tiny fraction of its potential. Yet two of the biggest problems of the small firm are the pressures on the proprietor's time and lack of current financial information, both of which can be greatly eased with the intelligent use of micro-computers.

There are just two more examples of small firms as a growth business for bigger suppliers. The insurance industry has certainly put a lot of effort into selling self-employment pension plans, but did you know that at least 75 per cent of those eligible do not have one yet? Portable pensions and other recent changes in the law will allow a tremendous growth in this business. Finally, the legal profession seems to be leaving the small business market increasingly to the accountants. Yet taxation is legally based and the continued growth and amendments of other legislation affecting small business provide plenty of opportunities for solicitors to sell their services to small firms. Your accountant probably sent you a note on the implications of the 1987 Finance Act, but when did you last get an unsolicited communication from your solicitor?

AN ESSENTIAL PART OF THE MARKET ECONOMY

Before getting into small business policy as such I want to make a plea for another change of viewpoint. For too long, though it was natural while long established blind-spots on small firms were being eradicated, we have been stuck in an adversarial stance for and against small firms. Small is beautiful, big is ugly, or, more specifically: small firms create jobs, earn a better return on capital, are more flexible and inventive, large firms offer better pay and conditions, export more of their output, are more technologically advanced, large firms are impersonal, do not identify with local communities, abuse their monopolistic power, and so on. Even where supported by the facts, these generalizations can be misleading because they draw attention away from the complementarity of firms of different size. We do not face a choice between one and the other, we need both and we have both.

NEUTRALITY

The real issue for small business policy is, should small firms be playing a greater or lesser role in the economy? In an economist's theoretical model, which among other things would assume profit maximization, perfect information, free mobility of resources, freedom of entry and neutral government policies, we should not need to worry. Subject to a few other assumptions, the national output would be maximized at the lowest cost level that could be achieved by a mix of producers. Each firm would be of a scale that could only be increased or reduced at the expense of higher costs or lower output. That mix, the optimum, would change as consumer tastes or technology, or the relative supply of the factors of production, changed. In other words, you could leave it to the market. But the real world is not like that.

There is no way of calculating what the optimum would, or should, be, but it seems clear to me, given that most of our assumptions do not hold in the real world and that deviations from them are mainly in a direction that would tend to depress the share of small firms in the mix, that this share is below the optimum in the UK and perhaps in other countries. Indeed the share of small firms in output and employment, though probably rising, is below that of most other developed countries, as it was when the Bolton Committee reported a decade and a half ago. So we cannot leave it to the market, and the fact that all parties in this and most other countries subscribe to special policies for small firms indicates that there is a general consensus that things cannot be left to the market.

The Bolton Committee agonized at some length on the issue of whether positive discrimination in favour of small firms could be justified. The conclusion was that it could not, unless there was clear evidence that the size of the small firms sector was diminishing to the point where its key role in providing a seed-bed for new enterprise was threatened. At the time the Committee was carrying out its research, and, unknown to it, in fact, the long decline in small business was in the process of reversal. This is a salutary fact because it means that the reversal started before governments in this country had a small business policy, though the pace of recovery since presumably owes something to changes in policy that have been more favourable to small firms. Equally, we may add, with the notable exception of Japan, the existence of explicit small business policies in other countries had not prevented a decline in the importance of small firms up to the 1960s, though the decline went further and faster in Britain than elsewhere.

In my view the Bolton Committee's conclusion remains correct, and the right policy for government is to try to remove imperfections in the market which work against small firms and to ensure that its own activities, as far as possible, are neutral in their impact on firms of different sizes. This leaves massive scope for small business policy as a part of overall economic policy and indeed I am more hawkish now than ever on the need for such a policy and one with real teeth (perhaps beak to get the metaphor right).

This concept of neutrality, as a guiding principle, does, I think, help in clearing away a lot of the dissension and confusion that surround small business policy issues. First, at a stroke it eliminates any necessity for us to define small business since we are concerned not with firms of any particular size, but with the degree of neutrality, or if you prefer it, equity of policies between firms of whatever size. Second, as a corollary of this, it should help to defuse the political (though largely unadmitted) resistance to providing assistance for this particular section of the business community. This will not alter the fact that trade unions, on the one hand, and some big business interests, on the other, will resist what they see as discrimination against their present interests, but it should at least help to make the debate less confused and more explicit. Who, after all, can argue against the principle of equity and neutrality? It may be, of course, that neutrality towards size of business and social equity conflict. If that is so and it is desired to correct it, then it would be economically more efficient to deal with it explicitly, for example through the tax system, rather than in ways which distort the economy and reduce output and efficiency.

WHAT REMAINS TO BE DONE?

Much has of course been done, and there were signs under the previous Conservative government (1983–7) of a shift away from those special schemes for parts of the small business, that the mass of small business proprietors have never heard about, towards a more fundamental approach tackling root causes and which generally help business as a whole.

Six years ago I set out a schema for a fundamentalist approach to small business policy (Figure 2.1) (Bannock, 1981). Some of the things on that list have been tackled and in some respects with subsequent experience the list could be improved on, but it is clear that there is a long way to go. Here are the five main areas where action is still required.

1 *Taxation* appears several times on the list and remains, in my view, the most important area for reform. Our present system not only dampens incentives, it distorts the capital market and it places heavy compliance burdens on small firms. It also encourages evasion and avoidance. In all these ways our tax system discriminates against small firms.
2 The *compliance burdens* of government activities are highly regressive, that is to say they are proportionately much greater on small firms than on large ones. This needs to be corrected.
3 *Purchasing*: the public sector is a major consumer of goods and services. We do not have even rough estimates, but we do know that about 95 per cent of defence purchasing is from large firms (some of it is subcontracted). If

Figure 2.1 Small firm problems and their solution

Problem area	Diagnosis	Action needed on:
Supply of entrepreneurs	Social and economic bias in favour of employment	Social security system Education Tax system
Lack of capital	Distortions in capital market	Tax system Subsidized lending Monopoly policy Credit guarantees
Labour shortages	Imperfections in labour market	Social security system Social environment Housing policy Training and education Monopoly policy
Lack of premises	Imperfections in market	Urban redevelopment Planning regulations Infrastructure investment Tax system
Bureaucracy	Growth of government	Simplification, exemption, changes in local taxation and the organization of central and local government
Purchasing	Imperfections in supplier markets	Monopoly policy, tax system
Marketing	Imperfections in seller markets	

Source: Bannock.G (1981) *The Economics of Small Firms*, Basil Blackwell, Oxford

government buys a larger share of its requirements from large firms than does the private sector, then this is a depressing force on the small business economy.

4 *Competition policy*: our largely discretionary system of competition policy inevitably favours vested interests and larger firms.
5 *The educational system* at primary and secondary level does little or nothing to give young people an understanding of small enterprise. Progress is now being made at the level of higher education, but we need urgently to ensure that entrepreneurs and small firm employees in the 1990s are better prepared than the present and earlier generations.

There are, of course, several other matters that require attention but these, I suggest, are the five priorities.

It may be that organizational changes in government are required for really effective action to be taken on all these fronts. They are all difficult and involve several government departments. Wherever the small business minister is located in government, he or she faces problems in getting the necessary commitment from other ministers and their civil servants. The same problems exist in Brussels and confront the SME Task Force.

ATTITUDES OF THE POLITICAL PARTIES

One of the most promising changes in the British political scene is that a consensus seems to be emerging on the importance of, and the necessity for, small business policy. In West Germany, Japan and the United States, there appears to have been a greater degree of consensus on these issues in the past than in Britain and their economies have benefited from that.

All three manifestos for the major parties in the 1987 General Election were, nonetheless, rather vague on the subject of small business policy. Only the Alliance had an explicit section on small firms. The Conservative manifesto set out no new policies, but of course we have plenty of information on what the government has done in the past. The Labour manifesto does not mention small business as far as I can see, but Barry Sheerman has issued a paper on the subject, the first from his party that I know of.

In measuring their policies against the criteria I have been talking about, a number of things come across fairly clearly. Only the Conservatives are committed to reducing taxation. Lower taxation is good for small business because it allows people to retain more of their own money, which they are free to invest in their own or other businesses or consumption as they wish. Financial institutions can never completely fulfil small firm investment needs, particularly for small amounts and for riskier purposes, nor do small business owners wish to concede control of their enterprises to institutions if they can avoid it. The lower the rate of taxation, the less distorting effects it can have on consumption and investment decisions. However, there is no sign yet that the Conservatives will go much further in pursuing tax neutrality: they have removed initial allowances for corporation tax, but they have actually increased distortions in the allocation of savings by promoting investment in quoted securities.

The expenditure tax, the long-term aim of the Alliance, is the best available instrument for achieving a more neutral tax system. Under such a system, all forms of saving, not simply those which channel funds principally to large firms, property and government securities, would be free of tax. This would increase the flow of funds into the small business sector.

The previous Conservative government (1983–8) did set up a Deregulation Unit, but progress has been slow. None of the parties shows much evidence of real enthusiasm for reducing the compliance burden, although this is one area where the government could actually do something rapid and tangible to release more resources in small business for productive effort. The Labour party programme for small business does mention the possibility of making available computer software for tax administration; this would be a welcome development.

Education and training were of course given prominence in all the manifestos in a general sense. The previous Conservative government had begun minor initiatives on the small firms front for primary and secondary education, but it is not clear what any of the parties have in mind in detail. All of them are, however, more explicit about training for small business managers and their employees.

Competition policy and government purchasing are dead areas in all the parties' programmes. There is a need for fresh thinking on both of these issues. We have much to learn from other countries on both subjects. Experience overseas is, for example, that passive approaches to making more purchasing information available for small firms are not very effective. Pressures for more subcontracting and even set asides are more likely to work, but other approaches such as decentralization and computerization of public purchasing need to be tried. Pushing more purchasing authority to a local level would inevitably help small firms who are essentially local in their sphere of activity. Electronic purchasing systems could help to reduce administrative costs and widen the catchment area for purchasing activity. A useful first step would be to publish information on the percentage of public purchasing from small business as the Ministry of Defence has already done.

SOME PREDICTIONS

I think some broad but confident predictions can be made. Outcomes will not be determined as much as you might think by the present policies of political parties, these change in response to the realities of economic forces and electoral wishes. Those who are unhappy about the shift towards small business may blame the Thatcher government, but in fact that government has gone with the grain of change in that respect; it did not anticipate it, it responded to deep forces in the world economy and in our own society. These trends will continue for some time yet.

Some trends in small business policy have already been mentioned: the emerging all-party consensus and the shift away from specific schemes for particular sectors towards general measures which tackle root problems. Another trend, which is already identifiable and which will accelerate, is a shift towards local emphasis in small business policy. This will happen because it must happen given the decentralized nature of small business and because regenerating inner cities and other disadvantaged areas is a political imperative. Private initiatives, I am thinking particularly of the enterprise agencies, are leading the way, but are already beginning to be reinforced by government despite its moves in the opposite direction over the control of local authority expenditure and its ill-advised policies on local taxation. Our steadily closer links with the rest of the European Community will help influence this result and indeed other aspects of small business affairs. The Enterprise Agency, Local Enterprise Trust and Enterprise Board movement may, as it receives more public funds and perhaps develops closer links with Chambers of Trade and Commerce, in a unique British way, end up performing more of the functions in training, advice and representation which the public law chambers perform in several other member states.

I am very confident indeed that in time we and all EC member states will move towards taxing expenditure, reducing tax expenditures (allowances) and removing taxes on all forms of saving. This process has already started with the rise of indirect taxation (VAT) in Europe, the elimination of investment allowances in Britain and the United States, and the move towards lower tax rates in Britain and soon in West Germany. The process has been confused (for example, by the removal of life assurance premium relief and the introduction of personal equity plans by the previous Conservative government) but the trend is there. Eventually the logic of necessity will reassert itself. Europe cannot indefinitely pursue tax policies which are incompatible with those in the stronger economies of Japan and the United States. The move towards lower tax rates is everywhere being driven by the need to stimulate private expenditure and investment in an ageing and deflationary era. All this will be good for small business. We may even eventually abolish altogether business taxation, which rests on the myth that companies, as distinct from their owners and customers, bear taxes, but that is more of a hope than a forecast.

What is more likely is that there will be a gradual acceptance of the principle that the compliance burden that business taxation imposes should be roughly proportionate to the size of the business. Perhaps the best way of dealing with that would be to allow small firms to retain a proportion of the taxes they collect on behalf of government as partial compensation for the compliance costs they bear.

This proposal will no doubt be received with horror by the Treasury and the tax authorities, but there are precedents for it in West Germany and elsewhere. Furthermore, if the government actually were bearing part of the compliance cost and the deduction were related to real costs, it would have a stronger incentive to get these costs down. Can you believe that if the collection of taxes were privatized it would not rapidly find ways of getting compliance costs down? I hasten to say I am not suggesting that, but simply making the point that where there is a will, there is a way.

REFERENCES

Bannock, Graham (1981), *The Economics of Small Firms*, Graham Bannock, Basil Blackwell, Oxford.

Bannock, Graham (1985), *New Business Formation, Unemployment and the Role of Small Business in Economic Growth*, Paper presented to the 30th Annual World Conference of the International Council for Small Business, Montreal, June 1985

Bolton Committee (1971), *Small Firms*, Report of the Committee of Inquiry on Small Firms, Chairman J. Bolton, HMSO, London.

Curran, James (1986), *Bolton Fifteen Years On: A Review and Analysis of Small Business Research in Britain 1971-1986* Small Business Research Trust.

Galbraith, J.K. (1967), *The New Industrial State*, Hamish Hamilton, London.

Ganguly, Pom and Bannock, G (ed.) (1985), *UK Small Business Statistics and International Comparisons*, Paul Chapman Publishing, London.

Small Business Research Trust (1985), *Quarterly Survey of Small Business in Britain*, no.3.

Chapter 3

SMALL FIRMS AS EXPORTERS*

INTRODUCTION

Terms of Reference and Background

The three main objectives of the study which will be considered here are:

1 to help establish the extent of untapped export potential among smaller and medium-sized manufacturing companies;

2 to ascertain the barriers and obstacles to exporting and their relative significance;

3 to help to establish what would encourage companies with export potential, but not exporting actively, to become active exporters.

This is an important but hitherto little researched subject. We refer in the next section (p.26) to some work carried out for the Committee of Inquiry on Small Firms which reported in 1971 (Bolton Committee, 1971), and in 1983 a survey of small firm exporters was carried out for SITPRO (Pickett et al, 1983) on which we draw in the third section (p.27). Apart from these, little survey work on small firm export activity seems to have been carried out in Britain, and we have come across only two other studies in other countries (NMB, 1979; National Federation of Independent Business, 1985).

Although it is known that many small firms do export, for many, exports may account for only a small percentage of turnover and they will export only occasionally or in response to unsolicited orders from abroad. After Cannon and Willis (1982) we refer to these as *passive exporters*. *Active exporters*, in contrast, will regard the planned expansion of exports as important to the survival and growth of their business, will sell a substantial proportion of their output abroad and will be actively seeking new markets for existing products and new products for which a market exists abroad. Active exporters account for the bulk of exports and it is this group which the British Overseas Trade Board (BOTB) wishes to foster and enlarge by bringing more firms into active exporting.

---

* An edited version of the report of a study commissioned by the British Overseas Trade Board (BOTB) and completed in October 1986. We are grateful for the Department of Trade and Industry's permission to reproduce this material from the report.

Previous studies have shown that the proportion of the number of firms exporting increases with the size of firm and exporters may be expected to be more numerous in the manufacturing sector where most products are, in principle, tradable between countries. For these reasons, the BOTB decided that the present study should focus on manufacturing companies with a turnover in the range of £1m to £10m per annum (the *target group*). In fact, according to statistics compiled from VAT returns and supplied to the Board by HM Customs and Excise, 50 per cent of the 12,000 or so firms in this selected group do not export at all and many of the remainder can be expected to be passive exporters.

Field Work

To explore the nature of the barriers to export and differences between exporters and non-exporters, we carried out personal interviews with the chief executives of 41 firms in the target group. Interviews were mainly confined to three parts of the country (the North-west, Dorset/Hampshire and London) and to three sectors (clothing, printing and electronics).

The impressions gained in the interviews were validated, selectively, in a large scale postal questionnaire survey addressed to 3,000 firms, or 25 per cent of the target group. Full responses were received from 920 firms, a response rate of 31 per cent. In addition, questions on export activity were included in the Small Business Research Trust's *Quarterly Survey* for June 1986. These responses from some 900 firms, mainly with a turnover of less than £1m, in all sectors of the economy have helped us to fill out the general picture of small business export activity presented in the next section. Further details of these three field surveys are included in Appendix 2.

THE EXPORT PERFORMANCE OF SMALLER FIRMS

Export Performance by Size of Firm

In terms of aggregate value, exports are dominated by a small number of large firms. We have calculated from export data from company accounts regularly published by the *Financial Times* (1986) that the 100 largest exporters accounted in 1985 for about 55 per cent of UK exports of fuels, basic materials and manufactures, while the top 50 alone accounted for about 47 per cent. This compares with a share of the 100 largest enterprises in total net output in manufacturing of about 41 per cent (Prais 1976).

If, however, allowance is made for the fact that virtually all exports of fuels and basic materials will be made by the 100 largest enterprises, it is not clear that the share of these enterprises in exports of manufactures alone is greater than their share in manufacturing net output. We show later (p.53) that on the basis of our postal questionnaire survey, firms in the £1m to £10m band are estimated to account for about 9 per cent of total UK exports of manufactures.

We are not readily able to make even a rough estimate of the share of smaller firms — say those with a turnover of less than £10m — in manufacturing exports, but it is certainly significant. There are many exporting firms with a turnover of less than £1m.

In fact, we know from figures derived from VAT returns that the percentage of all firms which export tends to increase with the size of firm measured by turnover. In the less than £1m turnover band, 14 per cent of manufacturing firms and 3 per cent of VAT registered firms in other sectors export. In the over £100m band, the corresponding figures are 72 and 35 per cent.[1] (Figure 3.1).

Evidence from earlier studies on the relationship between the percentage of turnover exported (the export ratio) and size of firm is limited and conflicting. In a 1969 study carried out in the North-west region for the Committee of Inquiry on Small Firms (Bolton Committee, 1971), small exporting firms employing 200 or fewer persons on average exported 32 per cent of their turnover while the average export ratio for larger exporting firms was 36 per cent. According to the

Figure 3.1 Number of exporters as percentage of number of firms, manufacturing and non-manufacturing, 1983–4.

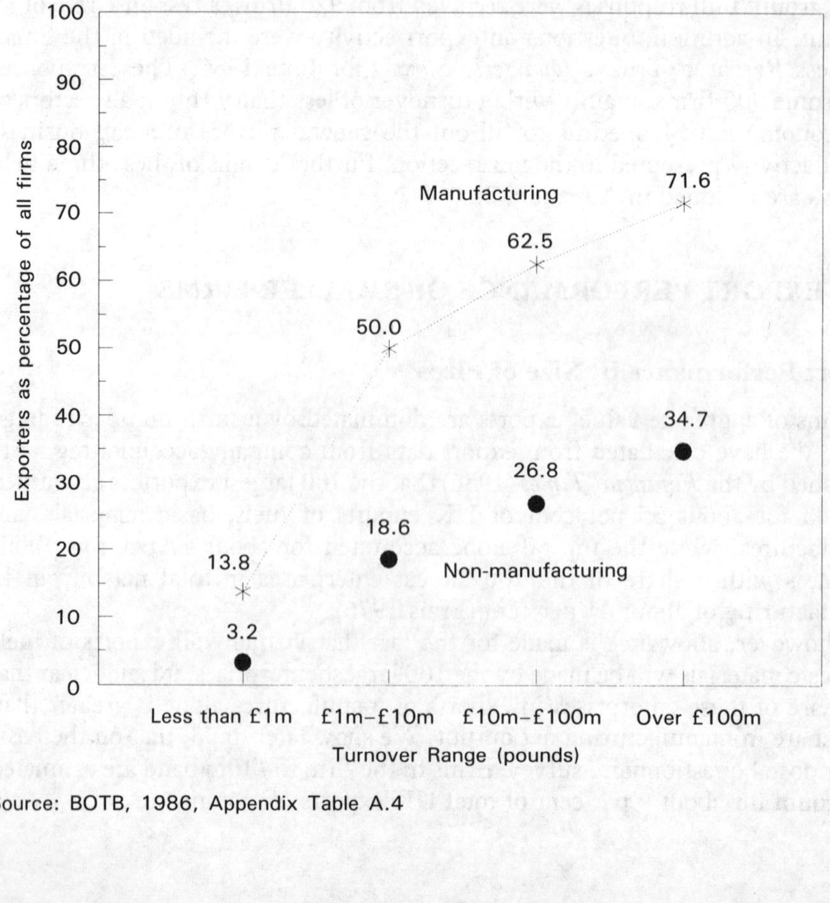

Source: BOTB, 1986, Appendix Table A.4

accounts for larger manufacturing companies analysed by the Department of Trade and Industry for 1973, the relationship between size and exports was negative rather than positive (Hannah and Kay, 1977). It may well be that the positive relationship between size and exports levels off and then becomes negative for the larger firms which have the option of producing locally in major export markets.

In Figure 3.2 we combine the results of the Small Business Research Trust (SBRT) Survey covering mainly firms with a turnover of less than £1m and our postal questionnaire survey of manufacturing firms in the £1m–10m size band. This chart does suggest that there is some relationship between size and export ratio, but the numbers of respondents in some of the size bands are very small and we cannot be sure that the result is unaffected by sampling error. The SITPRO study (Pickett et al, 1983) (where the sample was also open to criticism) also showed a positive relationship between size and the export ratio and we conclude that there probably is such a relationship, although it may not be a very strong one.

There has hitherto been very little information available on the sectoral pattern of export activity among small firms. The VAT statistics in Table A2.4 (p.56) show that there are a surprising number of small exporting firms, both in manufacturing and non-manufacturing. In manufacturing, as mentioned in the Introduction, 50 per cent of the 12,000 firms in our target group were exporters, but there were nearly 14,500 small firm manufacturing exporters with a

Figure 3.2 Export ratio of exporters by turnover size band, manufacturing, 1986.

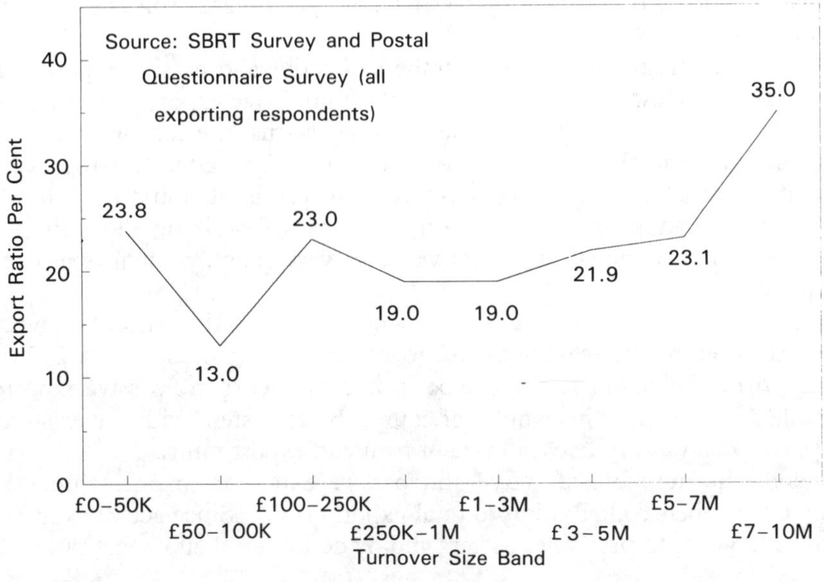

turnover of £1m or less. There were also another 34,000 non-manufacturing exporting firms with a turnover of less than £1m (17,000 of them in the distributive trades) and over 6,000 in the £1m–£10m size band. The widespread extent of exporting among small firms was confirmed in the SBRT survey (Small Business Research Trust, 1986), which included exporting respondents in agriculture, forestry and fishing, construction, transport and business and other services as well as in manufacturing. The data from the SBRT survey, like the VAT statistics, indicate a surprising number of exporters in the distributive trades, which we assume include retailers making VAT-free sales to tourists from abroad. Given the rapid growth of invisible exports, the predominance of small firms in the service sectors and the lack of information about their overseas sales, there is clearly scope for deeper inquiry into the role of small firms in non-manufacturing exports.

Active and Passive Exporters

As mentioned earlier (p.24), the distinction between active and passive exporters is a useful one in analysing the activities of exporters. Although many firms, large and small, export, the commitment to exporting and the success achieved vary considerably. In analysing the results of our postal questionnaire survey we have defined *active exporters* as firms which have exported more than 15 per cent of turnover in at least one of the past three years. *Non-exporters* are firms with export ratios of 1 per cent or less. *Passive exporters* are the residual of these two categories.

Our *core sample* excludes respondents which, including their parent or subsidiaries (if any), had a group turnover below or in excess of the £1m–£10m turnover band of the target group. We analysed 463 responses in the core group. *All respondents* analysed numbered 848; these include the core sample together with respondents with a group turnover below, or in excess of, the turnover range of the target group.

There were approximately equal numbers of active and passive exporters in the core sample. However, the response rate from active exporters was almost certainly higher than that from passive exporters so that the core sample is not an accurate guide to their relative proportions (see Appendix 2). (It does not seem that our conclusions are very sensitive to the precise definition of active or passive exporter adopted. The proportion of firms describing themselves as experienced and occasional exporters was also very roughly equal; see Table A2.5, p.56).

There was a clear tendency within the core group for the ratio of active to passive exporters to increase with turnover. In other words, the larger the exporting firm, the more likely it is to be an active rather than a passive exporter (see Table A2.5, p.56). This would, of course, be consistent with the existence of a positive relationship between size of firm and export ratios.

Although the numbers of active and passive exporters in our sample are roughly equal, their contribution to total exports is not. Since active exporters tend to be larger than passive exporters and by definition their export ratios are higher, active exporters make a disproportionate contribution to total exports. We estimate the active exporters contributed 80 per cent of the total exports of the firms in the target group.

Conclusions

We conclude that the larger the firm the more likely it is to be an exporter. Among firms which do export there also seems to be a positive relationship between the export ratio and the size of firm, though it may become negative for the largest firms. This suggests that there are economies of scale in exporting. In the next two sections, we show that small firms do experience difficulties in their access to information and capital necessary for exporting. Common sense suggests that the larger firm with greater administrative and financial resources — and perhaps sales offices and subsidiaries overseas — has great advantages in the development of export business. Despite this, many small firms do overcome the obstacles in the way of exporting and we also show that within our samples of smaller firms, differences in approach between exporters and passive or non-exporters were very great. Attitudes to exporting, therefore, play a very important part in success, irrespective of the size of firm.

THE BARRIERS TO EXPORTS

The Personal Interview Survey

In general, exporting is less straightforward than selling in the domestic market. Goods leaving the UK have to pass through the British and foreign customs procedures. Even within the EC, different legal and currency regimes will be involved, tastes and languages may be different and costs will be higher. Even in the simplest case of delivery by vehicle using a roll-on roll-off ferry, transport costs on a journey including a trip across the Channel can be at least 50 per cent higher than on a journey of similar distance inland.

Our personal interview survey was intended to explore the nature and scope of the obstacles in the way of exporting as perceived by manufacturing exporters and non-exporters, and to see if there appeared to be any systematic differences between the two. This section concentrates on the responses which emerged in our personal interviews (see Appendix 2 for details of the sample).

Product/Sector Barriers

In some sectors, the nature of the product itself imposes a barrier to exports. This is most common and obvious outside manufacturing, for example in much of the service sector where the provision of the service has to be where the customer is, as in a restaurant meal or the encashment of a cheque. However, even in these cases the implications for the scope for overseas trade are not necessarily clear cut. The food itself could be a frozen ready-made dish and the cheque could be a travellers' cheque issued abroad, and both the meal and the banking service might be provided to foreign visitors to the UK by a local subsidiary of an overseas-based business. Such an apparently simple aspect of domestic activity can therefore give rise to a range of visible and invisible imports and exports.

In the manufacture of tangible goods, where the goods do not have to be consumed where they are produced, things are more clear cut, though manufacturing can also give rise to invisible as well as visible trade. Goods may be manufactured under licence and by foreign-owned establishments in the UK, resulting in invisible exports of profits and royalty payments and in imports of components and raw materials for subsequent re-export in the form of finished goods. Virtually all types of manufactured goods enter into international trade to some extent, though scope for foreign trade may be limited by heavy transport costs or other factors. It is in fact very difficult to think of manufactured products with no exports — freshly baked bread is one — but there are many cases where the value-added ratio is low and transport costs high and where there is nonetheless a significant export-import trade such as mineral water and basic steel products.

The UK as an Export Base

The small size of the domestic market was cited by several respondents as an obstacle to the development of export markets, as well as a spur to exporting, and it was universally agreed that products had, as far as possible, to be proven before exporting could begin. Smaller firms also needed to build up their capital and administrative resources before tackling markets abroad. This applied particularly to quality products where, in some fields, domestic consumers seem to have traded down to low-cost imports leaving a tiny quality market also swamped by imports from Switzerland, West Germany and Scandinavia. Producers in these richer (though not larger) countries benefited from economies of scale.

Others blamed British conservatism which made it more difficult to develop and launch new products in the UK as a precursor to exporting. Finally, several respondents pointed out that British manufacturers' poor reputation for meeting delivery dates meant that they had to move faster than their foreign competitors since 'we are all tarred with the same brush and lack credibility'.

Against these problems, which present a picture of a vicious circle of poor export performance and were mainly confined to passive or non-exporters, the successful, confident exporters claimed that the UK was a good export base. Most felt that labour costs were lower in Britain than in other developed countries and where they were not they could be got down by further investment. Very few exporters mentioned the strength or volatility of sterling exchange rates as a serious problem. Political stability, a favourable tax regime, improving labour relations, a good supply of labour, the availability of creative research and development staff, in some instances, lack of strong domestic competitors, good international communications, were cited as advantages for the UK by many firms, including those with overseas subsidiaries and therefore in a position to make international comparisons.

Net export margins among active exporters, particularly in Europe, were often as high or higher than at home though, as in the home market, business with some customers was more profitable than that with others. One active exporter of electrical instruments and control systems expressed clearly in a letter a widespread attitude to profitability among the more aggressive firms:

> When we have invested a great deal in developing a new product, we will only make good profits by selling it worldwide. The UK market is very small and shrinking. Although exporting is more difficult than home sales and although it is less profitable on a unit sold basis, it is absolutely necessary to export in order to increase production quantities to amortize the initial investment over a greater volume ... There is an attitude in the UK that if you are exporting more than 50 per cent of production you are doing well. I will not be satisfied until we are exporting at least 90 per cent of production. If you talk to manufacturers in Scandinavia, they would consider this as a minimum.

Risk Aversion

It is often said that many small business owners are risk averse and that if growth, including export growth, involves undue risk they will opt for a comfortable life and stay as they are. Small firms that lack ambition are, in fact, in a minority. An international survey of 11 countries a few years ago (which included businesses which were predominantly smaller than those in our samples) found that 71 per cent wanted to expand, while the UK had a much higher percentage than this wanting to grow, and indeed had the highest percentage among the developed countries in the sample (Bannock, 1984).

Obviously some individuals are more risk averse than others and successful business people seem to be those who take carefully calculated risks, not gambles. By its very nature, however, working in a small firm tends to involve greater risks than working in a large firm or in the public sector and people who are really risk averse would not set up in small businesses at all. Among our sample, most, if not all, of the chief executives (we did not ask all of them) were major shareholders in the business, and in the smallest firms several mentioned that they had personally guaranteed bank borrowing or other obligations of the firm and were exposed to considerable personal risk. (Several firms volunteered the view that large financial institutions were highly risk averse.)

All the firms in our sample were motivated to expand, though not all judged that exports were the appropriate route for expansion, at least for the time being. In some of these cases we felt their judgement was correct, given the financial and administrative resources needed for exporting; in other cases we felt that exaggerated fears about the problems of exporting had clouded their judgement. This was not so much risk aversion, however, as uninformed judgement. In a few other cases, proprietors perhaps sensed that the firm had grown near to the limit of their ability to control it. In these few instances, the solution might have been to bring in other shareholders and talent. It was really only in these instances that we detected risk aversion in the usual sense of the term.

Export Operations

Other inquiries into the problems of selling abroad have given prominence to the sheer mechanics of exporting. In the Small Business Research Trust Survey, which predominantly covered firms smaller than those interviewed in our survey and included non-manufacturing businesses, 'Finance' received nearly twice as many mentions as 'Export paperwork', 'Product suitability' and 'Market information' which were all about the same (Table 3.1). There were indications within the sample, however, that 'Export paperwork' was regarded as more difficult by the smallest firms.

It has been well demonstrated that official administrative burdens such as tax compliance costs fall much more heavily on small firms since there are economies of scale in administration (Chapter 7).

The list of items to be covered under export operations is indeed formidable, but it was not our impression from the interviews we conducted that they present a significant barrier to exporting for firms in the £1m–10m turnover range in practice, though the prospect of administrative problems may well deter some non-exporters and passive exporters from exporting.

Table 3.1: The greatest difficulties in exporting

	Per cent of mentions
Factors	
Finance/delays in payment	26.2
Export paperwork	14.4
Market information	14.4
Product suitability	14.3
Suitable overseas representation	10.1
Costs/profitability	8.3
Language	2.9
Other	9.4
Total	100.0
Base	908

Source: Small Business Research Trust (1986[b]).
Question? Whether you export or not, what would you say the greatest difficulties are?

It was quite striking that the successful exporters in our sample, almost without exception, dismissed such matters as customs procedures and export documentation as nothing more than an administrative nuisance which, once the learning process had been gone through, were easily dealt with by routine office procedures and the use of intermediaries such as forwarding agents.

Non-exporters and occasional passive exporters who are not properly organized do find the complexities of bills of lading, EUR 1s, customs entry forms and other documents baffling or burdensome at first, but soon discover that if what cannot be dealt with by an intermediary is given the same practised and meticulous treatment as the more familiar cheques or VAT invoices used in domestic business, then the difficulties soon disappear.

This is not to say that the details of export operations are easily mastered or unimportant. Despite the efforts of SITPRO and some progress in streamlining international customs procedures in recent years, these procedures do remain complicated and errors or failure to observe the rules can result in costly delays, which can result in lost business. There are several minefields for the inexperienced. Failure to obtain forward cover against currency changes, which it may prove difficult to do for the Irish Punt for example, can result in margins being eroded or even eliminated. Some currencies in developing countries cannot be converted or exported through exchange control. Irrevocable letters of credit confirmed on a UK bank are not as good as cash (a common fallacy this for the beginner) and can be rendered void through misspellings of the names of ships or, in one case put to us, through the lack of a comma. Some agency agreements do not state that agent's commission is forfeited if the customer defaults. Most exporting firms bear the wounds of experience in these matters and the beginner is right to be wary of them.

Problems can be minimized by the careful selection of markets, as well as by the use of specialized intermediaries, especially in the early days. France was mentioned by many respondents as being a particularly difficult country to export to, requiring, for example, certificates of origin stamped by a recognized international Chamber of Commerce in addition to the CT forms used in the EC to permit free circulation of goods within EC boundaries. Some Middle East and African countries have incredibly slow and tedious border control procedures and in many cases there will be severe payment problems in these markets.

Views on export pricing were forthright from experienced successful exporters. The market sets the price and the method of pricing. If customers wanted the price CIF and in their local currency that was how they got it. One electronics exporter explained: 'If it is a regular customer, say in Germany, then if you price in sterling he will welcome that since he will assume that over time the DM will appreciate against the £ sterling. If you price in DM you have to make an allowance for the same factor. Either way he will come back to you and re-negotiate if he feels the deal has moved against him.' What exporters should not do is simply to take UK prices and add a margin for transport costs. In some cases they will be able to do better than this, in others they will be out of line with competitors unless they charge less.

The proper organization of export administration is clearly important, but the precise form this organization takes seems to be related more to the size of the firm and the volume of exports than to its relative success in exporting. For all but the largest firms, a separate export department was unusual, though it was common for one or more persons to specialize in export paperwork. Indeed, several respondents said that the separation of domestic and export sales management and administration was counter-productive. The best exporters were those that recognized that exporting was the responsibility of everyone in the company and that only at a relatively junior level of administration was specialization in exporting justified.

Export development as distinct from export administration was clearly seen in all successful exporting firms as a board level responsibility. The assessment of markets and risk, the selection of distributors, decisions on export product specifications, were too important to be left to the sales manager or export manager (if there was one) or even to the sales director. In every case, the chief executive with support from the sales or marketing director, and often the production and technical director, was involved in these decisions, and for major markets the chief executive personally carried out a major part of the work in the field. Many of our respondents did not seem to be aware how common this was and expressed surprise when we told them that their own story was repeated many times over in other companies. In all the successful exporting companies the chief executive and other board directors spent several months of the year travelling abroad. Some mentioned that in developing export markets they had been forced to neglect domestic customers at some risk to their home business.

Finance

Both exporters and non-exporters emphasized the obstacles placed in the way of exporting by financing problems, but their viewpoints were rather different. Non-exporters and passive exporters were well aware that entering the export market or increasing their export business would place heavy demands on working capital resources, but many of them, judging by the problems experienced by exporters, underestimate the difficulties. In contrast, non-exporters seem to overestimate the problems arising from credit risks and delays in payment and are not well informed about the facilities available for assisting with these problems.

The main source of increased working capital requirement in exporting is generally simply the time and money it takes to develop a new market. First, there will be heavy travelling expenses in researching the market, finding and negotiating with local representation. There may then be expenses and delay in modifying the product and perhaps in testing it for local conditions and acceptability. Examples of product changes in clothing (special collections) and medical equipment (re-engineering) were given earlier. One printer had to carry out a great deal of research to ensure that his printed material was suitable for the paper-feed and optical recognition characteristics of the equipment used by his export customer. Then it may be necessary to exhibit the product at a trade fair and certainly to show it to distributors. In some industries where product ranges are very wide (as in clothing where there may be large numbers of combinations of colours, materials, trims and sizes) or where transport costs are high (as in heavy machinery) it may be necessary to get prospective buyers to visit the factory, perhaps at the exporter's expense. All this will probably take at least a year and very often significant sales will not be made, if they are made at all, until the second or subsequent years.

Several non-exporters we talked to had embarked on this process and had given up fairly early on. One printer travelled to a Middle East country and spent several days waiting to see a buyer only to find when he got out of the waiting room and into the buyer's office that there were several people there all trying to sell different products to the same man at once! We were told several stories of distributors appointed after lengthy search or negotiation who sat on expensive consignment stock for months without selling anything or even responding to telexes. In more than one instance, distributors once appointed simply disappeared. Experiences of these kinds are quite commonplace and were recounted by exporters and non-exporters alike; the former group, however, had persisted. Only one of the non-exporters we saw who had tried to export seemed to have given up for good. The rest intended to try again, though in most cases not until they had a stronger balance sheet.

Many passive and non-exporter respondents said that the commercial clearing banks were not sympathetic to applications for loans to finance export development ahead of receipt of orders. They believed that even when orders had been secured, banks were reluctant to finance more than a proportion of the working capital requirement. This was particularly so in the clothing industry where margins are small (5–7 per cent is regarded as normal), trade credit from supplying mills tight or unavailable, and many firms habitually overtrade. But there were a few other examples in the other sectors where non — or passive exporters believed that development might be frustrated by lack of loan finance for working capital, though there were no actual cases of finance being refused.

The financing of export debtors does not in fact seem to be a serious problem for experienced exporters, though there is evidence that there are difficulties in obtaining loans for export development. On the other hand we also found cases of extreme caution on the part of borrowers. One successful non-exporting firm which had grown slowly but steadily over a 30-year period had never had *any* borrowings 'even from day one'. It seemed likely that the firm would enter the export market soon, though it had several advantages and could have done so earlier. The company's bank was 'falling over itself to lend' said the proprietor. In general, there seemed to be a widespread belief that, because of the greater risk, export development should be financed from retained earnings and not by bank overdraft.

Several experienced exporters said they had difficulties in raising working capital in the early days of export development. In several cases finance had been refused. This seems to be size related: none of the larger, profitable firms was now experiencing difficulty. One clothing firm said: 'Now that our turnover has reached £5 million, the bank is much more accommodating, but earlier on they didn't want to know'. A small and expanding publisher said that his rate of export growth was constrained by inability to raise bank finance for the development of a new series of books for an overseas market. This was because it lacked fixed assets against which the loans could be secured, though its export business was highly profitable.

Another larger firm, which had recently set up a subsidiary to handle explosive export sales growth to the United States for a technically advanced product, said that its UK bank would not lend to finance stocks and products on evaluation trials with prospective customers abroad since the assets were outside the country. At the same time the British bank's US subsidiary would not lend on the same assets without a guarantee from their client's UK parent company. Local US banks would not lend to a company without at least a three year track record in the United States. This seemed to be a case where a British bank was not able to provide a true multinational service to a smaller firm. The same company had found that a US bank in the UK was willing to sell dollars forward without the 10 per cent deposit required by the company's own bank, thus saving a substantial amount in financing costs. It seemed possible that the company might later transfer the whole of its business to that bank. Although passive and non-exporters were very apprehensive about credit risk and delays in payment from customers abroad, there were few worries about these matters among the experienced exporters, at least as far as markets in the developed world were concerned.

Credit risk assessment for customers abroad is carried out by bank and trade references and the use of credit rating agencies in much the same way as it is in the domestic market. There are several methods used by experienced exporters to minimize risk. One is to leave it to the distributor or agent, although this can obviously only be done after confidence in that person has been built up over a period of time. Another is to use credit insurance. Views were divided on the Export Credits Guarantee Department (ECGD): some firms felt it was too costly to insure all their business (which ECGD requires) in order to obtain cover for the few cases where risk was significant. Some firms felt that ECGD was too slow and the administration too time consuming, particularly for small customers. Others, however, and all of those that currently used ECGD that we talked to, were extremely satisfied with ECGD cover and would not export without it. These responses were probably largely influenced by the size of firm, type of export business carried out and the markets served. Some firms, particularly those which traded only in the USA, Japan and Europe, did not feel the need for insurance cover and had stopped using it many years ago. Some larger firms, particularly those with small unit orders, felt they could 'self-insure'.

Factoring, where the factor, instead of the exporter, obtains ECGD cover is a useful service used by several firms in our sample. The factor normally pays 80 per cent of the invoice value immediately to the exporter and charges interest at the same rate as a commercial bank plus a small premium of about 2.5per cent. Since the factor can obtain the insurance cover, this method relieves the exporter both of the credit risk and the administrative burden and simultaneously provides debtor finance. Factoring has a poor image 'People think you are going bust if you use it' said the chief executive of an electronics company and it is not widely understood, particularly among non-exporters. Confirming houses, which will also take the risk of non-payment by the customer but act for the buyer rather than the seller, perform a similar function, though they were not mentioned in any of the interviews.

In fact, only a minority of our exporter respondents found that customers abroad were slower to pay than domestic customers. A clear majority said that their customers overseas required significantly shorter credit periods on average than those at home. Only for certain developing countries, especially Nigeria, India and in Latin America, were there severe payment delays.

One well-known problem in export finance is encountered in competition from overseas suppliers in the provision of medium and long term finance for customers. This problem seems to be restricted to large unit value export business. Examples are defence or construction contracts or the supply of capital goods such as textile machinery to customers in developing countries with restricted capital markets and international payments difficulties. As such, export customer finance did not come up in any of our interviews in printing and clothing, though one electronics manufacturer mentioned it in the context of his role as a subcontractor.

Most respondents, exporters and non-exporters alike, complained about the high level of UK interest rates which they cited as an obstacle to the development of their export and domestic business alike.

Information

As might be expected, non and passive exporters complained most about information problems. For the smallest firms of this type in our survey, the problem was to know where to start. Almost all of the passive and non-exporting firms we talked to expressed an interest in developing exports, but many were inhibited from doing so by their self-confessed lack of confidence and experience, fears about the difficulties and lack of awareness of sources of information. The main needs are for information about markets and market requirements, how to find overseas representation and a whole range of detailed queries about tariffs, law, standards and regulations, translations, documentation, transport, payments and finance.

We detected a fairly clear pattern in the sources of information used and attitudes to them. At the bottom of the nursery slope, smaller non-exporters use a very wide range of sources: their friends and business acquaintances, bank, trade association, Chamber of Commerce, the trade press, libraries and, for start-ups, their enterprise agency, but put some emphasis on official sources, particularly the BOTB, in those cases where they are aware of the service it offers. A common misconception is that foreign embassies in Britain are the best place to go for information and help on export markets. Consultants and most other charged-for services are ruled out on grounds of cost. Higher up on the slope of export experience and corporate growth, firms seem to place more emphasis on personal visits to markets and on intermediaries such as forwarding houses; they also become increasingly selective about the sources of information they approach. Some continue to use the BOTB and a surprising number had used the Statistics and Market Intelligence Library.

Experienced exporters rely principally on their representatives or subsidiaries or other sources of information overseas, including foreign trade press, and on personal visits. Generally speaking, they disdain the use of official sources of information (other than statistics) and are sceptical of advice given by banks and professional advisers on export matters. The only information problems to which experienced exporters admit concern intelligence, for example on competitors' prices and forthcoming new products. All our respondents valued personal experience over everything else, and in several cases export success by proprietors was attributed to experience they had gained in export markets in earlier employment with a much larger multinational firm.

Distribution Channels

There are really only two ways of achieving export distribution on a significant scale in most sectors: one is to appoint an agent or distributor in each export market and the other is to establish a local subsidiary or joint venture. Other alternatives are direct exporting, the use of export houses and piggy-back exporting. No examples of the second and third of these alternatives were encountered in our sample. Direct exporting was, of course, the usual method employed by passive exporters, but is typically viable only for dealing with occasional orders, for goods which can be sold by direct mail or high value or contract work and lower value products which do not require after sales service.

Although some of the passive exporters used agents and some active exporters used agents in minor export territories, the principal export channels used by exporters in our sample were distributors. (Agents act on behalf of the exporter and introduces the exporter to sales opportunities against commission. Distributors operate on their own account, normally holds stocks and, unlike agents, add value to the product.) When export volume was large enough, and particularly in the electronics sector, then the preferred method was an overseas subsidiary, which allows greater control and the possibility of local production in whole or part. Several of the larger firms in our sample had experience of joint ventures with partners abroad. Some had been successful and some not. One printer found that a similar firm in a different branch of the business in Belgium proved to be an ideal partner in developing his overseas sales. However, there is a need for caution in embarking on joint ventures with actual or potential competitors.

One of the greatest difficulties in the early stages of exporting is finding the right distributor or agent. All respondents with experience agreed on that. Indeed, even if the exporter can produce an acceptable product, has the necessary finance and has mastered the administration of exporting, nothing will come of these efforts without good distribution. As mentioned, the distributor will help with information, credit risk and product modifications to suit local tastes. The distributor will promote the product and, where appropriate, handle after sales services, and plays an essential role in the whole marketing function of the exporter.

Good distributors are not easily found. A variety of methods can be used: advertising, visits to trade fairs and exhibitions, correspondence with prospects selected from directories, assistance from British embassies and the BOTB. However, success typically involves personal recommendation and personal visits and, in most cases, trial and error. One of our respondents had used a commercial intermediary to find a distributor and was satisfied with the results. Once appointed, a distributor or agent requires continuous support. All this is costly.

Languages

All the active exporting firms we talked to had staff and directors with some foreign language capability. All of them had some foreign language sales literature and agreed that importers liked to deal with people who spoke their language, however imperfectly, and that it was courtesy and good business practice to make the effort to do so. Passive and non-exporters were mostly apprehensive about their language capabilities. Several chief executives in these companies were taking language courses. Experienced exporters, however, with only one exception (a fluent French and German speaker) did not think that language was a significant obstacle to exporting. After all, day to day local contact was the prime responsibility of the distributor or agent.

Many pointed out that one advantage the British have is that English is increasingly the common language in international trade, especially in new industries like electronics. English-only speakers would suffer no disadvantage in the Low Countries, Scandinavia, and little in West Germany. Among the major markets only in Japan and France were languages of considerable importance.

Other Barriers

It might have been expected that the lack of skilled export personnel would be an obstacle to the development of exports, but the recruitment of export staff was not an issue with any of our respondents.

There was ample evidence of skill shortages at various levels in some firms, but the limiting factor was a lack of technical or industry knowledge and experience rather than of skills in export administration. It was pointed out to us several times that it was much easier to train an existing employee who was familiar with the company and its products in exporting than to train experienced export staff from another company. This was particularly so in electronics; an experienced sales engineer recruited from outside would not be productive for at least nine months unless he or she had worked for a very close competitor.

Several firms complained about delays and unnecessary complexity in the procedures for obtaining import duty drawback or VAT repayments on imports. These taxes can result in cashflow penalties for exporters. Many exporters are also importers of raw materials or semi-finished goods most of which, for example cloth or chemicals, are subject to VAT at the point of entry and, for goods of non-EC origin, customs duty also. Although inward processing relief and, for regular imports, complete suspension of customs duty where goods are re-exported within six months, are available, the regulations, we were told, are complex and not easily understood or, for small and new exporters, widely known.

The Lessons of Experience

We asked each of our respondents what they had learned from their mistakes and what advice they had for new exporters. Much of that material has been incorporated in the early parts of this section and is summarized in Appendix 3.

Conclusion

In analysing the results of our interviews we found that very clear patterns emerged. The most serious barriers to success in export markets in the tradable goods sector were not so much lack of competence as lack of knowledge, commitment and persistence within the firms themselves. Successful exporters had very different management attitudes to non- and passive exporters. In part this may reflect differences in management ability: there was an apparent tendency for almost all the most successful and rapidly expanding firms beyond about £5m in turnover to be active exporters, at least in clothing and electronics.

It would be tautological to say that successful exporters are those who have overcome the barriers to exporting, but the differences in approach between exporters and passive or non-exporters were systematically different, and different enough to indicate that chance plays little part in success.

Despite the clarity of the patterns which emerged (summarized in Appendix 3), there are obvious dangers in drawing firm conclusions from such a small sample. We were, however, sufficiently impressed with the strength of the evidence to focus our large scale postal survey on attitudinal factors and on the collection of hard statistics rather than to collect further information on the perceived difficulties of exporting.

EXPLAINING SUCCESS AND FAILURE IN EXPORTING

Why Exporters Start

Our exporter respondents were asked to select from a list the reason why they started exporting in the first place. Very clear differences emerged between active and passive exporters (Table 3.2). Forty-five per cent of active exporters started because they saw market potential abroad and this reason received far more mentions than any other. The corresponding figure for passive exporters was only 30 per cent. For them, proportionately, the most mentions were given to unsolicited orders.

The pattern of responses reveals clearly the more purposeful, aggressive attitudes of the active exporters; for example, implementation of long-term policy received twice as many mentions proportionately for active as for passive exporters, and the percentage of mentions of spare production capacity was over 2.5 times higher for passive than for active exporters. Declining domestic sales

Table 3.2: Why did exporting start?

	Percentage of all exporters	Percentage of active exporters	Percentage of passive exporters
Factor selected as most important			
Saw market potential abroad	37.92	44.70	30.37
Unsolicited inquiry/order from abroad	32.12	22.17	43.19
Implementation of long-term policy	9.22	12.01	6.12
Spare production capacity	6.83	3.91	10.07
Technological/product advantage	5.72	6.42	4.94
Declining domestic sales	3.97	5.36	2.43
Home market saturated	1.76	2.79	0.62
Encountered foreign competition in UK	1.29	1.26	1.33
Government encouragement	1.18	1.40	0.93
Total	100.00	100.00	100.00
Number of respondents	283	149	134
Non-respondents	35	11	24
Base	318	160	158

Source: Core sample, exporters only.
Question 12: Why did exporting start?

Note: This table shows the percentage of exporter respondents marking each factor as the most important. If a respondent marked more than one factor, the mark is split equally between the factors marked.

and saturation of the home market accounted for a higher proportion of mentions for active than for passive exporters, though encountering foreign competition in the UK was of little importance for either group.

How Exporters Start

Our exporting respondents were asked in a similar way to select from a list the ways in which they actually started exporting. Again, among passive exporters, unsolicited orders received by far the most mentions (Table 3.3). For active exporters, appointing overseas representation received the largest percentage of mentions — twice as many as that for passive exporters. A special sales visit and exhibition at an overseas trade fair received a much higher proportion of mentions for active than for passive exporters. Active exporters were somewhat more likely to start with a planned meeting with an overseas buyer in the UK and by acquiring equity in an overseas company, while a slightly higher percentage of passive exporters mentioned chance meetings. Market research, in contrast, received more mentions among passive than active exporters, perhaps reflecting a greater reliance on research than on personal visits to overseas territories.

Although a large proportion of all exporters mentioned initially selling direct

Table 3.3: How did exporting start?

	Percentage of all exporters	Percentage of active exporters	Percentage of passive exporters
Factor selected as most important			
Unsolicited inquiry/order from abroad	28.84	20.12	38.37
Appointed agent/distributor	18.80	24.66	12.40
Special sales visit	17.68	20.50	14.60
Exhibited at foreign trade fair	8.62	10.83	6.20
Planned meeting with overseas buyer in UK	8.23	8.74	7.69
Market research	6.84	5.84	7.95
Others	5.12	3.55	6.84
Chance meeting with overseas buyer in UK	5.10	4.70	5.56
Acquired equity in overseas company	0.75	1.09	0.39
Total	100.00	100.00	100.00
Number of respondents	270	141	129
Non-respondents	48	19	29
Base	318	160	158

Source: Core sample, exporters only.
Question 13: How did exporting start?
Note: This table shows the percentage of exporter respondents marking each factor as the most important. If a respondent marked more than one factor, the mark is split equally between the factors marked.

to customers, the proportion who did so was higher for passive exporters (Table 3.4). A much higher number of mentions was given to the use of agents and distributors by active than by passive exporters, and, in both cases, agents received more mentions than distributors at this initial stage. Considerably more active exporters mentioned the use of ECGD and the ECGD bank guarantee scheme. More passive exporters used export houses to bring their goods before the market, but none used debt factors. More active exporters used their own overseas companies or joint ventures.

Exporters were asked both for the date their company started trading and the year in which they started exporting. The interval between these two dates was surprisingly long, on average, in 58 per cent of cases it was over 10 years. However, active exporters started exporting significantly earlier, 38 per cent of them in the first five years, compared with only 20 per cent of passive exporters (Table 3.5).

Perceptions of the Difficulty and Profitability of Exporting

The difficulties of exporting are widely recognized, though perceived more acutely by passive and non-exporters than by exporters. An overwhelming proportion of respondents thought exporting to be the same or more difficult than domestic sales. Only 1 per cent, all of them active exporters, thought

Table 3.4: Methods used by new exporters

	Percentage of all exporters	Percentage of active exporters	Percentage of passive exporters
Method or methods used initially			
Sales direct to customers	64.66	60.67	69.17
Agents	38.52	46.67	29.32
ECGD insurance	30.74	36.00	24.81
Distributors	14.49	18.67	9.77
An export house	7.42	6.00	9.02
ECGD bank guarantee scheme	6.71	9.33	3.76
Own overseas company/joint venture	3.53	4.00	3.01
Debt factors	0.71	1.33	0.00
Total	166.78	182.67	148.87
Number of respondents	283	150	133
Non-respondents	35	10	25
Base	318	160	158

Source: Core sample, exporters only.
Question 14: Initially, did you use ...?
Note: This table shows the percentage of exporter respondents marking each factor.
Some respondents marked more than one factor, so the scores add up to more than 100 per cent.

Table 3.5: Lead time to export

	ALL RESPONDENTS		ACTIVE EXPORTERS		PASSIVE EXPORTERS	
	Number	Per cent	Number	Per cent	Number	Per cent
Lead time (years)						
Nil	19	7.4	13	9.6	6	4.9
1 year	12	4.7	8	5.9	4	3.3
2 years	16	6.2	13	9.6	3	2.5
3-5 years	29	11.3	18	13.3	11	9.0
6-10 years	33	12.8	16	11.9	17	13.9
Over 10 years	148	57.6	67	49.6	81	66.4
Respondents	257	100.0	135	100.0	122	100.0
Non-respondents	61		25		36	
Base	318		160		158	

Source: Core sample, exporters only.

Question 1: In what year did your present business start trading? Question 11: In about what year did your business start exporting?

exporting was easier (Table 3.6). As might be expected, the percentage of respondents thinking exporting to be more difficult fell from 91 per cent for non-exporters to 82 per cent for passive exporters and 74 per cent for active

Table 3.6: Exporting versus domestic sales (difficulty)

	All respondents Number	All respondents Per cent	Active exporters Number	Active exporters Per cent	Passive exporters Number	Passive exporters Per cent	Non-exporters Number	Non-exporters Per cent
Difficulty								
Exporting is:								
More difficult	362	81.7	119	74.4	126	81.8	117	90.7
Same	76	17.2	36	22.5	28	18.2	12	9.3
More difficult or same	438	98.9	155	96.9	154	100.0	129	100.0
Less difficult	5	1.1	5	3.1	0	0.0	0	0.0
Respondents	443	100.0	160	100.0	154	100.0	129	100.0
Non-respondents	20		0		4		16	
Base	463		160		158		145	
Profitability								
Exporting is:								
More profitable	89	20.6	39	24.5	33	21.4	17	14.3
Same/cannot distinguish	177	41.0	63	39.6	54	35.1	60	50.4
More profitable or same	266	61.6	102	64.2	87	56.5	77	64.7
Less profitable	166	38.4	57	35.8	67	43.5	42	35.3
Respondents	432	100.0	159	100.0	154	100.0	119	100.0
Non-respondents	31		1		4		26	
Base	463		160		158		145	

Source: Core sample.
Question 9: In general, how do you think exporting compares with domestic sales in difficulty and profitability?

exporters. Nearly 23 per cent of exporters thought exporting was the same as domestic sales in difficulty, more than twice the proportion for non-exporters.

Views on the comparative profitability of exporting were less clear cut. Just over 50 per cent of non-exporters thought the profitability of exporting and of domestic sales was the same or could not distinguish between the two, given their lack of experience in exporting. A sizeable proportion of active exporters, almost 40 per cent, also considered it to be the same or could not distinguish between the two, but from our personal interviews we know that this is because many active exporters consider that exporting contributes to overall profitability, even though it may be less profitable in unit terms. The percentage of respondents who thought that exporting was or could be more profitable rose from 14 per cent of non-exporters to 21 per cent of passive exporters and nearly 25 per cent of active exporters. This meant that nearly two-thirds of active exporters considered the profitability of exporting to be the same as, or indistinguishable from, domestic sales.

The Experience of Non-Exporters and Reasons for not Exporting

Fifty-five per cent of the non-exporters, spread through 10 of the 14 subsectors of manufacturing, had never tried to export, or even seriously investigated the possibility of doing so (Table 3.7). A further 20 per cent (approximately, there were a few double mentions to question 16) had investigated, but decided against exporting. Thus, approaching three-quarters of the non-exporters had

Table 3.7: Past export activities of non-exporters

	Number	Per cent
Company's past export activities		
Ceased exporting after occasional activity	28	24.8
Tried active exporting but not worth while	2	1.8
Previously successful in exporting, but no longer company policy	2	1.8
		0.0
Investigated but decided against exporting	22	19.5
Never tried to export	62	54.9
Respondents	113	102.7
Non-respondents	32	
Base	145	

Source: Core sample, non-exporters only.
Question 16: Which of these corresponds most closely to your company's past export activities?

Note: Figures add up to more than 100 per cent because of multiple responses.

not tried and failed, they had not tried at all. Twenty-five per cent of the core sample of non-exporters had ceased exporting after occasional activity and the vast majority of these were firms with a turnover of less than £5m. Of the non-exporters over that size, most had never tried to export. Although our sample of non-exporters is relatively small, it seems that many non-exporters, and particularly those at the top end of our target group, have no experience in exporting.

In selecting their reasons for not exporting, the most mentions, 32 per cent of the total, were given to 'products unsuitable for export markets' (Table 3.8). These non-exporters were to be found in all the subgroups of manufacturing, except metal manufacturing, textiles, clothing, leather and footwear, ceramics. As a percentage of respondents, this reason was given by 50 per cent or more in food, drink and tobacco, chemicals, instruments and vehicles and transport equipment (though sample sizes in these cells were low). The absolute number of firms who considered their products unsuitable for export in the sample as a whole, not just the core sample, was heavily concentrated in mechanical engineering, clothing and footwear, timber and furniture and paper and printing, all quite fragmented sectors with large numbers of smaller firms.

The next most frequent mention after product unsuitability, though far behind with 13 per cent, was 'satisfied with home market opportunities', followed by 'lack of market information' with just under 13 per cent, and a further 4 per cent mentioning difficulties in finding distributors. Respondents

Table 3.8: Reasons for not exporting

	Number	Per cent
Reason for not exporting		
Satisfied with home market opportunities	14.62	13.1
Lack of confidence/experience in exporting	11.38	10.2
Exporting unprofitable	4.17	3.7
Cannot get suitable overseas distribution	4.60	4.1
Products unsuitable for export market	35.78	31.9
Lack of export demand	8.32	7.4
Lack of production capacity	2.87	2.6
Lack of management time	10.98	9.8
Lack of finance	4.90	4.4
Lack of market information	14.38	12.8
Respondents	112	100.0
Non-respondents	33	
Base	145	

Source: Core sample, non-exporters only.
Question 17: Which one or more of the following most closely matches your reasons for not exporting?

Note: Multiple responses have been counted as fractions.

mentioning lack of marketing information were a high proportion of the total in clothing, transport equipment and metal goods, though the sample sizes were small, especially in the latter two of these sectors. Ten per cent mentioned 'lack of confidence/experience in exporting'. This last group did not lack experience in business, they were typically older firms in the whole sample, over half of them started trading over 25 years ago and none was less than 10 years old. Lack of management time and finance and production capacity received mentions, and together these resource deficiencies accounted for nearly 17 per cent of total mentions. Lack of export demand received 7 per cent of mentions.

The Keys to Success

The basic conclusion from the personal interview survey work was that it was primarily attitudinal differences that distinguished active from passive and non-exporters, rather than differences in organization or the impact of external obstacles. Question 8 in the postal survey which asked respondents to score the key factors in success in exporting on a five-point scale, was, therefore, especially important. Table 3.9 presents the overall response to this question in terms of the percentage of respondents ranking each factor first.

The first thing to remark about Table 3.9 is that although there was a good measure of agreement on the first few factors, the first three were mentioned by 52 per cent of the active exporters compared with only 42 per cent of passive and 43 per cent of non-exporters. Active exporters, it seems, have clearer cut views on what is important. For them, finding the right overseas representation is paramount, followed by commitment, confidence and persistence, and choosing the right markets. A near equal proportion of both passive and non-exporters

Table 3.9: Keys to success in exporting

	Percentage of all respondents	Percentage of active exporters	Percentage of passive exporters	Percentage of non-exporters
Most important factor				
Finding the right agents or distributors	17.55	22.22	14.96	15.46
Choosing the right export market(s)	15.21	14.72	14.94	16.04
Being committed, confident and persistent	12.81	15.18	11.82	11.37
Reducing costs to match foreign competition	9.30	6.58	12.06	9.03
Understanding customers and competitors	9.22	9.53	10.70	7.17
Getting sound outside initial advice	6.94	5.01	5.67	10.51
Modifying products/packaging for market	6.61	5.73	4.50	10.03
Using fast communications (telex/fax)	5.38	5.25	5.74	5.09
Having foreign language abilities	4.65	3.25	6.40	4.15
Taking a long view on costs and returns	3.39	3.63	3.35	3.18
Coping with transport, customs & payments	3.19	3.11	3.30	3.13
Recruiting experienced export staff	2.95	2.55	3.66	2.58
Training existing staff	2.65	3.17	2.77	1.94
Respondents	394	132	141	121
Non-respondents	69	28	17	24
Base	463	160	158	145

Source: Core sample.
Question 8: Whether you export or not, what would you say are the keys to success in exporting?

Note: This table shows the percentage of respondents marking each factor as the most important. If a respondent marked more than one factor the mark is split equally between the factors marked.

mentioned choice of distribution and markets. Commitment fell in fourth position for passive exporters and received only 1 per cent more mentions than understanding customers. For non-exporters, although commitment came third, it was only narrowly ahead of several other factors.

The measure of agreement on the importance of some other factors was also interesting. A smaller proportion of active exporters gave reducing costs as their first choice, especially compared with passive exporters who seem to give less weight to marketing factors. Both active and passive exporters made fewer mentions of getting sound initial advice than did non-exporters (reflecting confidence in their own judgement). Foreign language abilities were first choice for twice as many passive as active exporters and there were somewhat fewer mentions of technical matters and recruitment problems among active exporters, who give more emphasis to training existing staff.

There were similar percentages of mentions of the use of fast communications. Twice as many non-exporters as exporters gave modification of products as a first choice. This is, of course, consistent with the large proportion who mentioned product unsuitability as their reason for not exporting. In most instances, differences are quite small (and often not statistically significant) though in general they support the conclusions reached in the personal interview phase of the study. An examination of the rankings in a few subsectors did not suggest major differences at that level.

ASSISTING SMALLER EXPORTERS

The Justification for Intervention

Success in export markets is often important for the achievement of individual objectives at the level of the firm, but it is also of great importance in the achievement of national and international economic objectives. The great expansion of world trade in the post-World War II period, through allowing countries to specialize in those activities in which they have a comparative advantage, has helped to raise standards of living everywhere. For those smaller countries with limited internal markets, such as Switzerland and Scandinavia, exports have been essential in achieving and maintaining high standards of living. Export growth played a vital role in the industrial revolution in Britain in the nineteenth century, in West Germany and Japan in the 1950s and 1960s and in the newly industrialized countries such as Hong Kong and Singapore in the 1970s. In all these cases, smaller firms also played a crucial role in economic development.

In all countries governments have adopted measures to promote exports within (and sometimes outside of) the scope of international agreements to reduce barriers to trade and eliminate unfair competition in the form of subsidies. Most economists are agreed that trade barriers and subsidies, except possibly in the short run, reduce welfare. Intervention to promote exports, if any, must take other forms dependent on the identification of imperfections in internal markets which obstruct shifts of resources into exports. Measures to assist particular groups of firms must be justified by the same type of argument.

There has been extensive and continuing discussion in Britain about the case for promoting small business, particularly since the publication of the Report of the Committee of Inquiry on Small Firms in 1971 (Bolton Committee, 1971). Opinion began to shift in favour of intervention in this field with the Committee's discovery that the small firm sector was declining and was relatively smaller in Britain than in other countries. The reversal of that decline with the onset of slower economic growth, faster inflation and rising unemployment around 1970 was later followed by a second discovery, that of the major role which small firms play in employment creation in all countries. More recently still, there has been a growing realization of the ways in which some aspects of public policy, particularly taxation and regulation, distort capital markets and place greater relative burdens on small firms than on larger firms. Reducing these distortions and burdens can only help to promote exports, although these barriers are not specific to exporting and are outside our terms of reference.

Market Imperfections

This study has found evidence of three sets of obstacles to the realization of the untapped export potential which we have concluded exists among smaller manufacturing firms in our target group (and probably also in other firms and other sectors). The first and second — and probably most important — of these obstacles lie in what we are calling imperfections in the *market for information.* Although many passive and non-exporting firms would like to develop export business, they were deterred from doing so either by uninformed fears about the difficulties or by an inability to obtain the necessary information even though, as we shall show, some were willing to pay for it. There are, therefore, two more or less distinct aspects to the information problem. The first and prior difficulty is lack of awareness of the nature of exporting and the real character of the difficulties in entering export markets. We have been able to show that many of the problems that deter passive and non-exporters from developing export business, for example fears about delays in payments, lack of skill in languages, the complexities of export procedures, are either unjustified or relatively easily overcome. The second difficulty is that inexperienced exporters do not know how to go about exporting, for example how to select distributors, use intermediaries, do not appreciate the importance of selecting markets, winning customer confidence and so on and do not know where to seek specific information.

The third set of obstacles to the expansion of exports by smaller firms is concerned with imperfections in *capital markets.* These problems are less widespread than those to do with information, and because of this and the extreme pressure of space in our postal questionnaire, we did not attempt to investigate them more fully in the second phase of our study. Moreover, postal questionnaires have only limited effectiveness for investigating problems in small business finance. Five per cent of non-exporters gave lack of finance as a reason for not exporting (see Table 3.8). We have no indication of how many passive exporters are limited in their export development by problems in finance, but our personal interviews indicate that their number will be significant.

From these interviews, it was certainly clear that lack of finance was an obstacle to export development for both exporters and non-exporters. It is not easy to interpret this, however, since finance limitations may be the result of a number of factors both internal and external to the firm. We list these factors below (not necessarily in order of importance):

1 lack of a well-researched and presented case;

2 an inadequate profit or credit record;

3 an inappropriate capital structure (insufficient equity);

4 lack of knowledge of the available sources of capital;

5 unwillingness to pay the market rate;

6 unwillingness to borrow;

7 unwillingness to consider raising external equity to finance export led expansion.

There are also capital market imperfections which could lead to:

8 commercially unjustified discrimination against small firms in collateral security requirements, in interest rates or in other loan terms and conditions;
9 insufficient suppliers of equity finance in amounts below £100,000–£150,000, perhaps arising from the operating costs of larger institutions.

We suspect that all these factors are at work and that the problem of export finance has two more or less distinct elements. The first is (again) lack of information among smaller firms about the facilities available and how to approach financial institutions, that is to say deficiencies in knowledge and perception on the part of smaller firms; and the second, deficiencies in financial institutions.

NOTES

1 These figures relate to VAT registered traders, which include mainly firms with a turnover of £18,000 or more, though many firms with a lower turnover register voluntarily. Some firms are not liable to register for VAT. We have excluded firms where it was not known if they exported or not; most of those excluded are probably non-exporters so the percentages given above will be overestimates.

2 It is interesting that the study of small firms in the United States (National Federation of Independent Business, 1985) found that exporting manufacturers are much larger on average than non-exporters and that regular exporters were larger than occasional exporters.

APPENDIX 1: THE EXPORT POTENTIAL

The Factors Affecting Export Demand

The purpose of this appendix is to demonstrate the scope for increased exports of manufactures which could be achieved by raising the export ratios of smaller non-and passive exporters nearer to the levels obtained by active exporters. This is a supply-side study at a high level of aggregation and we have not, of course, been able to assess at the micro level of the individual firm or sector whether or not unexploited potential exists for new or increased exports by smaller British firms. To do this would require extensive market research of export markets across the whole of manufacturing, which is hardly practicable. Even then there would be great difficulties arising from the need to assess the ability of firms to adapt their products to local requirements abroad where these differed from those in the domestic market.

There is also the question of the price-competitiveness of UK exporters. We would argue that the influence of exchange rates on exports has been overstated in the past and the importance of quality, design and service neglected. After all, countries with continuously appreciating currencies like West Germany and Switzerland have not found their parities an obstacle to increasing exports. As so often in economic questions, the direction of causality between export success and exchange rates is not obvious and other factors, notably capital movements, play a role in determining both. This question may, in any event, be less apposite in assessing the export potential for small firms, many of which operate in niche markets, than for large firms.

Certainly the scope for exports generally is growing. Over a long period the growth in world trade has been very much faster than the growth of world production. According to the GATT Secretariat (General Agreement on Tariffs and Trade, 1983) world exports of all commodities in volume terms grew at a rate 50 per cent faster than production, even in the period of slower output growth which began in the early 1970s. World trade in services has grown somewhat faster than world trade in commodities; according to figures published by the British Invisible Exports Council (BIEC), the percentage of invisible trade to total world trade on a payments basis rose from 26.2 per cent in 1969 to 27.6 per cent in 1984.

As a result, exports of goods and services have been increasing as a proportion of the gross domestic product (GDP) in most advanced countries. Although higher in the exceptional period after World War II, UK exports of goods and services were 18.6 per cent of GDP in 1964 (of which services 4.9 per cent). By 1974, UK exports had greatly exceeded 1950s levels at 27.4 per cent and by 1985 they accounted for 29.1 per cent of GDP (services 6.9 per cent) (Central Statistical Office, 1986).

These trends have been reflected both in an increase in import penetration of the domestic market for manufactures and in the export ratios of UK manufacturers. Import penetration rose from 30.5 per cent in the 12 months ending September 1983 to 34.7 per cent in the corresponding period ending September 1985. The export ratio of UK manufacturers rose from 26.6 to 30.5 in the same period (*British Business*, 1986). Data by sector of manufacturing from the same source show that there is a clear tendency for higher import penetration to be associated with higher export ratios.

In our postal questionnaire survey, 79 per cent of active exporters acknowledged competition from imports in the domestic market compared with 55 per cent of non-exporters. Within our sample, export ratios were increasing. Among all respondents, for example, the percentage of exporters had risen from 32 to 36 per cent over the past three years. Over the same period, the percentage of respondents exporting over 50 per cent of turnover had increased from 7.5 to 10.0 per cent.

Future Export Intentions and Scope

The number of exporters seems set to continue to increase. Almost two-thirds of non-exporting respondents in the core sample indicated that they intended to export at some time in the future. It is especially encouraging that the proportion of young firms intending to export was particularly high (Table A1.1). Non-exporters intending to export were to be found in all subsectors of manufacturing, but the sample size was too small to permit analysis at that level of detail.

The VAT figures in Table A2.4 (p.56) indicate that there are over 6,000 non-exporting firms in manufacturing with a turnover in the £1m–£10m size band. After correcting for unequal response rates, we estimate that there are about 3,750 passive exporters in the same group. Despite the size-related nature of export activity, all sizes of firm were represented among active, passive and non-exporters.

Table A1.1: Intention to export in future (non-exporters)

	Yes		No		Total	
	Number	Per cent of age group	Number	Per cent of age group	Number	Per cent of age group
Age of business (years)						
0 - 2	0	0.0	0	0.0	0	100.0
3 - 5	5	100.0	0	0.0	5	100.0
6 - 10	5	55.6	4	44.4	9	100.0
11 - 20	26	76.5	8	23.5	34	100.0
21 - 40	28	66.7	14	33.3	42	100.0
over 40	23	53.5	20	46.5	43	100.0
Respondents	87	65.4	46	34.6	133	100.0
Non-respondents	3		3		6	
Base	90		49		139	

Source: Core sample.
Question 18: Do you intend to export some time in the future?

There are probably over 550 passive exporters with a turnover of £5 million or more in our target group and some 600 non-exporters in the same size bracket. Many of these firms in this upper half of our target group in particular should have more realizable export potential.

Several ways of using our data to identify sectors in which there is particular scope for improvement in export performance suggest themselves, though in all cases it has to be borne in mind that our sample sizes are low and the sectors very broad. The following analysis is restricted to the activities of exporters (active and passive, we separate them out later, however) on the grounds that exporters have proved that their products are acceptable to at least some overseas buyers.

In Table A1.2 we show the average export ratios, unweighted by turnover, of the exporting respondents by sector (column 2) which range from 15 per cent in paper, printing and publishing to 32 per cent in instruments, electrical and electronics. The range of maximum and minimum export ratios within each sector is very much larger than between sectors (columns 5 and 6). Column 7 of Table A1.2 gives the ratio of export penetration to import penetration as measured by the official statistics from *British Business* (1986). Where the number in column 7 is greater than 1 this indicates that the export ratio is greater than the import penetration, and where it is less than 1 imports take a larger share of home demand than exports take of domestic output. On these two grounds there is evidence of plenty of scope for improved export performance; the gap between the best and worst export performance is large in all 14 sectors and in only 3 of the 13 sectors for which data are available does the export ratio exceed the import penetration.

Columns 5 and 6, however, measure extremes which could be isolated instances. A more helpful measure for our purpose is the standard deviation which is a statistical measure of dispersion about the mean (column 3). In column 4 the standard deviation is given as a ratio of the mean. The higher the number in column 4 the greater is the dispersion of export ratios of firms within the sector and apparently the greater the overall scope in that sector for improving export performance.

There seems to be particular scope in timber and furniture, paper, printing and publishing, and clothing, leather and footwear where there is wide dispersion of export ratios and

Table A1.2: Analysis of average export ratio of exporters by sector

	(1) Number in sample	(2) Mean export ratio	(3) Standard deviation	(4) Ratio of SD:mean	(5) Maximum	(6) Minimum	(7) Export/import ratio
Sector							
Food, drink & tobacco	17	23.71	16.09	0.68	50	2	0.58
Chemical industry	27	26.96	22.56	0.84	75	2	1.21
Metal manufacturing	10	20.50	21.48	1.05	80	2	0.88
Mechanical engineering	125	29.90	24.28	0.81	90	1	1.19
Instruments, electrical and electronics	83	31.90	24.28	0.76	90	2	0.89
Vehicles and other transport equipment	20	29.60	26.58	0.90	75	1	0.95
Metal goods n.e.s.	66	20.77	21.79	1.05	90	1	1.14
Textiles	36	21.97	19.33	0.88	84	2	0.73
Clothing, leather, footwear	47	20.89	21.52	1.03	85	1	0.53
Timber and furniture	19	18.95	18.98	1.00	67	2	0.19
Paper, printing, publishing	28	14.86	17.61	1.19	84	1	0.50
Ceramics, glass and other non-metallic products	19	24.26	10.87	0.45	50	5	N/A
Rubber and plastics	40	17.15	18.14	1.06	85	2	0.88
Other manufacturing	13	28.92	25.43	0.88	84	2	0.74
Total	577	25.01	22.63	0.90	90	1	
Unclassified	17	26.88	29.27	1.09	90	2	
Base	567	25.07	22.86	0.91	90	1	0.88

Source: All respondents which were exporters in 1986.

export/import ratios are well below average, but metal manufacture and textiles also suggest themselves. It will be noticed that most of the sectors identified might be described as 'low technology' sectors, but these are sectors perhaps where more firms need to move up market to escape import competition and exploit niche markets with high value-added products overseas. Obviously there is scope in all other sectors and particularly in those where the world market is expanding rapidly such as in electronics.

The Implications of Higher Export Ratios in the Target Group

From our sample, we estimate that the total annual value of exports of manufactures by firms in the £1m–£10m size band (including subsidiaries) was £4.4 billion to mid-1985, about 9 per cent of total UK manufacturing exports. Widespread improvements in the export performance of firms in this group could, therefore, have quite a significant impact on total UK exports. To assess what this impact could be, we have calculated the increase in exports that would be achieved if the average export ratios of passive exporters in the group could be raised to equal those of active exporters. On these assumption, exports would have been £5.2 billion higher, an increase of 117 per cent. This increase compares with a total non-oil deficit on visible account of £10.2 billion in 1985.

While no doubt an upper limit of what is achievable, it will be noted that the scope for increased exports has been calculated on the basis of an assumed improvement in the export performance of passive exporters alone. These are firms for which there is evidence that their products already have achieved at least limited acceptance in overseas markets. There will also be scope for exports among at least some non-exporters. If we assume that the export ratios of non-exporters — excluding those that gave product unsuitability as a reason for not exporting — could be raised to equal those of passive exporters, however, then exports of the target group as a whole would increase by only £0.6 billion.

APPENDIX 2: FIELD WORK

The Personal Interviews

Details of the personal interview sample are shown in Table A2.1. The sampling frame was the Market Location (ML) Ltd Database. ML were asked to produce a random selection of 200 names and addresses of firms in the target group in the three selected geographical areas and within specified Standard Industrial Classification (SIC) groups (electronic components and capital equipment; men's and women's outerwear, jobbing printing and book printers and publishers). Selections were made at random from these lists within geographical clusters. There were very few refusals. Six firms were selected by other means, including export award lists and the services of local chambers of commerce. Interviews were mainly carried out between 12 and 28 May 1986.

The Main Postal Questionnaire Survey

The ML Database does not include information on turnover, but the target group could be identified approximately from numbers employed using factors for turnover per employee supplied to us by the Business Statistics Office. The resulting numbers of firms tallied well with numbers of firms by turnover range shown in the VAT statistics (see p.561). Questionnaires were mailed to a random 25 per cent sample of manufacturing firms in the (estimated) turnover range of £1m–£10m.

After a follow-up reminder, a total of 920 questionnaires were returned, a response rate of 31 per cent. Of the returned questionnaires 848 (28 per cent of those sent out) were in time to be included in the analysis for this report (see p.245 for a description of the various subsamples analysed). On the assumption that 50 per cent of the population of firms surveyed were exporters (based on the VAT statistics) instead of the 31 per cent indicated by the actual responses, we can

Table A2.1: Personal interview sample

	North-west			London			Dorset/Hants			Total
	A	B	C	A	B	C	A	B	C	
CLOTHING										
Active			1		2	1				4
Passive	2		1		2	1				6
Non-				3						3
Total										13
ELECTRONICS										
Active		1				2			4	7
Passive	1			2	2					5
Non-							1			1
Total										13
PRINTING										
Active				1	1		1			3
Passive	1				2	1	1			5
Non-	1							1	1	3
Total										11
Others										4
Total	5	1	2	6	9	5	3	1	5	37 41

Note: A = Turnover under £1m.
B = Turnover between £1m and £5m.
C = Turnover over £5m.

calculate that the response rate from exporters (for those analysed) was nearly 40 per cent, while that for non-exporters was only 17 per cent. Table A2.2 compares the percentage of all respondents and non-exporters by sector with those in the population. It can be seen that, except for coal and petroleum products and vehicles, all subsectors of manufacturing are represented in the sample though the absolute numbers are very small in some sectors, while non-exporters are under-represented in all sectors except paper and printing. For these reasons, we have been very cautious in drawing conclusions at the subsector level.

In Table A2.3 we have reweighted the responses for the core sample so that non-exporters represent 50 per cent of the number of respondents. In this table we have not reweighted the proportions of active and passive exporters to allow for unequal response.

The Small Business Research Trust Postal Questionnaire Survey

The Small Business Research Trust carries out a regular quarterly survey of small business in all sectors of the economy. In the seventh survey, carried out in April 1986, questions were included on export activity (see Small Business Research Trust, 1986, for details). Well over 90 per cent of respondents to the regular SBRT surveys have a turnover of below £1m. In this survey, responses from 1,052 small firms were analysed, of which 266 were exporters, 104 of them in manufacturing.

Table A2.2: Sectoral analysis of sample (1986) and population (1983–4)

SIC code	Sector	Percentage of Core sample	Percentage of Total population	Percentage of non-exporters in sample	Percentage of non-exporters in population
41,42	Food, drink & tobacco	5.0	9.7	73.9	83.5
	Coal and petroleum products	NIL	0.4	NIL	67.3
25	Chemical industry	3.7	5.0	17.6	33.6
22	Metal manufacturing	1.1	3.5	20.0	43.4
32	Mechanical engineering	18.6	15.5	23.5	38.5
33,34,37	Instruments, electrical and electronics	13.2	9.4	21.7	33.3
35	Shipbuilding, boatbuilding etc.	5.0	1.1	34.8	50.8
36	Vehicles		1.8		44.4
31	Metal goods n.e.s.	12.5	9.8	31.6	41.9
43	Textiles incl.man-made fibres	8.1	7.0	16.2	37.5
44,45	Clothing, leather, footwear	8.8	6.5	30.0	43.6
46	Timber and furniture	6.8	6.7	54.8	76.7
47	Paper, printing, publishing	6.8	11.6	67.7	68.0
24	Ceramics, glass and other non-metallic products	2.0	2.6	11.1	59.8
48	Rubber and plastics	6.4	4.2	20.7	42.7
49	Other manufacturing	2.0	5.2	NIL	41.8
	Classified respondents	100.0	100.0	30.9	50.2

Source: Sample = core sample plus subsidiaries; Population = H M Customs & Excise VAT Statistics.

Table A2.3: Analysis of respondents by turnover size, weighted

	ACTIVE EXPORTERS Number	ACTIVE EXPORTERS Per cent	PASSIVE EXPORTERS Number	PASSIVE EXPORTERS Per cent	NON-EXPORTERS Number	NON-EXPORTERS Per cent	ALL RESPONDENTS Number	ALL RESPONDENTS Per cent
£1 - 3 million	57	50.0	66	57.0	159	68.3	282	
Per cent of row	20.2		23.4		56.4			100.0
£3 - 5 million	31	26.3	32	27.8	49	21.4	112	
Per cent of row	27.7		28.6		43.7			100.0
£5 - 7 million	16	13.8	15	12.7	14	6.2	45	
Per cent of row	35.6		33.3		31.1			100.0
£7 - 10 million	12	10.0	3	2.5	9	4.1	24	
Per cent of row	50.0		12.5		37.5			100.0
Total	116	100.0	116	100.0	231	100.0	463	
Per cent of row	25.0		25.0		50.0			100.0

Source: Core sample reweighted from VAT statistics to adjust for low response from non-exporters.

Table A2.4: Number of UK exporters and non-Exporters by VAT trade classification and turnover size, Sept 1983–Aug 1984

	Turnover less than £1m	Turnover £1m - £10m	Turnover £10m - £100m	Turnover over £100m	Not known	Total
Number of exporters in turnover band						
Agriculture etc.	826	46	6	0	45	923
Mining and quarrying	16	29	13	13	7	78
Manufacturing industry	14,459	6,011	1,254	154	2,389	24,267
Construction	961	284	55	12	175	1,487
Transport and communications	1,769	360	69	15	488	2,701
Distributive trades	17,252	3,876	530	84	2,922	24,664
Services	13,590	1,729	392	124	2,728	18,560
Utilities, public administration	2	9	5	4	-	20
All exporters	48,875	12,344	2,324	406	8,754	72,700
Number of non-exporters in turnover band						
Manufacturing Industry	90,497	6,052	752	61	27,091	124,453
Other Sectors	1,050,918	27,781	2,925	474	241,533	1,323,631
All non-exporters	1,141,415	33,833	3,677	535	268,624	1,448,084

Source: H M Commissioners of Customs and Excise.

Table A2.5: Self-classification as exporters

	All respondents Number	Per cent
Occasional	103	32.6
Experienced	117	37.0
Expanding	97	30.7
Declining	15	4.7
Respondents	316	105.1

Source: Core sample
Question 10: How would you classify your company as an exporter?

Note: Percentages add up to more than 100 because 16 respondents marked more than one answer. Of these, 12 marked both Experienced and Expanding.

Table A2.6: Export percentages now and three years ago

	This year Number	Per cent	Three years ago Number	Per cent
Nil	154	32.2	173	36.1
1 - 10%	131	27.3	131	27.3
11 - 20%	60	12.5	60	12.5
21 - 30%	38	7.9	37	7.7
31 - 40%	36	7.5	21	4.4
41 - 50%	12	2.5	21	4.4
Over 50%	48	10.0	36	7.5
Respondents	479	100.0	479	100.0

Source: Core sample.
Question 5: What percentage of sales, if any, comes from exports (1) currently, (3) three years ago?

APPENDIX 3: PROFILES OF ATTITUDES OF SUCCESSFUL AND LESS SUCCESSFUL EXPORTERS

Key Issues

	Successful	**Less successful**
Finding right distributors	Regard this as *the* prime issue. Board director involvement in vetting	Respond to inquiries Expect distributors to be found easily via directories, embassies, etc.
Commitment to export	Regard exporting as inevitable and necessary in a growing business. Persistent, professional and go forward to their customers. Concern of whole company.	Insular, unprofessional, unaware of issues. Exporting seen as solution to problem and concern of part of company only.
Learn by doing	Assume responsibility for building in-house expertise on the whole process of exporting. Automatically assume mistakes will be made.	Overwhelmed by early obstacles and blame others. Defeatist.
Selectivity in markets	Ranking process according to rational criteria, progressive focus.	Spreads effort too thinly, go for high cost/risk markets too soon, e.g. France, US. Restrict efforts to passive response to unsolicited inquiries.
Financial investment	Prepared to look at projected returns on long-term basis.	Exporting seen as gamble with spare cash. Short-term view.
Long-term horizon	Several years effort necessary to lay foundations for solid success. Expect hiccoughs.	Expect quick results with meagre resources.
Confidence	Do not export until confident of success. Control growth	Start too soon in haphazard way. Take on too much.

Respect for customer	Assumes the customer will be at least as good at business as you are. Careful study of customer's needs and sensitivity to them.	Adopts take it or leave it attitude. Underestimates the customer.
Attitudes to intermediaries	Use advisers at start of export process, but thereafter only very selectively	Either over- or under-rely on external advice. Insufficient range of potential advice sought.
Fast communications	Use telephone, fax, telex, electronic mail as appropriate.	Rely on letters. Unaware of importance of speed of response.

Less Important Issues

	Successful	**Less successful**
Languages	Simply part of looking after the customer. Normal in-house skill.	Overestimate importance leading to excessive timidity or ignore altogether.
Credit risk	Regard as no worse than domestic in general. Use of ECGD, letter of credit, proper investigation etc. Obvious exceptions (some Less Developed Countries (LDCs)).	Fear of risk prevents action.
Export documentation and procedures	No problem to professional. Handled expertly in-house or by forwarding agent externally.	Lack of professional approach: tries to cut corners.
Export pricing	Accepts that market determines the price and exporter has to control costs. Quote in foreign currency where customer requires it. Hedge if necessary. Aware of volume/unit cost relationships.	Inflexible attitude. Tries to price at UK levels plus freight. Worries about currency problems.
Export staff recruitment	Good people can be trained in house.	Believe good people are very difficult to find and prohibitively expensive
Technical standards/legal systems	Can be a non-tariff barrier but usually surmountable.	Overestimate importance.
Organization of export function	May have separate export organization or not, but whole company committed to export. Usually separate staff handle detailed documentation.	Exporting not integrated sufficiently with total business.
Payment delays	Generally similar or Believed to be a better than UK. Some exceptions (LDCs).	Believed to be a high cost of exporting

REFERENCES

Bannock, Graham (1984), *Surveys of Forum Members*, Forum of Private Business, Washington DC.

Bolton Committee (1971), *Small Firms*, Report of the Committee of Inquiry on Small Firms, HMSO, London.

British Business (1986), *Import penetration and export performance for September 1985*, *British Business*, 8 August.

British Invisible Exports Council, *World Invisible Trade, BIEC,* Successive editions
British Overseas Trade Board (1986), *Bringing More Manfacturers into Active Exporting,* HMSO, London.
Cannon, T. and Willis, M. (1982), *The Smaller Firm in Overseas Trade,* European Small Business Journal.
Central Statistical Office (CSO) (1986), *United Kingdom National Accounts,* HMSO, London.
Financial Times (1986), *The Top 100 Exporters 1985,* Financial Times, London. (These figures drawn from company accounts are not strictly comparable with the other data used and include re-exports).
General Agreement on Tariffs and Trade (1983), *International Trade 1982-83,* GATT.
Hannah, Leslie and Kay, John (1977), Quoted in *Concentration in Modern Industry,* Macmillan, London.
National Federation of Independent Business (NFIB) (1985), *Small Business in Export Markets,* National Federation of Independent Business, Washington DC.
NMB (1979), *Export Promotion and Medium Sized and Small Companies,* NMB, The Netherlands.
Pickett, Shirley et al (1983), *Small Firm Exporter Survey,* for SITPRO.
Prais, S.J. (1976), *The Evolution of Giant Firms in Britain,* Cambridge University Press.
Small Business Research Trust (SBRT) (1986[a]), *Quarterly Survey of Small Business in Britain,* Vol 2, no 1.
Small Business Research Trust (SBRT) (1986[b]), *Quarterly Survey of Small Business in Britain,* Vol 2, no 2.

Chapter 4

NEW BUSINESS FORMATION, UNEMPLOYMENT AND THE ROLE OF SMALL BUSINESS IN ECONOMIC GROWTH*

The past 15 years have seen a major expansion in the volume of research on small business. We know a great deal more about small firms, demography, financing, the problems they face, management and training issues, their role in innovation and employment creation, their use of part-time workers and many other things. Very little work, however, has been done on what might be called the macro-economics of the small business sector (is that a contradiction?) and on the role of that sector in the process of economic growth. The growing recognition that economic growth requires continuous structural adjustment, and that this in turn requires a lowering of institutional, regulatory and social barriers to change (the shift in emphasis from demand to supply-side economics), has not been reflected in any really fundamental reassessment of the role of small firms.

Yet the accumulating body of research on small business raises many questions about the role of small firms that have yet to be asked, let alone answered. We know, for example, that small firms are very efficient users of resources: they achieve high rates of return on capital in relation to large firms and they survive in all countries in large numbers in competition with large firms in all but the most large scale capital intensive industries (Bannock, 1981[a]). Regular surveys, such as those carried out by the Confederation of British Industry (Ancrum, 1985), show that small firms compared with larger firms have 'maintained their capacity at more efficient levels, responded to economic recovery earlier and adapted more quickly to changing business conditions'. These surveys also bear out one of the key distinguishing features of small business: their capital constraints. Small business, it has been shown, is a much more efficient user of research and development (R&D) resources than are large firms and accounts for a disproportionate number of innovations.

Why is it then that the share of small firms in employment and output, and in many countries the total number of firms, declined in the long post-World War

* A paper presented to the 30th Annual World Conference of the International Council for Small Business, Montreal, June 1985.

II economic boom? Why is it that, since that sustained period of economic growth ended in the earlier 1970s, the numerical importance of small business has been increasing again? Now that in Japan (where the small business sector did not decline) and the United States and more latterly elsewhere, economic growth has been resumed, will we once again see a renewed decline in the small business sector? Another interesting question is, does the major role of small business in job creation, demonstrated first in the UK by Gudgin and subsequently Gallagher and later by Birch in the USA, simply reflect a temporary phenomena not seen in earlier periods and do basic changes in economic structure (the shift to services) and technology affect the role of small firms or is that role largely independent of these changes (Birch, 1979; Fothergill and Gudgin, 1979; Gallagher and Stewart, 1984)? Are there, in short, any economic laws of permanent validity about the role of small firms in long-term economic growth?

The purpose of this paper is not to attempt to answer these questions but simply to pose them and remind the reader of some of the previous research which is relevant. My real object is to stimulate interest in this neglected but vitally important branch of our subject.

There have been three obstacles to the development of thought on the macro-economics of small business, two of them have diminished and continue to diminish. The third remains. (I do not include lack of research funds — literally millions of pounds are available for research on macro-economics of the conventional kind but very little for the subject of this paper.[1])

The first obstacle to research has been the unavailability of statistics. I need not elaborate on this. For well known reasons all small business statistics are poor. Some progress has, in recent years, been made in the use of commercial databases. The Small Business Administration (SBA) is also laying the groundwork for future researchers in its Small Business Database Project while private organizations like the Forum of Private Business, the National Federation of Independent Business (NFIB), the Canadian Federation of Independent Business (CFIB) and the Small Business Research Trust are quietly accumulating data which will eventually prove to be of considerable value.

The second obstacle to research progress in this field has been that small business has for too long been looked on more as an alternative to big business, rather than as complementary to it. We have regarded small firms as more efficient, more innovative, more likely to promote competition and more likely to create jobs than large firms and therefore something to be promoted at the expense of large firms. It is as if more output by small business would result in less by big business. If we list the relative strengths of large and small firms, we can see that they are actually complementary:

Small firms	*Large firms*
Local	International
Client tailored products and services	Market tailored products and services

Specialist	Conglomerate
Innovation	Diffusion
Labour intensive	Capital intensive

In fact, small businesses carry out services which it would not be economic for large firms to perform and as a generalization we can say that they do not compete directly. If and when a small business innovates in an area with mass-market potential, either the firm will grow to exploit that potential or, more commonly, the firms or the idea will be taken over and exploited on a large scale by a big firm. Sometimes innovation — as distinct from invention — will only be possible for a large firm; photocopiers were invented by a small firm and commercialized by a large one, for example.

The dynamic function of large firms is to reduce the labour content of mass-marketed consumer products, processes and services and major capital goods, and by so doing to create the increased added value per employee which generates the higher incomes and more diversified demand that leads to more opportunities for small firms.

The interaction between small and large firms is a two-way process. Small firms are both customers of large firms and important subcontractors to large firms. Indeed, in a less well-known way, much of the so-called deindustrialization in the advanced countries (the shift to services) actually represents a spinning-off of specialized functions from large firms to small. Gershuny (1978) has shown how much of the growth of services is, in fact, manufacturing related — factory cleaning, recycling waste products, computer software services, consultancy, R&D, marketing services and business services generally represent work carried out by small businesses in the service sector which was previously carried out by large firms in the manufacturing sector. Even within US manufacturing, which is an increasingly information-intensive sector, at least half of new jobs created between 1969 and 1979 were white collar jobs (Kirkland, 1985). The third obstacle to the development of thought on the macro-economic role of small business has been the adoption of perspectives which have been too short and too policy oriented.

We discuss the role of small business in growth as if it were a new problem and as if small business did not provide a major driving force for the first industrial revolution in the nineteenth century, and indeed for the development of the newly industrialized countries (NICs) in the 1960s.

The recent interest in employment creation has done a great service to the cause of small business by demonstrating that small firms create jobs, but it has done little to help our understanding of the role of small business from the longer term point of view of this paper. The contribution of small firms to employment creation in the 1970s (the period to which the employment change studies were mainly confined) largely, though not wholly, reflects the shift to service industries that was going on rapidly at that time.

As mentioned, much of this shift was probably an intersectoral movement from manufacturing. This process might not last as certain services become more capital intensive. (There are reports from the USA that the capital stock per employee is already higher in the service sector than in the manufacturing sector (Kirkland, 1985).) If this happens, will small businesses cease to be regarded as important to the economy?

The value of a longer term perspective is suggested by the fact that there do, in fact, seem to be long-term ebbs and flows in the quantitative weight of small business in the economy. In analysing these, we are greatly hampered by lack of long-term data series. Work by Prais (1976),[2] however, together with more recent information, enables us to see that the share of small business in employment and output in the UK and the USA has probably gone through the very approximate phases:

Period	*Share of Small Business*
1910–35	Downward
1936–50	Upward
1951–70	Downward
1971–	Upward

I will not, in a brief and largely non-technical paper of this kind, spell out all the many qualifications that need to be attached to the above information. However, it is clear that in the post-war period, the small business sector actually increased in weight during the period of stagflation from the 1970s onwards and decreased in the earlier period of sustained economic growth.

This weight increased during the World War II period when the growth experience of the UK and the USA was rather different and fell during 1910–35, which was a mixed period which included the recessions of the 1920s and 1930s.

An econometric study by Johnson and Darnell (1978) for the period from 1950 to the early 1970s found, in fact, that new business formation was positively and closely related to the unemployment rate. In other words, new business formation tended to increase when unemployment increased and vice-versa. Data for the United States suggest that over the same period there was a similar relationship between the number of business concerns (i.e. not new business formations but the number net of failures) and the unemployment rate.

The figures for the pre-war period show some evidence of a similar if weaker relationship for the UK but not for the US. This may partly reflect data deficiencies,[3] partly the lower concentration of economic structure, but possibly changes in the availability of finance for small business. We have yet to run a regression analysis on these data and to test for lags, but the post-war relationship at least is quite striking.

At first sight, it is surprising that new business formation should increase with unemployment but the reason could be that those unable to get a job as an employee have to choose between working for themselves or unemployment. There may, however, be other reasons; a recent study suggested that recession actually creates new business opportunities for small firms while periods of economic boom restrict the availability of resources such as premises and skilled labour (Bannock, 1981b). The greater buoyancy of new business formation in the post-war period can certainly be partly explained at least by the higher levels of income, greater redundancy compensation and improved availability of finance and technical assistance and for incentives which have eased the financial obstacles to new start-ups.

The issues raised in this paper provide considerable scope for further research. First, the apparent relationship between unemployment and new business formation could be more systematically investigated on a longitudinal basis with broader international coverage. Second, cross-sectional analysis both as an international and a nationally disaggregated basis might be used to throw more light on the role of small business in economic growth in several other ways.

Many years ago, for example, I carried out some preliminary work on the relationship between the size of the small business sector and the rate of economic growth for a large number of countries (Bannock, 1975). The relationships were complex because it seemed that both the trend rate of economic growth and the importance of small firms declined with the level of GDP per head. It was clear that the achievement of high levels of wealth does not depend on the reduction in the importance of small firms. There was some tendency for countries which had a larger small business sector than would be predicted from their level of economic development, for example Japan and the USA, to have a faster rate of growth than those that had a smaller small business sector than would be expected (the UK notably). The size of the public sector also seemed to be relevant to the determination of the size of the small business sector and the trend rate of growth.

My belief is that small and large firms are complementary in the long-term economic growth process. The former tend to be motivators of growth and the latter consolidators and accelerators, but a balance between them is necessary. The optimal balance will no doubt be affected by many factors and will vary from country to country and perhaps over time, but there is a possibility — I put it no more than that — that when small business formation and growth get out of balance compared with big business, then economic growth will sooner or later be less than optimal. This may well be what happened in the 1960s. In the post-war period at least, there seems to be some evidence that small business formation does have a strong tendency to recover when economies are in recession and structural readjustment back to the growth path is necessary.

Those who have read Mancur Olson's important book, *The Rise and Decline of Nations* (Olson, 1982), will find an echo in all this of his thesis that differences between, and the timing of, periods of economic growth can be explained by the power and prevalence of special interest groups which subvert market forces and delay the processes of change necessary for economic growth. The interests of small business, largely unorganized and under-represented, compared with big business and the State itself, tend to suffer from the activities of other groups. If their interests can come to the fore only in recessions, then this is a brutal and costly way of reasserting balance that would repay further study.

NOTES

1 In the early summer of 1988 the Economic and Social Research Council announced the availability of £1 million over a period of four years for a coherent body of research on small firms.

2 There is ample evidence on the upsurge of small firms since the early 1970s (Small Business Administration, 1984; Ganguly and Bannock, 1985). For the earlier periods we have relied on Prais' (1976) work on the obverse — the share of large firms — though our conclusions are supported by research carried out by the UK Committee of Inquiry on Small Firms.

3 For the United States, the Dun and Bradstreet series for the number of business concerns reproduced in *Historical Statistics of the United States* (US Department of Commerce) do not cover all sectors, and exclude enormous numbers of smaller businesses. For the UK, our analysis and that of Darnell relied mainly on incorporated businesses only. Most start-ups are unincorporated.

REFERENCES

Ancrum, Libby M. (1985), *Smaller Firms in the CBI Trends Survey* CBI, London.

Bannock, Graham (1975), *The Economics and Politics of Small Firms*, International Symposium on Small Business, Tokyo, November 1975.

Bannock, Graham (1981a), *The Economics of Small Firms*, Basil Blackwell, Oxford.

Bannock, Graham (1981b), *Enterprise West*, Shell UK Ltd.

Birch, D.L. (1979), *The Job Generation Process*, MIT Press, Cambridge, Mass. (mimeo).

Fothergill, S. and Gudgin, G. (1979), *The Job Generation Process in Britain*, Centre for Environmental Studies.

Gallagher, Colin and Stewart, Henry (1984), *Jobs and the Business Life Cycle in the UK*, University of Newcastle.

Ganguly, P. and Bannock, G. (eds) (1986), *UK Small Business Statistics and International Comparisons*, Paul Chapman Publishing Ltd, London.

Gershuny, Jonathan (1978), *After Industrial Society*, Macmillan, London.

Johnson, P.S. and Darnell, A.C. (1976), *New Firm Formation in Great Britain*, Durham University.

Kirkland, Richard I.,Jr (1985), *Are service jobs good jobs? Fortune*, 10 June 1985.

Olson, Mancur (1982), *The Rise and Decline of Nations*, Yale.

Prais, S.J. (1976), *The Evolution of Giant Firms in Britain* Cambridge University Press.

Small Business Administration (1984), *The State of Small Business*, Small Business Administration (SBA), US Government Printing Office, Washington.

Chapter 5

BRITAIN IN THE 1980s, ENTERPRISE REBORN?*

INTRODUCTION AND SUMMARY OF CONCLUSIONS

3i commissioned this research paper because experience over the past six years in their principal activity, investing in growing companies, leads them to believe that the most profound changes in attitudes to enterprise are now taking place in Britain since the establishment of the Industrial and Commercial Finance Corporation (ICFC) in 1945.

Our answer to the question posed in the title is an unqualified 'yes', but the path to that conclusion has not been an easy one. Although they may be guided by intuition, economists have to anchor themselves firmly in facts if they are not to be carried away by the strong political emotions and issues raised by national economic performance, especially in the aftermath of a bitterly contested General Election. Given the central importance of enterprise (which we define as 'new entrepreneurial activity including diversification and product, process and organizational innovation') to economic development, it is surprising how little reliable information we have to work with.

There is no shortage of macro-economic data, but these measure only what is going on the surface and at that level there is plenty of room for doubt about whether or not anything fundamental has really changed to affect Britain's long term growth prospects. That is the conclusion of Section 5.1.

Section 5.2 shows that what really counts, however, is the turmoil going on beneath the surface. In the recent past, in terms of the 29 broad industrial sectors in the National Accounts, 60 per cent of the economy has been growing and 40 per cent declining. At a finer level of detail, each of these sectors is divided into growth and decline at varying rates, right down to the individual firm. Both growth and decline are equally important to the rate of economic growth, since growth requires a continuing shift in resources between the two, and enterprise can be reflected as much in contraction to achieve profitability, as in expansion.

Section 5.3 sets out briefly our central thesis that if a fundamental change in enterprise were taking place we should expect to find:

— a resurgence of new business formation accompanied by a high failure rate;

---

[1] A study commissioned by Investors in Industry — 3i and completed in August 1987. We gratefully acknowledge 3i's permission to reproduce the report here.

- some decline in the share of the largest existing firms in output and employment;
- an increasing rate of organizational change, especially in large firms and an increase in the size mobility of all firms;
- an upsurge in activity in capital markets, especially in the provision of venture capital for growing companies and in the reallocation of resources among large firms;
- geographical disparities in the rates of these changes, largely determined by variations in the historical pattern of industrial structure, but nevertheless the existence of some signs of change everywhere.

Sections 5.4–5.6 assemble evidence that shows that all these things are in fact happening. Increases in the rate of net new business formations have, since the mid-1960s, reversed the long decline in the numbers of small firms. For the first time this century (except during World War II), the increase in the share of the 100 largest enterprises in net output stabilized in the late 1960s and now seems to be showing signs of a reversal in the mid-1980s. There seems to have been an increase in the rate of organizational change in big companies, the slimming down of the labour force, management buy-outs and other acquisitions and disposals. The growth of unlisted securities markets and a massive increase in venture capital activity since the early 1980s are perhaps the most convincing evidence of change in enterprise activity. Many of the companies recently floated or receiving venture capital are in advanced sectors of manufacturing (such as stainless steel or high specification nylon bolts, or powder metallurgy) which are substituting for the lower added value products (such as mild steel fasteners and castings) in which Britain was losing out to foreign competition a decade or more ago.

Finally, in Section 5.7 we argue that although it is not possible to pinpoint precisely the date when things started to turn, or indeed to measure enterprise statistically at all, there has clearly been a revolution in social attitudes over the past two decades. The changed social standing of small business as an occupation, the number of new publications on business and investment, developments in business education and the attitudes of the young and, of course, the election to a third term of a government proclaiming the virtues of enterprise, are evidence of that.

This paper covers a broad canvas, at some points sketchily, and we have not attempted to document every statement. Some waivers also need to be made. It is not concerned with exactly why or how the change has occurred, nor does it deal at all with the continuing controversies about macro-economic policy which we believe, although important, are largely irrelevant to the issues covered here. Nor are its conclusions necessarily relevant to the short-term economic outlook (though they presage a better long-term outlook). Nor do we pretend that the developments discussed are confined to Britain, in fact many of them are international in scope and can be traced back to the sea change in world economic affairs which took place at the end of the 1960s.

THE MACRO-ECONOMY

Britain's economic growth rate, as measured by changes in the real gross domestic product (GDP), has lagged behind that of other industrialized nations since World War II. Between 1950 and 1970, Britain's average annual growth rate was less than two-thirds of that for the OECD countries as a whole, and even in the period of slower international growth in the decade 1970–80 it was relatively no better (Table 5.1). Since 1980, when growth rates for the OECD countries as a whole have still not recovered to their earlier levels, Britain has moved up to near the OECD average of the growth league, and indeed will probably substantially exceed its own long-term trend rate of growth in 1987. This year the UK's growth rate may be over twice that of the Federal Republic of Germany and is expected to be at or near the top of the growth league with Japan.

Even so, the depth of the 1979–80 recession was so great in Britain that by 1986 real GDP was still only 10.5 per cent above the 1979 level and manufacturing production alone was actually still 4.5 per cent below it (Figure 5.1).[1] It could be argued that Britain's relatively faster growth than that of most other countries in the 1980s simply reflects the process of its recovery towards the long-term trend which, when reached, will slope upwards as it has for most of this century, less steeply than that of its overseas competitors.

Figure 5.1 United Kingdom GDP and index of manufacturing output (1980 = 100).

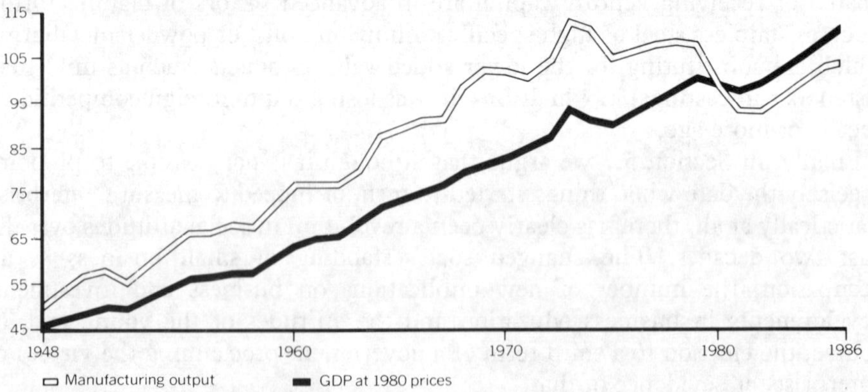

Source: Economic Trends, HMSO, London.

Yet many people believe that something fundamental has changed in the British economy during the past decade or so, that the depth of the 1979–80 recession and the ensuing record levels of unemployment represented a permanent shake-out of overmanning and obsolete capacity and the adoption of a more aggressive approach to economic enterprise, which have laid the groundwork for faster future growth. It is certainly not difficult to find macro-economic data to cast doubt on that view. Despite improving real rates of

Table 5.1: Average annual growth rates in real GDP (OECD and UK)

	Per cent change per annum			
	1950-70	1970-80	1980-6	1986
Total OECD	4.5	3.1	2.2	2.5
UK	2.8	1.9	2.0	2.7

Source: Calculations from OECD and other sources by Angus Maddison for the author.

return on capital employed (now back to the levels of the late 1960s, for all industrial and commercial companies; see Table A.10, p.93) fixed investment has been sluggish and, for manufacturing industry, it was in real terms still 22 per cent below 1979 levels in 1986 and total gross fixed investment was only 6 per cent up over the same period.

Many other indicators present the same picture. Employment in research and development (R&D) fell sharply from 1981, though real expenditure on R&D was 5.5 per cent above 1981 levels in 1985, the latest figure available. Applications for patents are down in total over a similar period, though there was a small increase in applications by UK residents. Commercial planning applications are down heavily from the early 1980s. Although total and manufacturing output continues to expand rapidly and unemployment had declined every month for 12 months in the period up to mid-1987, unemployment is still only just below 3 million and manufacturing employment continues to decline. Import penetration of domestic sales continues to increase slightly faster than the proportion of domestic output which is exported.

Thus, although the recent indicators mostly point to continuing growth and some features of the economy are worse or better than expected (the balance of payments and the rate of inflation for example), there is little really convincing evidence in the macro-economy that we are experiencing anything other than a prolonged recovery from a severe recession. Even this recovery, it is feared, may be threatened soon by a deterioration in the level of world activity, or overheating under growing domestic capacity constraints. The recent strength of the stock market and the pound simply, from this stance, reflects the present view that consumer credit, public expenditure and inflation are more or less under control, while continuing economic growth is expected to maintain the growth in corporate earnings for some time yet.

THE MICRO-ECONOMIES

Macro-economic data, however, are not able to capture the answer to the question posed in the title of this paper. Changes in enterprise are not necessarily reflected in overall economic performance in the short, or even medium term, nor are its manifestations easily measured at all. Changes in enterprise are not to be found by a study of data on the macro-economy. Overall data on the economy reflect the net result of different degrees of activity at the regional and local level and at the level of the industry and the firm. It is quite possible for GDP or employment to be declining while massive beneficial change is taking place in particular sectors and places that will only show through at a macro-economic level after a delay of a decade or more. The economy is changing all the time, but all sectors of it in all parts of the country are not changing in the same direction, or at the same rate.

Table 5.2 gives the rate of change in GDP by sector for the decade 1974–85. It can be seen that some sectors have grown and some declined. Agriculture, energy and most service sectors expanded while manufacturing and construction contracted. Overall manufacturing output declined at an average rate of 0.8 per cent per annum; food and tobacco, chemicals, electrical and electronic engineering grew and all other sectors of manufacturing declined. Within each of these broad aggregates there were also contrary movements of course. At the level of disaggregation shown in Table 5.2 which, of course, is still a broad one, sectors accounting for 60 per cent of output in the base year were expanding while 40 per cent of the economy was contracting. Differential rates of change of this kind are not restricted to the particular period chosen, while changes in output do not always move in the same direction as changes in employment (and vice versa) because of differences in productivity levels and rates of change. Over time, massive changes take place in the economy. In 1907, for example, textiles accounted for one-quarter of manufacturing employment; by 1970 it had fallen to less than one-third of that figure.

In shipbuilding, leather goods, clothing and footwear the employment contributions were halved. As against that there was an eight-fold increase in the employment share of electrical engineering over the same period. Industries which declined in output shed jobs at a rapid rate but not all growth industries, chemicals for example, have increased employment in the recent period, though employment in services (though not of domestic servants) has increased spectacularly.

Evidence of enterprise is not, of course, only to be found in expanding sectors and firms. Those which close existing capacity and dispose of it or convert it to new uses are showing enterprise, so are those which find new and more efficient ways of organizing activities on a large scale. Nor is enterprise revealed only in introducing new products or in starting new firms; the introduction of new processes that will make existing products more cheaply reflects enterprise, while large firms may diversify into new products just as new firms may be started up for the same purpose. But although enterprise is difficult to measure and perhaps for that reason has received little attention from economists, it is essential for economic growth. That growth can only take place if resources are continuously being shifted from declining activities to expanding activities and from the less profitable to the more profitable. Once this process stops, once the turmoil beneath the surface diminishes, there is a risk of ossification and decay.

Table 5.2: Output by industry, 1974–85

	Weights per thousand, 1980	Annual per cent change, 1974-85
Agriculture, etc.	22	2.5
Coal and coke	15	-3.1
Oil and natural gas extraction	44	194.4
Mineral oil processing	5	-2.1
Other energy and water	31	1.8
Energy and water	95	7.9
Metals	9	-2.0
Other mineral products	15	-2.1
Chemicals	24	1.5
Man-made fibres	1	-6.2
Metal goods n.e.s	16	-2.9
Mechanical engineering	38	-2.6
Electrical and electronic engineering	24	2.4
Motor vehicles	15	-3.5
Other transport equipment	14	-0.9
Food	24	0.6
Drink and tobacco	12	0.4
Textiles	9	-2.9
Clothing, footwear	10	-0.3
Paper, printing, publishing	24	-1.0
Other manufacturing	21	-0.9
Manufacturing	266	-0.8
Production industries	361	0.9
Construction	63	-0.5
Production and construction	424	0.7
Distribution, hotels	128	0.8
Transport	46	0.6
Communication	26	3.6
Transport and communication	72	1.7
Banking, insurance, business and professional services	116	6.2
Dwellings	62	1.6
Public adminstration	69	0.1
Education and health	87	1.8
Other services	61	3.0
Financial adjustment	-4.1	5.3
GDP	1,000	1.5

Source: Ray, George F. *The changing structure of the UK economy, National Institute Economic Review*, November 1986.

SMALL FIRMS AND LARGE FIRMS

Although both small and large firms engage in new enterprise it is small firms that historically have almost always pointed the way in sectoral change, even though once new markets are established large firms may do so, through converting what was a minor activity into a mass produced, mass marketed one, as with most products from the motor car to the micro-computer. This is not to deny the importance of large firms (often in Britain, for example, the activities of large foreign multinational firms) in initiating industrial change but excessive domination of an economy or a sector by large firms does in general seem to dampen enterprise. This is not only because large firms are more inflexible and bureaucratic, or because they drive out smaller competitors through their market power or greater productive efficiency. There is evidence, for example, that in parts of the country dominated by large branch plants there are fewer start-ups of new firms (Sweeney, 1987). And since over-mature declining industries tend to be dominated by large firms, this lack of start-ups tends to make regional decline self-reinforcing, as in Scotland (shipbuilding) and the North-west (textiles).

The best conditions for self-reinforcing growth appear to be where there are large numbers of small and medium-sized firms in a wide range of activities. A large number of different enterprises increases the chance that there will be a few firms that grow to substantial size, while a large pool of small enterprises stimulates the combination of technologies from different fields in new ways. Such a pool also promotes the exchange of information and provides a training ground for large numbers of people to obtain direct experience of small business, some of whom will splinter off to start on their own. These phenomena were to be seen in the Midlands in the past and can be seen in the Cambridge area and other parts of the South where large-scale industry is relatively rare today.

For all these reasons, and others which lie outside the scope of a short paper, if there were a resurgence of enterprise in Britain we should expect to find it to be accompanied by a resurgence of new small business formation and an increase in the number of failures as more people take risks. We should also expect, as a consequence, a decline in the domination of large firms in output and employment, evidence of the spinning-off of non-mainstream activities from large firms and changes in management attitudes in these firms. An increase in the size mobility of firms, resulting from expansions and contractions, is also to be expected. This would result in an upsurge in activity in capital markets to supply finance for these developments. We should expect there to be quite pronounced regional disparities in the rate of change depending on the location of concentrations of large firms and declining industries, but if the change in enterprise were really fundamental we should expect to find signs of it in most parts of the country. We should also expect these changes to be stimulated and reinforced by changes in social values.

The remaining sections of this paper contain evidence to show that all these things are, in fact, happening in Britain today though their roots can be traced much earlier than the early 1980s and in fact from the middle 1960s or before.

NEW BUSINESS FORMATION

The Committee of Inquiry on Small Firms, which reported in 1971 (Bolton Committee, 1971), found that the numbers of small businesses and their share of output and employment in Britain had declined up to the mid – 1960s (they had little statistical information after that date). This decline had taken place in most sectors of the economy and had been going on at least since before World War II. The Committee expressed concern about the consequences for the dynamism of the economy if the declining rate of small firms should continue. It is ironic that at the very time these concerns were being put down on paper the long decline, as we now know, had already stopped. Such are the lags in the availability of comprehensive statistics on economic structure.

It is not just that statistics inevitably lag behind events, however, it is also that our economic statistics are not designed to answer the sort of questions posed in this paper. We have no regular census of all enterprises in the economy and, for understandable reasons, all information about the older, declining industries is more complete and more easily interpreted than that on new industries, the newest of which tend to be buried under the labels 'other services' or 'not elsewhere classified'. Information on trends in small businesses and their activities is especially sparse and of suspect quality. This is because many small firms are born and die before they even appear on a database, because small business proprietors have little time or inclination to provide information and the authorities are, for laudable reasons, increasingly loath to trouble them with statistical inquiries.

Some information is available, however, and it shows clearly that the rate of new firm formation turned upwards in the mid- to late 1960s and that the number of surviving small firms is now increasing in most sectors of the economy. This is evident from the numbers of new company registrations shown in Figure 5.2, which have increased continuously since 1968, except for the period of the second oil crisis in 1973–4. Of course not all new companies survive and large numbers of companies are struck off the register each year. The number of liquidations has in fact risen faster than the number of new registrations since 1980, though not in the longer period since 1970 (see Table A.1, p.87). A high failure rate, provided it is matched by a high rate of new business formation (as it usually is except in times of recession), is a healthy sign because it is an indication of change (bike shops closing, computer and health food shops opening) and of risk-taking, both of which are absolutely necessary for economic development. The total number of surviving companies on the register has risen strongly since the late 1960s to reach around one million, although probably no more than 350,000 are actively trading. Some new companies are simply formed from unincorporated businesses, perhaps for tax reasons or as subsidiaries of larger enterprises.

However, not all businesses are incorporated, certainly well under 35 per cent of the total, which is the proportion of VAT registered firms which are not partnerships or sole proprietorships. Our information about the self-employed in small business is also unsatisfactory, but their numbers have also been rising.

Figure 5.2 New company registrations and numbers of self-employed.

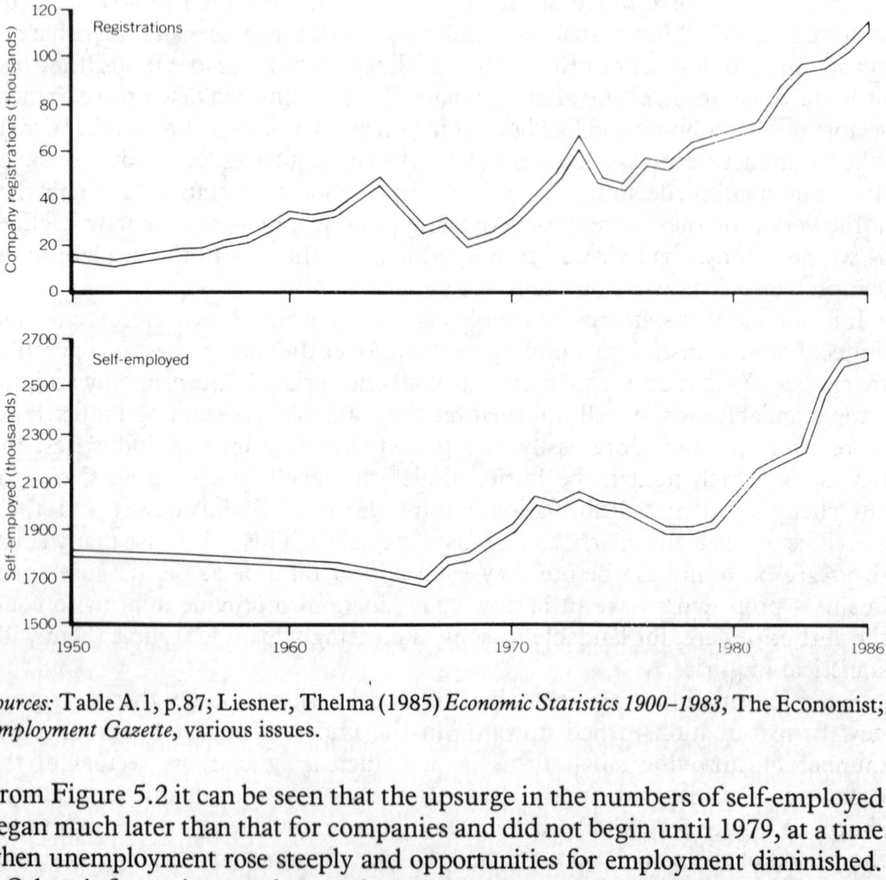

Sources: Table A.1, p.87; Liesner, Thelma (1985) *Economic Statistics 1900–1983*, The Economist; *Employment Gazette*, various issues.

From Figure 5.2 it can be seen that the upsurge in the numbers of self-employed began much later than that for companies and did not begin until 1979, at a time when unemployment rose steeply and opportunities for employment diminished.

Other information we have relates to small manufacturing firms from the regular censuses. Figure 5.3 shows how the numbers of establishments with 10 employees or fewer fell from 93,400 in 1930 to only 32,900 in 1963 but since appears to have recovered back to the 1930 level. Much of the subsequent increase may well be the result of statisticians 'discovering' more firms as registers, aided later by VAT sources of information, improved, but there can be no doubt about the reversal that occurred in the 1960s. Data to be published in the August issue of the *National Institute Economic Review* show that there has been a clear tendency for plant sizes in manufacturing industry to fall in recent years both as a result of closures of very large plants and the opening of new small plants. In interpreting these changes, however, it should be understood that losses of jobs in large manufacturing plants have swamped the increase in employment in the very smallest plants. In plants employing under 100 people, total employment fell slightly between 1979 and 1986 though almost one million jobs were lost in plants employing 1,000 people or more over the same period.

Figure 5.3 Number of establishments with 10 employees or fewer, 1930–84.

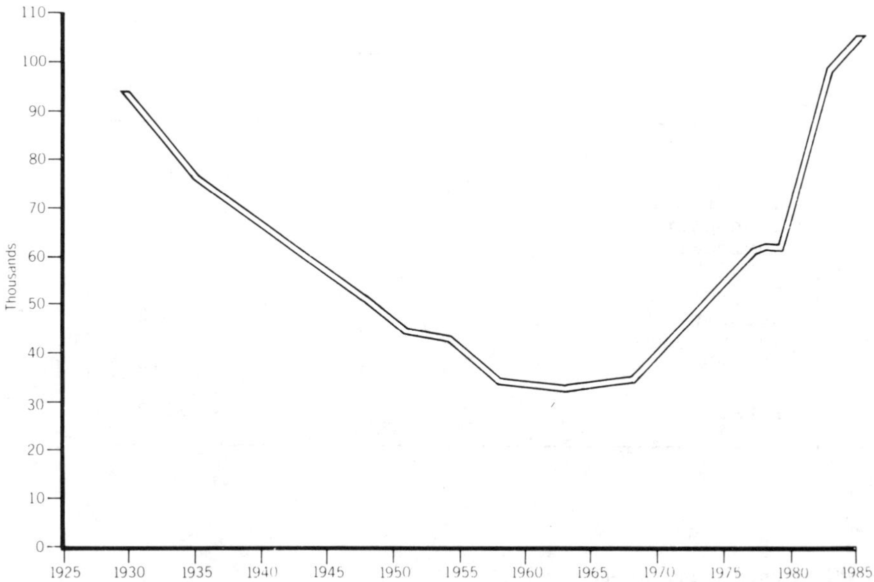

Sources: To 1986, adjusted data from Prais, S.J (1976) *The Evolution of Giant Firms in Britain*, Cambridge University Press; from 1976, *Business Monitor,* PA 1003.

A relatively new source of data on numbers of businesses is that opened up by the introduction of VAT in 1973. Not all businesses are registered for VAT (it is voluntary where turnover is less than £21,300 and firms in a few trades are not required to register at all), but changes in the numbers of VAT registered traders provide a good indication of the numbers of significant businesses. Since the vast majority of VAT registered businesses are small (at least 96 per cent on updated Bolton definitions), then increases in the number of traders reflect an increasing small business population. This is what has been happening: the total number of traders increased from 1,225,800 in 1975 to 1,468,000 in 1986 (see Table A.2, p.88). The overall change was the product of a great deal of churning as new firms are formed and others go out of business. In 1986, for example, the stock of traders increased by a net 29,000 after 193,000 new registrations (not all of them new firms) and 164,000 deregistrations (not all failures).

Increases in the net number of businesses have taken place in all sectors of the economy except for a small decline in the number of retailers (Table 5.3). It is particularly interesting, and encouraging, that increases in the production industries were well above the average for all sectors. The number of firms increased in all the regions during the period 1980–5, but was markedly lower in the northern parts of the country (Table 5.4).

A recent issue of the *Quarterly Survey of Small Business in Britain* (Small

Table 5.3: Net change in the number of VAT registered traders as a percentage of the total in 1985, by sector

Region	Net Change
Agriculture	2.3
Production	15.9
Construction	16.5
Transport	6.4
Wholesale	19.8
Retail	-3.3
Finance etc	32.2
Catering	4.2
Motor trades	7.2
Other	38.5
Total	11.7

Source: Department of Employment.

Table 5.4: Net change in the number of VAT registered traders as a percentage of the total in 1985, by region

Region	Net Change
South-east	14.9
East Anglia	12.3
South-west	11.7
West Midlands	11.2
East Midlands	12.0
Yorkshire and Humberside	8.6
North-west	6.6
North	8.7
Wales	9.0
Scotland	9.7
Northern Ireland	14.8
UK	11.7

Source: Department of Employment.

Business Research Trust, 1987) suggests that these trends have continued into 1987 and that the growth of output and employment in small firms may be accelerating. The same survey also includes evidence that firms employing over 20 employees may now be showing a greater rate of growth. In the past small firms in Britain seem to have run out of steam at a much earlier phase than similar firms in, say, the United States.

THE DECLINE IN CONCENTRATION

There are several ways of measuring concentration. One is to look at changes in the shares of the leading firms in each industry in terms of sales, output or employment. Over the long term, say since the inter-war period, average concentration in Britain has increased by all available measures and continued to increase slowly until the late 1970s. Since 1979, the average share of the five largest firms in all sectors of industrial employment has declined somewhat (Hart and Clarke, 1980; and recent information supplied to the author by Professor Hart).

Another way of measuring concentration, the so-called aggregate measure, is to take the share of the 100 largest companies in some measure of overall economic activity. This helps to capture the effects of the increasing diversification of large companies into each other's markets and their broadening hold on economic activity as a whole (another characteristic of the past 50 years or so) since in many different industrial sectors the same companies appear again and again in the top five (Bannock, 1971).

Figure 5.4 shows how the share of the 100 largest private sector enterprises in manufacturing output rose fairly steadily from the early part of the century until 1968, then stabilized until 1983. In 1984 there was a small but probably significant decline. In terms of employment where data are only available since 1980, there has been a more pronounced fall, as might be expected given the reductions that have taken place in employment in many of the largest firms (see

Figure 5.4 Share of the 100 largest enterprises in manufacturing net output and employment.

Source: Table A.3, p.88

Table A.3, p.88). These changes, if confirmed and continued after 1984, as we should expect, are of great importance, representing as they do a break in the long process of concentration which continued up to the late 1960s.[2]

There are some indications that the cessation and beginning of a reversal in the process of concentration reflect widespread changes in the structure of economic organization and a welling up of growth among medium-sized firms as well as increased numbers of small firms, though comprehensive data are rarely available to measure these things. The number of businesses in wholesaling, for example, rose by 20 per cent between 1980 and 1985 in dramatic contrast to the massive decline noted by the Bolton Committee in this sector in the period 1950–65. There has been much comment on the growth of employment and numbers of businesses in the service sector, but the real growth has not been in the 'froth of the consumer society'.

It is true that the numbers of businesses in catering and allied trades grew by nearly 8 per cent between 1980 and 1985 (mostly snack bars and restaurants); there was even an increase in the number of filling stations and the motor trades (another dramatic reversal) and in road transport, but these changes are dwarfed by the 50 per cent increase in the numbers of business services from under 43,000 in 1981 to over 64,000 in 1985. Property businesses, hairdressing and launderettes declined in number. The expansion of numbers of firms (and output) in business services, in wholesaling and in road transport, as well as that of the numbers of firms in the production industries noted earlier, is encouraging. Some of the growth in wholesaling will be connected with the growth in imports, but some may be related to the growth of small firms in manufacturing, which are more dependent on wholesalers than are larger firms.

The expansion of business services reflects not only the movement of small firms to meet new opportunities, for example in data processing, software development and training, but also the spinning out of activities by large firms to the market-place. This is a healthy development because it indicates a more aggressive approach both in the management of large firms and their suppliers.

To the extent that declining employment in manufacturing is being compensated for by growth in employment in manufacturing related business services, the picture in the manufacturing sector is not as gloomy as it appears. There is some evidence, for example, that although employment in industrial R&D establishment has been falling, contract research is booming. Cost pressures and the uncertainties of the 1970s and early 1980s have greatly stimulated contracting out. A survey of industrial and commercial companies by the *Financial Times* in 1986 found that in the previous three years, 35 per cent of respondents in Britain had contracted out work on a regular basis to other companies which had previously been done in-house. This trend was expected to continue and the proportion of those contracting out was two and a half times higher for firms employing over 1,000 people compared with those employing 50 or fewer.[3]

Another trend which reflects a new spirit of enterprise and changes in organisation is the management buy-out (MBO); virtually unknown before the mid – 1970s, MBOs have become increasingly commonplace. 3i was a pioneer in this field and still accounts for almost a half of the total number, which has increased fivefold since 1979 (Table 5.5). It is widely expected that high and rising stock market prices will in 1987 have pushed the control of more buy-outs out of reach of their managers. The same factor has kept up the number and value of all corporate sales and acquisitions, often by the largest companies, but none of that alters the conclusion we are drawing here, which is that new forces, reflecting new pressures, attitudes and methods of organization, are at work.

Even though the number of acquisitions has been on a rising trend since 1984, the total number has yet to reach the levels of the early 1970s. The expenditure (inflated by some very large and often bitterly contested take-overs) was nevertheless twice as high in 1986 as in 1972, even after allowing for the increase in ordinary share prices over the period (see Table A.4, p.89). Big company management is being much more discriminating about retaining the components of the acquisitions it makes, sectors of business which do not fit in with corporate objectives seem more likely to be floated off or otherwise disposed of than was the case a decade or so ago. This indeed is part of the rationale for the growth of MBOs.

Productivity at all levels has improved markedly in large companies since 1979. Almost 2.5 million people have been made redundant by large employers in Britain since 1980, a process which has continued at a declining rate into 1987 even though overall demand and output have been rising quite strongly since 1981 (see Table A.5, p.90). Sixty-five per cent of these redundancies were in the production industries in 1956, which in the same year accounted for only 28

Table 5.5: Estimates of the total number and value of management buy-outs

	Total	Value £ m	Average value (£ 000s)
1979	52	26	500
1980	107	50	467
1981	124	114	919
1982	170	265	1,550
1983	205	315	1,534
1984	210	415	1,976
1985	229	1,150	5,020
1986	260	1,210	4,654

Sources: *Trends in UK Buy-out*, *Venture Economics* and the Centre for Management Buy-Out Research, 1987.
Wright, M., Coyne, J. and Mill, A. (1987). *Management Buy-out* Woodhead-Faulkner
Estimates by Graham Bannock & Partners Ltd based on information supplied by 3i.

per cent of employees in employment. Only 17 per cent of the redundancies were in the South-east, which accounted for 35 per cent of employees in employment. Employers, including small firms, are also making much more use of temporary and part-time workers than in the past. All this reflects a more determined approach to competitiveness and profitability which are, after all, aspects of enterprise.

ACTIVITY IN THE CAPITAL MARKETS

It is doubtful if the bull market run since 1981, even now, fully reflects the fundamental changes which have taken place in the prospects for the UK (and the world economy) in the past decade or so. In real terms the FT Index of Industrial Ordinary Shares is, after adjustment for inflation, still well below the levels of the 1960s. If we look at the constituents of the index, however, we find that in the past decade it is the industrial group of shares, and particularly the consumer group, which have made the running, not the financial group or oil and gas, which saw the biggest increases in the previous decade and a half (see Table A.6, p.91). As with the economy, the overall market valuations reflect the net effect of differential movements. Compared with the base year of 1962, the Industrial Group Index in March 1987 stood at 1206, but while metals and metal forming (564) mechanical engineering (520), motors (374), packaging (715) and textiles (818) were pulling that figure down electricals (2544), food retailing (2573), health and household goods (2529) and publishing and printing (experiencing a take-over boom at 4527) were pushing it up. Behind the changes of the 'Big Bang', the internationalization of capital markets, privatization and the bull market itself, solid achievements are being made in the provision of finance for growing companies. The number of new listings on the Stock Exchange has been growing: in the 1970s it looked as if they were drying up (Tables 5.6 and 5.7).

The launch of the Unlisted Securities Market (USM) in 1981 and developments in 'unofficial' unlisted markets, culminating in the introduction of the Third Market in January 1987, are events of great importance (see Bannock, 1987). The Third Market has had a relatively slow start compared with the USM, but some 16 companies had been floated by mid-1987 and it is expected that The year 1988 should see faster growth in the Third Market as early investments under the Business Expansion Scheme (which cannot be disposed of in under five years without loss of tax between 30 and 40 companies will be quoted by the end of 1987. relief) move towards flotation. The new unlisted markets are important not simply because they have allowed a number of rapidly growing companies to raise finance, but because their existence is stimulating the flow of capital to companies which are not yet ready for flotation and because they have provided entrepreneurs with something to aim for. By June 1987, 567 companies had been admitted to the USM.

Soon after the World War II there were only two venture capital management groups in Britain, including the Industrial and Commercial Finance

Corporation (ICFC, now within 3i) set up in 1945. The work of the Bolton Committee helped to encourage other financial institutions and independent groups to enter the field and by 1979 there were 20, though ICFC, which had by then expanded considerably, still dominated the venture capital market. Since 1979 the growth of venture capital groups has been spectacular. By 1986 there were 126 groups, which in that year invested a total of £671 million in 1,583 situations, 3i still accounting for over half of the number of situations and catering for somewhat smaller companies than the average for the industry as a whole (Tables 5.8 and 5.9, see also Table A.7, p.91).

3i's venture capital investments are spread throughout the country through its extensive network of 25 local branches. Although the pattern is affected by the regional disparities in levels of activity and new firm formation mentioned earlier (see Table A.8, p.92) there is little sign that over time the pattern of these investments is shifting dramatically.

For example, the share of the South-east in 3i's total investment barely increased between 1977–8 and 1985–6, despite the relatively rapid increase in new firm formation in that area. (Though this is not true of most of the rest of the venture capital industry which has a weaker branch network.)

3i's investments are also spread throughout all sectors of activity. Investments are, in fact, very disproportionately concentrated in manufacturing as compared

Table 5.6: Number of companies obtaining full listings and USM quotations on the Stock Exchange, United Kingdom and Irish Republic

	Official List	USM
1973	96	
1974	14	
1975	19	
1976	18	
1977	24	
1978	35	
1979	48	
1980	35	23
1981	61	61
1982	59	60
1983	79	85
1984	87	101
1985	80	98
1986 (provisional)	117	92

Source: Stock Exchange.

Table 5.7: Net new ordinary share issues by UK companies, USM and Official List

	USM	Official List (£ m)
1980	4	214
1981	54	965
1982	86	2,289
1983	161	1,422
1984	136	1,422
1985	163	4,234
1986	274	7,648

Source: Financial Statistics.

Table 5.8: Number of UK-based venture capital organizations

	Independent	Subsidiaries of other financial institutions	Total
1979	5	15	20
1980	8	19	27
1981	15	29	44
1982	22	35	57
1983	29	48	77
1984	41	59	100
1985	49	64	113
1986	55	71	126

Source: Venture Economics.

Table 5.9: Amount invested by UK-based venture capital organisations

	Total (£ m)
1981	195
1982	251
1983	342
1984	481
1985	553
1986	671

Sources: *Venture Economics* and estimates by Graham Bannock & Partners from data supplied by 3i.

either with total capital formation or the share of new or existing businesses in that sector (see Table A.9, p.92).

All this is unambiguous evidence of the enormous increases in investment which have been made in growth companies. Although some results are already coming through, there is much more to come. Of a sample of 53 start-ups in which 3i invested in 1980–1, 14 (26 per cent), had failed by 1985–6, 12 (23 per cent), had declining net assets and 51 per cent had growing net assets. Overall, the growth of net assets of those companies which survived was 95 per cent. Most of 3i's investments are held for long periods. It takes many years for most start-ups to reach flotation on the official list or USM. Many of the companies floated during the past three years, for example Octopus, Telecomputing, Body Shop, Laura Ashley and Control Techniques, were founded in the 1970s; the next largest group including Alphameric, Amstrad, Apricot and Superdrug were founded in the 1960s. A few were revitalized or reformed companies that started in the 1920s, such as Alexander Workwear, or even earlier, such as Reuters, in the 1850s.

Changes in the pace of economic development take time. If these patterns are repeated much of the economic consequences of investment activity in the mid–1980s will not be seen until the 1990s. After the war, for example, it took the Federal Republic of Germany 15 years to overhaul UK levels of output per head. We have seen that the roots of the change in enterprise in Britain go back to the mid-1960s, but the pace of change seems to have gathered speed from the early 1980s, especially in new growth business formation and financing. If the fruits of this are to continue and to be seen in a major way in the 1990s, then we should expect by now to be experiencing quite fundamental changes in social and cultural attitudes to enterprise.

CHANGES IN SOCIAL ATTITUDES

As Sweeney (1987) has recently reminded us, enterprise and economic development are as much social phenomena as technological or financial ones. Unless there is a widespread social will to produce and consume more, then little will happen. The differences in the degree of enterprise of different immigrant groups in Britain shows how important enterprise culture is in determining activity, and immigrants have to try harder than the established population because of their problems of social acceptance. Human societies are nearly always acquisitive: in Britain there have always been arguments about shares in the national product and plenty of rhetoric about the need for more output and greater efficiency, but there was no consensus about the painful changes that were needed to achieve it. Britain was willing to will the ends but not the means, and is still deeply divided about them. What has forced change seems to be a deep social realization that we could not go on as we were. Even the 'stop-go' of the 1950s and 1960s, and our progressively humiliating position near the bottom of the growth league, had been accompanied by rising standards of living. In the 1970s it was brought home to everyone that not even that could be taken for granted, though North Sea oil provided a cushion.

Deep down, in British society, however, things were changing. We have seen that new technological opportunities were grasped by a few entrepreneurs in the 1960s and have been brought to fruition by flotations in the 1980s. We also have seen that the long decline in small businesses came to an end about that time. As Clive Rassam writes in *Secrets of Success* on Britain's new entrepreneurs:

> By the spring of 1979 when Acorn Computers was set up by Hermann Hauser and Chris Curry, who had earlier worked with Clive Sinclair, the entrepreneurial revolution was almost complete. What this revolution needed was a voice that would acknowledge and recognize what had happened and enable it to flower further. They found that voice, imperfect as it was, in the shape of the soon-to-be-elected Thatcher Government, which in opposition seemed to personify their aspirations.

The growth of the enterprise culture accelerated after 1979 despite, perhaps in part because of, the savage retrenchment in the economy (unemployment seems to stimulate new business formation). We have noted the rapid expansion in the availability of venture capital which took place at that time and a number of tax changes introduced by the new government including the Business Expansion Scheme, the Enterprise Allowance Scheme (which spurred self-employment) and lower rates of personal taxation helped this process. The re-election of the Thatcher Government for a third term in 1987 on the same platform certainly confirms the wider, though (given the minority of the electorate that voted them into power), still incomplete, trend towards the revaluation of enterprise.

But apart from election results and the economic manifestations of the changes that have been traced in previous sections, can we actually measure the changes in attitudes which we assert took place? The answer is 'no': we can assemble other evidence that attitudes have changed, but we have not been able to find any statistical attitude measurement series that go back far enough in time for us to assess when the turning point was. Though the economic evidence points to the mid-1960s, the trend in attitudes must have turned earlier. However, in the 1960s and indeed, until politically motivated polls on the subject began in the 1970s, no-one seems to have bothered to measure attitudes to enterprise at all and even today we can find no systematic measurement. (3i are going to plug at least part of this gap and will be announcing an 'Enterprise Barometer' shortly.)[4]

Apart from the rapid growth in self-employment, including part-time employment, which itself is an indication of cultural change, most of the evidence is anecdotal. The *Times Educational Supplements* in the 1970s, for example, contain articles that indicate concern about the small number of students who wanted to enter industry. Then, as now, there were complaints about the relevance of education to the needs of commerce (similar complaints were recorded in the 1890s). Certainly in the 1960s and earlier, more well to do parents than now wanted their children to go into the civil service or into teaching or the professions rather than into industry. Corelli Barnett, in his book *The Audit of War*, documents the unfavourable attitudes of the older British universities, the Church and other parts of the establishment to wealth creation. This has certainly changed. A Fellow of Balliol College, Oxford, writing in *The Observer* on 26 April 1987 on the 'brain drain' (subsequently published and careful research by the Royal Society found little evidence of this phenomenon) complained that '...there is the siphoning of newly trained brain-power out of academia. Smart graduates look for brilliant careers elsewhere. Graduate scientists take (often non-scientific) jobs in industry and commerce. Many of the best and brightest go into the City.'

It used to be a very unfashionable thing in Britain to start up in one's own business, a route taken predominantly by the untrained and uneducated. Now it is all the rage. Large numbers of graduates of bodies in higher education now express a desire to have their own firm and many start one straight away. In the early 1970s there were virtually no courses in entrepreneurship and small business management, now they are available everywhere.

The content of publications is one of the best indications of changes in social values. According to figures published regularly in *The Bookseller*, the number of new books classified to 'commerce' has increased at twice the rate of all new books since 1970 and the annual number doubled between 1975 and 1980.

In 1975 Bannock commented:

> Virtually all general bookshops in the United States offer a choice of manuals on how to become rich. These books are enormously popular and several have sold more than a million copies, evidence that they have at least gone some way towards fulfilling their functions, for their authors if not their readers. The very absence, or at least muted existence, of such books in Britain tells us something of the difference between the social basis of capitalism in the two countries.

This is no longer true of Britain today as a visit to any large general bookshop with its piles of books on business, management, investment, property renovation and dealing, successful businesspeople, small business guides and tax havens, will testify, though we have yet to see quite the same genre of *How I Made my First Million on the Stock-Market* that are so popular in the USA.

Table 5.10 shows the results of a rough count of the number of general business and investment-related weekly and monthly publications in Britain with their date of launch. We have excluded trade publications, such as computer magazines, which are also booming and more general economic/business publications such as *The Economist*. Of course some publications (such as *Venture UK*) have been born, died or reborn, all within the recent period, but there is a clear sign of increasing activity in the business publishing (and reading) world. Even though not all of the recently launched periodicals can be expected to survive, the upward trend (84 per cent were launched after 1974) is impressive. Information on circulations was not available for almost half of the publications analysed, but for the remainder it totalled almost 2 million, 85 per cent of which was accounted for by periodicals launched since 1980.

Other aspects of the enterprise culture include share ownership, the emergence and growing strength of new organizations to represent small business interests, the 'yuppy phenomena', successful small business competitions, the sponsorship of business promotion by large companies and local authorities, Local Enterprise Agencies and Business in the Community, the content of TV and radio. These are all aspects that could have been discussed and which clearly show that much has changed since the 1960s.

These aspects all reflect social values, and society values what is rare and what it needs. People do not value sun tans so much now that more people can travel abroad and they do not value what they are told to value, but what they really want. This is why posters in communist countries depicting lathe operators in heroic stances did little for productivity. Rhetoric is not enough, but more Britons than perhaps ever before this century now seem to want success in business.

Table 5.10: Number of small business, business, entrepreneurial and investment related publications in circulation in mid – 1987, by period of launch

	Business	Investment	Total
1985-7	15	8	23
1980-4	23	5	28
1975-9	10	2	12
1970-4	3	-	3
1965-9	2	-	2
1960-4	-	2	2
pre 1960	4	1	5
Total	57	18	75

Sources: *Willings Press Guide*, 1987; and estimates by Graham Bannock & Partners Ltd.

Our conclusion is that enterprise has been reborn and will not easily be extinguished again, though the transformation in British attitudes towards wealth creation has a very long way to go. Many of these changes, it is important to note, are not restricted to Britain, they are to a greater or lesser extent to be found elsewhere. But Britain, which led the industrial revolution, also suffered most from the accumulated consequences of that lead and may be throwing off some of these first as was suggested in the mid-1970s (Bannock, 1975). Other, newer countries, such as the United States, are in a somewhat different position, but a revitalization of entrepreneurship is to be found there also. Japan, which industrialized late and in the post-war period, has avoided the excessive concentration of industry that occurred in Britain, is another special case where the spirit of enterprise has yet to flag. But Britain (and perhaps Italy) has definitely changed for the better in that respect. Since there can be no changes in the rate of economic development without changes in enterprise, we should expect the improvements in attitudes and their manifestations discussed in this study to be reflected in an improvement in Britain's long-term rate of growth relative to that of other countries. The recent relative improvement in that growth rate, therefore, should be maintained for some time, provided there is no reversal in the transformation of British enterprise that has taken place and provided an equivalent change does not soon occur in other countries where these changes seem weaker (France and West Germany, for example).

STATISTICAL APPENDIX

Table A.1: New company registrations and liquidations, Great Britain, 1970–86

	New registrations	Liquidations
1970	30,262	8,782
1971	39,445	8,412
1972	54,456	8,215
1973	67,349	7,240
1974	42,496	7,885
1975	45,678	9,795
1976	56,085	10,640
1977	52,214	9,974
1978	63,566	9,205
1979	66,472	9,019
1980	69,374	11,481
1981	72,416	12,920
1983	96,188	17,978
1984	97,908	18,250
1985	104,581	19,614
1986	114,831	

Source: Department of Trade and Industry, *Companies in 1986*, and earlier issues.

Table A.2: Total number of VAT business registrations, United Kingdom 1975–86

	000s, end year
1975	1225.8
1976	1248.8
1977	1247.8
1978	1241.8
1979	1288.3
1980	1304.2
1981	1335.7
1982	1356.0
1983	1390.0
1984	1419.0
1985	1439.0
1986	1468.0

Source: Department of Employment.

Table A.3: Share of the 100 largest private sector enterprises in manufacturing net output and employment, United Kingdom 1909–86

	By output (%)	By employment (%)
1986	39.1	33.2
1985	38.3	33.2
1984	38.7	33.1
1983	41.4	36.0
1982	41.0	36.5
1981	40.6	36.4
1980	40.5	37.2
1970	40.5	
1968	41.0	
1963	37.0	
1958	32.0	
1953	27.0	
1949	22.0	
1935	24.0	
1924	22.0	
1909	16.0	

Sources: 1909–70, Prais, S.J. (1976), *The Evolution of Giant Firms in Britain*, Cambridge University Press. 1980–1985 *Report on the Census of Production*, Business Statistics Office (BSO), successive issues. There are some differences in coverage between Prais' data and those for later years which are for SIC(80) 2–4.

Table A.4: Company acquisitions excluding mergers, industrial and commercial companies, and ordinary share prices, 1970–86

	Number of acquisitions	Expenditure on acquisitions	Financial Times Index of Industrial Ordinary Shares (1935=100)
		£ million	
1970	787	1,080	361.0
1971	884	911	386.2
1972	1,203	2,523	503.8
1973	1,203	1,302	435.6
1974	503	500	251.2
1975	312	285	311.0
1976	352	448	368.0
1977	479	794	452.3
1978	564	1,090	479.4
1979	531	1,623	475.5
1980	469	1,475	464.5
1981	452	1,144	518.5
1982	460	2,177	574.7
1983	443	2,214	692.6
1984	566	5,373	854.9
1985	474	7,074	1004.6
1986(provisional)	694	13,047	1287.1

Sources: Acquisitions, Department of Trade and Industry, *Business Monitor*, MQ7: FT. Index, *Economic Trends, Annual Supplement*, 1985 and *Financial Statistics* (excludes financial companies).

Table A.5: Confirmed redundancies by region 1984, 1985 and in total, Great Britain, 1977–86

By region	1984	1985
South-east	42,051	34,926
East Anglia	2,356	3,585
South-west	15,054	13,615
West Midlands	29,678	29,803
East Midlands	24,017	17,660
Yorkshire and Humberside	26,570	33,319
North-west	37,935	35,784
North	25,727	24,834
England	203,838	193,526
Scotland	30,164	26,424
Wales	11,441	15,027
Total	245,443	234,977

Year	Total
1977	158,360
1978	172,563
1979	186,784
1980	493,704
1981	532,030
1982	400,416
1983	326,633
1984	245,443
1985	234,977
1986	224,841

Note: The figures are based on reports by companies under the Employment Protection Act 1975. Employers are required to notify redundancies involving 10 or more workers.

Source: Department of Employment.

Table A.6: *Financial Times*, actuarial indices by equity groups, July 1977 and July 1987

		Index		
		1 July 1977	3 March 1987	1977=100
1	Capital goods	183.40	976.43	532
11	Consumer durables	172.06	1345.24	790
21	Non-durables	168.55	1345.24	790
40	Other groups	255.13	1130.76	443
49	Industrial group	181.50	1205.73	664
51	Oil and gas	513.40	2354.29	459
59	500 share index	208.17	1303.26	626
61	Financial group	138.57	830.38	599
71	Investment trusts	168.58	1100.40	652
81	Mining finance	88.94	525.49	591
91	Overseas traders	271.48	1123.87	414
99	All share index	189.32	1179.69	623

Note: The base of the index is 10 April 1962 = 100.

Source: *Financial Times.*

Table A.7: Number of companies in which investments were made by UK based venture capital organizations and average amount of investment, 1981–86

	No	Average amount (£000s)
1981	1,177	166
1982	1,172	214
1983	1,252	273
1984	1,529	315
1985	1,520	364
1986	1,583	424

Source: *Venture Economics* and estimates by Graham Bannock & Partners Ltd from data supplied by 3i.

Table A.8: Investment by 3i during the year by region 1977–8 and 1985–6 and per cent of total number of all VAT registered traders by region

	3i investment (%) 1977-8	1985-6	VAT traders (%) 1985
Scotland	8.6	6.8	7.5
Northern Ireland	-	0.7	3.5
North-east	7.7	13.3	7.8
North-west	12.1	3.1	11.8
East Midlands	5.8	3.7	6.8
West Midlands	6.4	6.2	8.6
Wales	1.4	3.0	5.4
East Anglia	7.5	5.4	4.0
Greater London	26.9	30.5	
			33.4
South-east	16.8	13.4	
South-west	4.4	4.8	9.5
Channel Isles	2.3	2.1	-
Overseas	-	6.3	-
Total	100.0	100.0	100.0

Sources: 3i and Department of Employment.

Table A.9: Investment by 3i during the years 1981–2 and 1986–7 by sector

	1981-2 (%)	1986-7
Agriculture, forestry and fishing	0.6	1.1
Energy and water	1.7	0.3
Mining and quarrying	-	1.3
Manufacturing	51.4	42.6
Construction	3.9	2.6
Distribution	13.3	14.6
Hotel and catering	3.8	3.2
Transport and communication	9.4	3.6
Insurance, banking and leasing	4.1	11.9
Other business services	6.2	11.5
Health, education, community services	2.9	5.3
Recreation and personal services	2.7	1.9
Total	100.0	100.0

Note: Totals include investments in assets other than equity or loan capital, for example in property.

Source: 3i.

Table A.10: Real rates of return on capital employed, United Kingdom, 1960–86

	All industrial and commercial companies (ICC)	ICC excluding North Sea oil
1960	12.9	12.9
1961	11.1	11.1
1962	10.2	10.2
1963	11.2	11.2
1964	11.9	11.9
1965	11.3	11.3
1966	9.9	10.0
1967	10.0	10.1
1968	10.1	10.2
1969	9.9	10.0
1970	8.7	8.7
1971	8.9	9.0
1972	9.4	9.4
1973	9.0	9.1
1974	5.3	5.5
1975	4.2	4.4
1976	4.5	4.5
1977	7.6	6.9
1978	8.0	7.2
1979	7.5	5.8
1980	6.3	3.8
1981	6.2	2.9
1982	7.3	3.6
1983	9.1	4.8
1984	11.1	6.1
1985	11.6	7.5
1986 (est)	9.5	8.0

Note: The data are accounting rates of return calculated as profit before interest and tax but after depreciation as a percentage of net capital employed at current replacement cost.

Source: *British Business*, 10 October 1986 and 22 May 1987.

NOTES

1 This report was completed in mid-August 1987. 1979 levels of manufacturing output were in fact reached in July 1987.
2 As this book went to press, figures for 1985 and 1986 became available, which suggest that the aggregate concentration has not changed much since 1984 (see Table A.3, p.88).
3 There are other ways in which statistics designed to reflect earlier economic structures can be misleading in times of rapid economic change. For example, data on fixed investment on which great credence is placed in assessing industrial confidence understate total investment, which includes investment in working capital, contracted-out research, investment in much computer software and hardware, training and so on. In an increasingly knowledge-based economy, data on investment in plant, machinery and buildings are of diminishing importance as an indication of investment in future growth. In the short period, existing statistical estimation procedures based on returns from larger enterprises is increasing. Some

invisible exports, to give another example, may be truly invisible to statisticians where, as is probable, exports of services by small firms are not picked up and lost in 'balancing items'.

4 3i's Enterprise Barometer was launched in February 1988 in the form of a quarterly survey of 3i clients. 82 per cent of respondents agreed that there is a 'new enterprise culture' in this country, only 4 per cent disagreed. In a MORI poll of the general public carried out for 3i at the same time, only 46 per cent agreed that there is a new enterprise culture, 14 per cent disagreed or had no opinion. It was concluded that public opinion, though on balance favourable to the idea that attitudes to enterprise are changing positively, is much more divided on the issue than those (3i companies) at the forefront of change. The Enterprise Barometer survey results are to be published in 3i's *Quarterly Enterprise Digest*.

REFERENCES

Bannock, G. and Doran, A. (1987), *Going Public*, Paul Chapman Publishing, London.
Bannock, G. (1971), *The Juggernauts*, Weidenfeld & Nicolson, London.
Bannock, G. (1975), *How to Survive the Slump*, Penguin, Harmondsworth.
Bolton Committee, (1971), *Small Firms, Report of the Committee of Inquiry on Small Firms*, HMSO, London.
Hart, P.E. & Clarke, R. (1980), *Concentration in British Industry 1935–1975*, Cambridge University Press.
Prais, S.J. (1976), *The Evolution of Giant Firms in Britain*, Cambridge University Press.
Rassam, C. (1988), *Secrets of Success*, Sidgewick & Jackson, London.
Small Business Research Trust (1987), *Quarterly Survey of Small Business in Britain*, Vol.3, no.2.
Sweeney, G.P. (1987), *Innovation, Entrepreneurs and Regional Development*, Frances Pinter, London.

Part II

Taxation

Chapter 6

TAX REFORM AND SMALL FIRMS: AN IMPOSSIBLE DREAM? A GLOBAL PERSPECTIVE

THE RISE OF TAXATION

At the beginning of Chapter 7 we document the striking increase in the ratio of tax revenue to the gross domestic product (GDP) (the tax ratio) which has taken place in all developed countries this century. This increase in taxation has been made necessary by the greatly expanded role of the State in the economy, as reflected by increased government expenditure on infrastructure, defence, education and, especially in the period following World War II, social welfare.

Although there remain large differences in tax ratios between individual countries (taxation is generally much higher in the member states of the European Community (EC) than in Japan, Switzerland or the United States for example) and in the relative contributions of different types of tax to total revenue, the general character of the tax systems used is remarkably similar. Personal and unincorporated business incomes are subject to progressive income tax, company income is subject to corporation tax while both employers and employees pay social security contributions. All countries tax expenditure as well as income. The EC does this primarily by value added tax (VAT) while outside the Community sales taxes are more commonly used, though as we show in Chapter 7 the use of VAT is spreading. All countries also tax gifts and wealth at death, although only a minority tax the wealth of the living except in the form of real estate taxes. All countries levy import duties and other specific taxes although these and other sources of revenue such as licences, fines or stamp duty, and indeed general taxes on wealth everywhere, contribute only a minor source of total revenue. All countries, and particularly those with a federal political structure, levy taxes at local as well as national levels of government.

With the rise in the tax ratio there has been a growth in the complexity of tax systems. Though not disputed this is less easily documented and is, in fact, difficult to measure with any precision. These two features of taxation are in fact related. The increasing tax ratio has led both to greater rewards for (legitimate) avoidance and (undetected) evasion and a parallel rise in concern for fairness. Measures to prevent the avoidance of taxation have taken the form of more complex regulations to close loopholes and to provide the necessary information and controls for tighter enforcement. Similarly, the alleviation of the burden of taxation on the least advantaged members of society has taken the form of complex exemptions and thresholds. Complexity in tax systems has been further increased by modifications designed to further particular policy objectives such as the encouragement of investment or saving.

The result of this process is that each year thousands of pages of tax legislation and administrative regulation are issued in all countries, and comprehension of the system has long passed far beyond the capacity of the average individual citizen. The tax authorities have been obliged to delegate the greater part of the administration of personal taxation to business, which is required to calculate and deduct income tax as well as social security contributions from the remuneration it pays to its employees. Businesses also collect all taxes on expenditure and deduct tax from dividends paid to shareholders. Even in countries with self-assessment income tax systems (which do not include Britain), probably the majority of citizens with anything but the simplest tax affairs need professional assistance if they are not to pay more taxes than they need. Virtually all businesses, even the smallest, use professional accountants or some other form of external assistance and large companies also employ tax expertise in-house.

THE EFFECTS OF TAX SYSTEMS ON SMALL FIRMS

Although it is uncertain precisely where the ultimate burden of taxation on business actually falls (most of it is probably passed on to consumers and perhaps employees rather than falling on the owners), there can be no doubt that taxation results in distortions in the pattern of savings, investment and output and in the organization of production. We can distinguish four classes of effects on the size distribution of firms.

The first of these effects of taxation arises from the greater dependence of small firms on the working proprietor as a source of funds and as a guarantor of borrowings as compared with large firms. Small firms do not have access to public securities markets for the issue of equity or long-term loan capital and are forced to rely to a greater extent than large firms on debt, particularly short-term debt (Table 6.1). The taxation of the incomes of working proprietors therefore directly depletes the principal source of equity capital for small firms and obliges them to use high-cost short-term debt, which has the further disadvantage of increasing their already high vulnerability to risk. In any event, borrowing capacity may be restricted by equity limitations.

The allocation of resources to small firms also suffers from two other features of modern tax systems: incentives for contractual savings and the high compliance costs arising from ever-increasing complexity. The second effect of taxation is that, while working proprietors obtain no tax relief on earnings invested in their own business, they and everyone else are eligible for relief on various forms of savings placed with large financial institutions. All the major developed countries provide some form of tax relief for savings in life assurance and almost all in the acquisition of pension rights. Since the capacity of financial institutions to invest in unquoted companies is limited by law, prudence and the high unit cost of small investments, the effect of these fiscal inducements to savings is to channel funds away from small and into large firms. The diversion of funds away from small and medium enterprises (SMEs) is further accentuated by the reliefs available on mortgage interest for the acquisition of dwellings in all countries. In many countries relief is also available for other investment in government securities or in equities in large firms such as the Personal Equity Plan (UK) of the *Loi Monory* (France). Taxes on personal wealth and capital also reduce funds available for investment in small firms.

Table 6.1: Balance sheet structure of small and medium companies compared with large companies, United Kingdom, end 1982

	£ million	
Small and medium-sized companies, all industries		
Shareholders' interest	20,528	(61.6%)
Minority shareholders' interest	72	(0.2%)
Deferred taxation	1,678	(5.0%)
Long-term loans	707	(2.1%)
Short-term loans (including bank loans and overdrafts)	10,364	(31.1%)
Total capital employed	33,349	
Total debt	11,071	(33.2%)
Total shareholders' interest	20,600	(61.8%)
Large companies, all industries		
Shareholders' interest	116,780	(61.4%)
Minority shareholders' interest	9,951	(5.2%)
Deferred taxation	7,216	(3.8%)
Long-term loans	17,431	(9.2%)
Short-term loans (including bank loans and overdrafts)	38,800	(20.4%)
Total capital employed	190,178	
Total debt	56,231	(29.6%)
Total shareholders' interest	126,731	(66.6%)

Source Department of Trade and Industry, *Business Monitor MA3* (17th issue, final year 1982).

Note: Large companies are defined to be those with capital employed of £4.16 million and over.

It should be noted that the tax-induced diversion of funds away from SMEs affects not only investment by the working proprietor but also by third parties. While working proprietors have to invest in their own business out of taxed income they may obtain tax relief on investment in large firms. It is true that in a few countries tax relief is now available for investment in unquoted companies, as in the Business Expansion Scheme in the UK, and similar reliefs are also available in a few other countries (France and the United States, for example). However, all these schemes are limited in extent and are not generally available either for investment in unincorporated business or for investment by (controlling) working proprietors.

Though the effects of contractual savings and institutional ownership of equities on industrial concentration were first identified as long ago as 1932 (Berle and Means, 1932), their more specific effects on small firms have received little attention until quite recently (Bolton Committee, 1971; Wilson Committee, 1979). It is difficult to see how the effects of fiscal capital market distortions on the role of SMEs in the economy can be quantified, but the magnitude of the diversionary effects of tax relief on savings flows is evident. There is also evidence that the role of small firms has been constrained in the UK where these distortions have been greatest. The SME sector has certainly been more buoyant over the long term in the low tax countries where these distortions have been least.

The third class of effects of taxation on small firms is associated with the rising compliance burden, that is to say the incidence of the cost of professional tax advice and tax administration borne by business both in assessing and paying its own tax and in collecting taxes from shareholders, employees and consumers. It is now well established that these compliance costs fall disproportionately on small firms. Value added tax (VAT) is probably the most burdensome and Chapters 7 and 8 are devoted to this subject. There is, however, little doubt that the compliance costs of other forms of taxation are also regressive with respect to firm size. This is certainly true of other forms of sales taxation (see Chapter 7). Professor Cedric Sandford has also demonstrated that the compliance costs of income tax are regressive with respect to size of income (Sandford, 1986). As is shown in Chapters 7 and 8, the regressive nature of tax compliance burdens follows from the existence of economies of scale in tax administration.

The foregoing does not exhaust the list of ways in which tax systems discriminate against small firms and reduce their role below the optimum. It may be that by taxing business success and failing to compensate for failure, taxation by its very nature discourages risk-taking and may, in this and other ways, reduce incentives to start up and expand a small firm. It is inherently difficult to assess the effects of taxation on motivation. However, it must be true that taxes unrelated to profit (such as property taxes) and tax allowances (for example, for investment) against profit, increase the tax rate and therefore deplete the resources of new enterprise, which is not yet in a position to earn a surplus and is at its most vulnerable. Death duties and inheritance taxes, where they apply to business assets as they do in all countries (although reliefs are available), must also threaten the continuation of some small firms whose ownership is not readily marketable. Finally, the general bias in tax systems towards favouring capital investment and penalizing employment through investment reliefs and social security contributions tends to favour large firms, which have easier access to sources of capital, and discriminates against smaller firms which tend to be more labour intensive.

TAX REFORM

What has been argued above is that modern tax systems work to deplete investment in small firms while favouring it in large firms. This arises principally because some forms of saving and investment receive more favourable tax treatment than others. The post-tax return on investment in small firms is artificially depressed relative to that in large firms or to investment in other tax-favoured assets such as property.

We should expect as a result that pre-tax returns on investment in small firms would be higher than in large firms. Since investors would select only the most profitable small firms post-tax returns on investment in small and larger firms would be equalized at the margin. In most countries, in fact, small firms do appear to earn higher returns on assets pre-tax though not, apparently, recently in Britain (Burns and Dewhurst, 1986). It could be argued that this is not necessarily conclusive evidence for our thesis for several reasons. One is that data on small firm profitability are suspect for well-known reasons, another is that since small firms tend to be more labour intensive than large firms, the use of return on assets as a measure tends to overstate their ralative profitability (Bolton Committee, 1971). Another factor, however, is that overall most equity investment in small firms is by working proprietors and in sectors with low barriers to entry. This depresses average returns because the investor's prime motive is not profit maximization alone, but independence and self-expression (see Goffee and Scase, 1987). These are important issues into which further research is necessary. We have also argued that the disproportionate burden of compliance costs also raises costs in small firms relative to those in large firms.

An obvious if incomplete solution to these problems would be either to restore business and personal income taxes to a true income base, that is to eliminate all tax reliefs on savings, or to tax expenditure only so as to remove discrimination between different types of savings media. Both these routes to reform would reduce artificial economic distortions in investment decisions and, by reducing allowances against tax ('tax expenditures'), would allow a major reduction in rates of taxation that would reduce the effects of remaining distortions. Which of the two alternatives is chosen would depend not only on whether or not tax systems should favour saving as against consumption (which is not obvious), but also on practical administrative considerations (see Peacock, 1978). Either route also has the potential for simplifying the tax system and reducing business compliance costs although this problem, to which we return later, could be alleviated though not solved by radical reforms of these kinds.

The prospects for widespread tax reform now appear more favourable than at any time since World War II. The era of higher unemployment and slower inflation-prone growth, which followed the early 1970s, has led to increasing concern about the effects of high taxation on economic growth and employment. There has also been growing concern about tax evasion, equity and the need for deregulation. In short, there is now 'a widely held view that tax systems in the western world are unfair and inefficient' (Pechman, 1987a).

To a varying degree, but as yet in a generally minor way, many countries have already started to simplify income tax schedules and reduce tax expenditures and tax rates and carry out other reforms or have announced their intention to do so. New Zealand and, following entry to EC, Portugal, Spain and Greece, have recently introduced value added taxes and eliminated other taxes; Japan announced but then deferred the introduction of VAT; plans for VAT in Australia and Canada seem to have been abandoned (see Chapter 7). Belgium plans to reduce the number of income tax brackets from 14 to 7 between 1990 and 1993 and The Netherlands, Sweden and Italy are considering similar moves. France has abolished its wealth tax and reduced corporation tax. West Germany and Japan plan tax reductions and both Australia and New Zealand have cut income taxes sharply. The UK anticipated the United States 1986 Tax Reform Act by two years in reducing investment incentives and lowering corporation tax rates and Canada has followed the United States in these aspects of reform.

On closer examination, however, with the important exception of the United States which we consider further below, none of these changes reflects a determined effort to simplify tax systems or a coherent move towards the removal of tax-induced distortions in savings and investment decisions. In some instances the changes were motivated more by macro-economic considerations and in most cases moves towards simplification in some aspects of tax law have been offset by more complication in other aspects. Nowhere, except in a limited way in the United States, has there been a move towards greater neutrality in the treatment of savings and investment.

British tax policy seems particularly confused in this respect. Life insurance premium relief was abolished in 1984 and, as mentioned, initial investment allowances with effect from April 1986, both moves towards a true income-based tax system. Incentives for personal investment in equities and unquoted companies have been introduced or extended, however, while the fiscal treatment of capital gains has been eased, a move in the opposite direction.

Nowhere, again with the possible exception of the United States, has any significant progress been made in simplifying existing tax systems. Value added tax in particular imposes heavy compliance burdens and distortions which are intensified by a variety of rates, exemptions and administrative complications. Recent attempts by the European Commission to reduce and harmonize VAT rates have met with strong resistance. It is true that all EC member states have measures to ease the tax compliance burden on small firms, not only for VAT but for other taxes, but, as demonstrated in Chapter 7, these measures do not match up to the size of the problem. It should be added that many countries both within and outside the Community also provide various fiscal incentives for small enterprise such as progressive rates of corporation tax in addition to the investment incentives mentioned above. However, these incentives do not comprehensively offset the basic distortions (but add others such as disincentives to growth) and certainly add to the complexity of the system.

Compared with developments in the rest of the world, the United States 1986 Tax Reform Act, however imperfect compared with the theoretical ideal, is a shining example of an attempt to tackle these problems at the root. The attempts at the removal of fiscal distortions in this Act have won the widespread approval of economists all over the world. Henry J Aaron, in a review for the Brookings Institution, describes the reforms as 'the impossible dream comes true' (Pechman, 1987b).

Basically, the United States reform increases thresholds for personal income tax and reduces or eliminates various deductions for both personal and business income taxes so as to allow major reductions in income tax and corporation tax rates without significantly affecting expected total tax revenues.

The number of personal income tax brackets has been reduced from 14, with rates ranging from 11 to 50 per cent, to 2, with rates of 15 and 28 per cent. The highest standard rate of tax is, therefore, only one point below the *lowest* UK rate of 27 per cent, although the highest effective rate is actually 33 per cent in the United States because some concessions are removed for high income taxpayers. The scope for sheltering personal income from tax has been greatly reduced, for example by the limitation of the deduction of interest on borrowings secured by first and second residences, and the exclusion of long-term gains from capital gains tax has been repealed.

Maximum corporation tax rates have been reduced from 46 to 34 per cent though lower rates on profits under $75,000 (formerly $100,000) to benefit smaller companies have been retained. The investment tax credit has been eliminated, depreciation deductions revised and various other business deductions reduced (for example, for business meals and entertainment) or eliminated. These changes apply of course to both incorporated and unincorporated businesses.

In the qualified judgement of the commentators in Pechman (1987b), the United States reform reduces economic distortions particularly in the after-tax returns for investment in different sectors and improves fairness. How much does it do to remove the particular distortions affecting small firms identified above? First of all and most important, by reducing marginal tax rates the reform reduces the effects of any distortions which remain. Second, the curtailment in the scope for tax sheltering should also improve the relative after-tax return of investment in all business as compared with real estate, tax-exempt bonds and other favoured savings media. Third, on balance, some simplification has been achieved if only because some six million people will no longer have to file returns and a further six million will not have to itemize deductions and will, as a result, face lower compliance costs. Many of these will be unincorporated businesses. After the reform, however, United States tax law remains very complex — the reform legislation itself covers some 1,600 pages.

A minority of taxpayers with higher incomes, many of these small business people, will experience increased complexity because of the complicated rules affecting the withdrawal of some tax concessions beyond certain income levels and because of the expanded provisions for a minimum rate of tax. Aaron (Pechman, 1987b) points out that 'because congress permitted some opportunities for tax avoidance to remain in the tax code, it was compelled to retain a minimum tax'.[1] These opportunities include reliefs for health and life insurance and mortgage interest relief on debt incurred to purchase first and second homes (this relief was limited to the first $1 million of debt in subsequent legislation following the October 1987 stock market crash!).

The advantage of radical reform of direct tax systems either in the direction of a move towards a wider income tax base, which is what the United States reform does, or towards a universal expenditure tax, has long been proclaimed by British economists (see Peacock, 1978; Bannock, 1981; Kay and King, 1986). By removing distortion in investment decisions such reforms can improve economic efficiency, not least by encouraging a shift of resources to expanding small firms. There would also be other benefits, for example, as Muellbauer (1987) has argued, fiscal advantages for house ownership hamper the mobility of labour. Just as important, reform is necessary to improve fairness and transparency in the tax system.

Radical reform also offers the best route to simplifying the tax system, the complexity of which is itself a major source of unfairness since it is the least advantaged who are least able to cope with complexity. Of course there is considerable scope for simplifying tax administration without new legislation and measures to do this are necessary whether or not there are radical reforms. Simplification is urgently needed to reduce the growing compliance burden on small firms and indeed on all business. In Chapter 10 it is shown that the costs of tax compliance borne by business are now of the order of 1.5–2 per cent of GDP, which represents a considerable waste of real resources over and above the losses caused by fiscal distortions. It is not clear why business should bear such a large proportion of the burden of tax administration. As Peacock (1978) has argued, a greater degree of self-assessment by taxpayers would improve tax transparency (the awareness by citizens of the taxes they pay) and it would reduce burdens on business and increase pressures for simplification.

The obstacles to tax reform are political but the short experience following the limited reforms in the UK suggests that the fears of unfavourable consequences were misplaced. The United States reforms will, it is to be hoped, provide further inspiration for believing that the political problems can be surmounted.

NOTE

1 Other criticisms made by Aaron include the loss of the opportunity to reform the United States corporation tax system, which is of the classical type, to eliminate the double taxation of dividends both in the company and in the hands of the recipients through income tax.

REFERENCES

Bannock, G. (1981), *The Economics of Small Firms*, Basil Blackwell, Oxford.
Berle, A.A. and Means, G.C. (1932), *The Modern Corporation and Private Property*, Harcourt, Brace & World, New York, 1967.
Bolton Committee (1971), *Small Firms*, Report of the Committee of Inquiry on Small Firms, HMSO, London.
Burns, P. and Dewhurst, J. (1986), *Small Business in Europe*, Macmillan, London.
Goffee, R. and Scase, R. (eds) (1987), *Entrepreneurship in Europe*, Croom Helm, Kent.
Kay, J.A. and King, M.A. (1986), *The British Tax System*, 4th edn, Oxford University Press.
Muellbauer, J. (1987), *The community charge, rates and tax reform*, *Lloyds Bank Review*, October.
Peacock, A. (1978), *Do we need to reform direct taxes? Lloyds Bank Review*, Vol.5, no.1.
Pechman, J.A. (ed) (1987a), *Tax reform prospects in Europe and Canada*, *The Brookings Review*, Vol.5, no.1.
Pechman, J.A. (ed) (1987b), *Tax Reform and the US Economy*, The Brookings Institution, Washington DC.
Sandford, C. (1986), *Taxing task in paying the Inland Revenue*, *Financial Times*, 28 November.
Wilson Committee (1979), *The Financing of Small Firms*, Interim Report of the Committee to Review the Functioning of Financial Institutions, HMSO, London.

Chapter 7

VAT AND SMALL BUSINESS: EUROPEAN EXPERIENCE AND IMPLICATIONS FOR NORTH AMERICA*

THE RISE OF VAT

Taxation and the Growth of the State

One of the most striking features of the international economic scene during the past two hundred years or so, in addition to the spectacular growth in wealth and international trade, has been the increase in the role of government in economic affairs. The share of the gross domestic product (GDP) accruing to employees of central and local government (but not including state industries) in Britain more than quadrupled from 3.0 per cent in 1907 to 12.9 per cent in 1973 (Bannock, 1975). Because of the growth of transfer payments (unemployment benefit and social security payments), the overall share of government in national expenditure is much larger. In Britain, it increased from 12 per cent of the gross national product (GNP) in 1790 to 53 per cent in 1982 (Sandford, 1984). We take Britain as an example, but government expenditure has risen everywhere and now accounts for between one-quarter and one-half of GDP in all the advanced countries.

The upward pressure on government expenditure has not been matched by as strong a pressure to keep down taxes. As a result, tax revenues as a percentage of national incomes have increased roughly in line with government expenditure. Figure 7.1 shows that today, looking at the whole range of democratic countries in the world economy, there is a clear tendency for taxes to rise with income per head. What has happened is that as countries have grown richer, governments have taken a larger share of the total. This relationship is not, however, a very close one; most of the richer European countries have a higher tax ratio (averaging 40 per cent) than might be predicted from the general relationship

---

* A study commissioned by the Canadian Federation of Independent Business (CFIB) and the National Federation of Independent Business (NFIB) in the spring of 1985 and completed in January 1986 at a time when the introduction of VAT was under consideration by the US and Canadian governments. We are grateful to the CFIB and NFIB for their permission to include the report in this volume. Two of the original six appendices have been omitted.

Figure 7.1 GNP–tax ratio and GNP per head, advanced and developing countries, 1982.

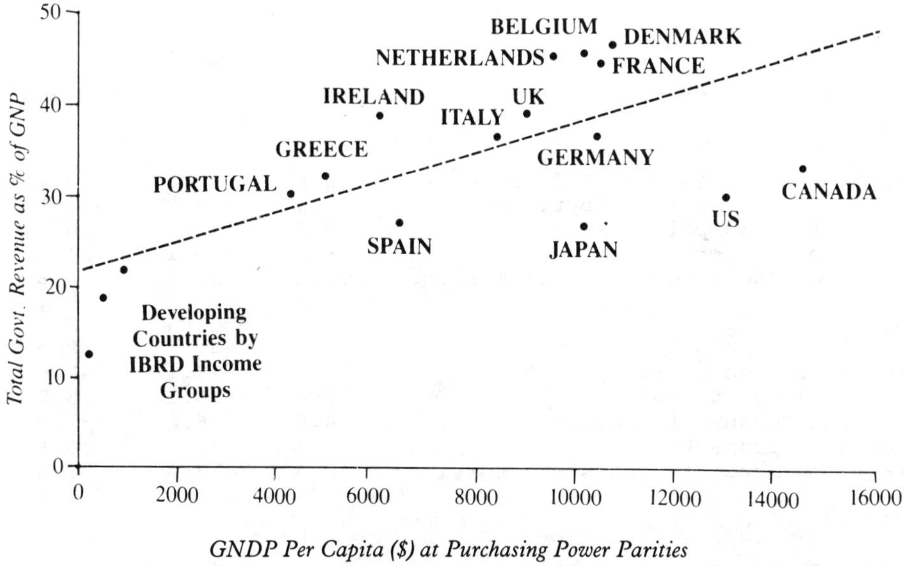

Source: OECD (1984) (1985) and IBRD (1985a). OECD GDP data (except Canada) are at current purchasing power parities. IBRD: Central Government Revenue as proxy for tax revenue.

between income and the tax-take, while North America, Japan and a few other countries not shown in Figure 7.1 (Australia, New Zealand, Switzerland) have lower tax ratios (averaging around 30 per cent) than might be expected.

Table 7.1: Total tax revenue as percentage of GDP

	1965	1980	1983
European Community	29.6	38.4	41.4
United States of America	26.3	30.4	29.0
Canada	25.9	32.0	33.0

Source: Organisation for Economic Co-operation and Development (1985a) (unweighted averages).

Table 7.1 shows the difference between average tax ratios in the EC, the USA and Canada and their evolution since 1965. There has been an increase in these ratios in all these areas, but they have actually fallen recently in the USA, and the gap between the EC and North American tax rates has widened significantly over the period.

Table 7.2: Groups of tax revenues in the EC and North America as percentage of total taxation

	1965	1980	1983
EC			
Taxes on incomes and profits	28.5	35.2	34.4
Social security contributions	24.4	27.8	28.8
General consumption taxes	13.0	17.2	16.7
Taxes on property	8.0	5.1	4.6
Taxes on specific goods and services	22.5	12.0	12.6
USA			
Taxes on incomes and profits	46.3	47.1	42.6
Social security contributions	16.4	26.1	28.7
General consumption taxes	4.6	6.6	7.0
Taxes on property	15.3	10.1	10.6
Taxes on specific goods and services	14.6	7.8	8.6
Canada			
Taxes on incomes and profits	39.3	46.6	43.7
Social security contributions	5.7	10.4	13.1
General consumption taxes	18.2	11.5	11.6
Taxes on property	13.2	9.1	9.1
Taxes on specific goods and services	17.1	13.0	14.4

Source: Organisation for Economic Co-operation and Development (1985a) (unweighted averages)

Note: Because of the method of averaging, omission and coverage, the percentages do not total 100.

Trends in Taxation

Table 7.2 shows the share of different types of taxes in total tax revenues in the EC, USA and Canada in selected years since 1965. Social security contributions have accounted for a rapidly increasing share of tax revenue in all three areas and now represent 29 per cent of the total in both the EC and the USA, though less than half that amount in Canada. The share of both taxes on property and taxes on specific goods (for example, excise duties) have fallen everywhere, while that of taxes on income and profits has fallen in the USA but risen in the EC and Canada.

We are discussing here shares in a rising total; both general consumption taxes and personal income taxes rose as a percentage of GDP in all three areas, though that of corporate income taxes fell sharply in the USA and Canada.

The subject of the present study, value added tax (VAT), is a general consumption tax levied, as explained in detail in Appendix 7.1 (p.158), on the retail price of goods and services in a similar way to a sales tax (which is also a general consumption tax). VAT differs from a sales tax, however, in that the revenue is collected at all stages in the process of production and distribution, including the retail stage, whereas a sales tax is collected only at the retail stage. Most US states have sales taxes, of course, and so do the Canadian provincial governments. In the USA general consumption taxes (sales taxes) have increased their share of total tax revenue quite considerably since 1965 and indeed have been second only to social security contributions as the most buoyant sources of revenue. The same is true of the EC. In Canada, where general consumption taxes were relatively more important as a source of revenue than in either the EC or the USA in 1965, the Federal Manufacturers' Sales Tax (levied at the wholesale stage) and provincial sales taxes have accounted for a declining proportion of revenue, although these general consumption taxes in Canada still yield relatively more than their counterparts in the USA.

It will be noted that in all three areas, the share of direct taxation (income and profits taxes and social security contributions) in tax revenues has increased while that of indirect taxes (taxes on expenditure) has fallen. Among indirect taxes, general consumption taxes are rapidly taking over from specific taxes on property, goods and services, especially in the EC but also in the USA. It is not surprising that federal governments in both the USA and Canada have looked with interest at the contribution of VAT to the large and rising take from general consumption taxes in Europe. This interest is particularly strong in Canada where the Federal Manufacturers Sales Tax has accounted for a declining share of general consumption tax revenue which, in turn, accounts for a declining proportion of GDP. The United States, of course, have no federal general consumption taxes, but general sales taxes have accounted for an increasing share of total state tax revenues (up from 19.3 per cent in 1949 to 31.3 per cent in 1984), as well as of total national tax revenue. These increases result partly from an increase in the number of states levying state taxes (45 now compared with 27 in 1949). In both the USA and Canada, average rates of local sales taxes have increased several-fold in the post World War II period (Table 7.3), though the increase in rates has been much faster in Canada.

The Rise of VAT

In the EC, VAT was introduced in Denmark in 1967, in West Germany and in France (in its present form) in 1968 and had been adopted by nine member states by 1973. VAT has accounted for an increasing, in some cases rapidly increasing, proportion of total tax revenues in all but two of the nine states (Table 7.4). Expressed as a percentage of central government revenues, the contribution of VAT is higher still, varying in the nine from 17.6 per cent in Luxembourg to 19.3 per cent in the UK, 34.7 per cent in West Germany (a federal state) and 42.2 per cent in France (1983).

VAT is levied at much higher rates than North American sales taxes and the tax base is wider, hence its great power as a revenue raiser. Figure 7.2 shows that

Table 7.3: Average rates of general sales tax, selected years, 1949–84, USA and Canada

	US state governments (%)	Canadian provincial governments (%)
1949	1.3	n.a.
1953	1.6	1.3
1957	1.8	1.5
1961	2.3	3.5
1965	2.6	4.2
1970	3.5	6.1
1972	3.8	6.1
1974	3.8	6.9
1978	4.1	7.0
1981	n.a	7.2
1982	4.2	n.a.
1984	4.5	n.a.
1985	n.a.	7.8

* Excludes Alberta, Yukon and the North-West Territories.

Sources: Current population weighted averages from *Statistics Canada*, Catalogue 68 – 201, Provincial and Municipal Finances, Canadian Tax Foundation. Selected issues of *The Book of the States*, Council of State Governments.

Table 7.4: VAT revenues as percentage of total tax revenues in the EC

	1965	1970	1975	1980	1983	1984 (est.)
Belgium	-	-	15.66	15.62	15.42	n.a.
Denmark	9.11	18.77	16.90	22.19	21.10	20.50
France	20.07*	25.41	22.97	20.74	20.22	21.50
West Germany	-	17.40	14.62	16.64	16.99	17.00
Ireland	5.68*	13.10*	14.68	14.76	21.07	21.30
Italy	-	-	13.68	16.25	14.92	n.a.
Luxembourg	-	6.78	11.86	10.92	12.08	13.60
The Netherlands	-	14.61	14.36	15.85	14.79	15.80
United Kingdom	5.92*	6.52*	8.78	12.41	13.86	14.60

* Sales tax subsequently replaced by VAT.

Source: Organisation for Economic Co-operation and Development (1985a); 1984 figures are estimates by Graham Bannock & Partners, based on national sources.

Figure 7.2 The rise of VAT.

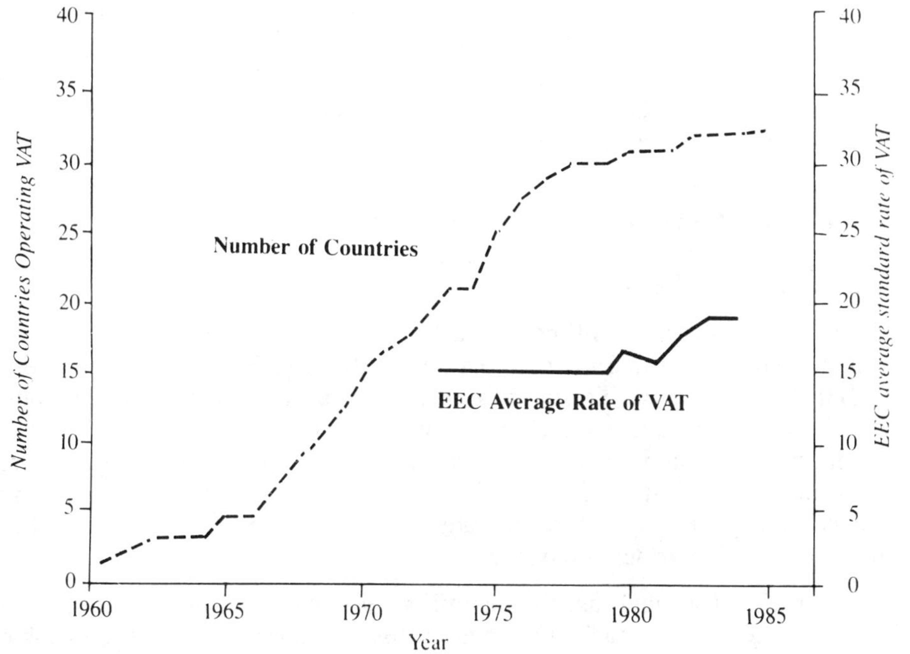

Sources: Appendices 7.2 and 7.3

the average standard rate of tax for the nine EC states has increased from 15 to nearly 20 per cent since 1973. As will be shown later (pp.117–8), the effective rate of tax is much lower than these standard rates (which are themselves not very precise indicators of changes in the burden of VAT) but there is no doubt that VAT rates, like sales tax rates in North America, have drifted upwards over a long period.

VAT is a complicated tax for both the tax authorities and the businesses which collect it, but its appeal as a source of revenue is obvious. VAT also has a number of theoretical advantages over other sales taxes; much of this report will be concerned with explaining and assessing these. Meanwhile, we may note that the spread of VAT has not been limited to the EC. By 1986, VAT was in operation in 36 states around the world, surprisingly, for such a complex tax, many of them developing countries, and the diffusion of this tax shows little sign of slackening (Figure 7.2). Appendix 7.2 (p.168) gives a full list of the countries with VAT. Although 15 of the 23 member countries of the OECD now have VAT, it is a striking fact that those that do not operate this tax, Australia, Canada, Japan, Switzerland and the United States, Turkey and Greece (temporarily), are relatively low tax countries (tax revenues averaging 29 per cent of GDP in 1983) compared with those that do (41 per cent).

The actual causal relationship between VAT and high total taxes is less clear. It is true that most European countries with VAT were already high tax countries relative to the USA, say, even before they adopted VAT. However, there is little doubt that in modern liberal democracies, public expenditures tend to rise to the limits of tax and borrowing potential. In this context, installing any new tax machinery, especially one as broadly based as VAT, will inevitably lead to higher overall taxation. The decision whether or not to introduce VAT needs to recognize these larger considerations just as much as the technical ones with which this report primarily deals.

VAT RATES AND COVERAGE IN EUROPE

The History of VAT

The consumption-type VAT now levied in the EC was recommended by the Neumark Committee in 1962 (International Bureau of Fiscal Documentation, 1983) five years after the Treaty of Rome agreement to form the customs union and affirmed as mandatory for member states in two directives in 1967. Douglas Dosser (in Peacock and Forte, 1981) wrote that the Committee 'reported against a "textbook background" that the VAT was the apotheosis of good indirect tax practice' and quoted the American academic, Carl Shoup (1969), whose earlier work influenced their deliberations:

> the turnover (cascade) tax, the manufacturer's sales tax, the wholesale sales tax, and the VAT . . . each of these taxes discriminates less than its immediate predecessors among types of business and methods of doing business . . . the VAT is the latest and probably the final stage in a historical development of general sales taxation at the national level that has eliminated the uneven impact of the turnover tax and the manufacturers and wholesalers sales taxes.

The Neumark Committee did not recommend that VAT should be applied at the retail stage. It seemed to be mainly concerned with the advantages of a more neutral tax than with the cascade taxes then widespread in Europe. Actually, VAT is not neutral with respect to large and small firms unless net compliance costs are fully compensated for, nor is it neutral with respect to consumption and production unless it is applied comprehensively at a uniform rate. Dosser points out that the aspects of neutrality which appealed to the Neumark Committee were that it did not distort the structure of firms by encouraging vertical integration and could be easily applied on either the origin or destination principle so that the administration of the tax would not depend on the continued policing of frontiers when tariffs were removed and VAT rates harmonized.

Both these considerations were rather specific to the EC. All the original six members of the Community had, or had at one time, experienced cascade turnover taxes, and in West Germany in particular there was great concern about the way this tax favoured industrial groupings. The cascade tax, like the Manufacturers' Sales Tax in Canada today, was patently inferior to the proposed VAT. VAT also clearly had advantages in a customs union. Tait (1984) points out that most of the countries in the Latin American regional groups — the Latin American Integration Association and the Andean Pact — have adopted value added taxes, in many cases to replace cascade taxes.

The origins of VAT go back much further than the Neumark Committee. According to the International Bureau of Fiscal Documentation (1983), proposals for a 'refined turnover tax', which in its essentials was an income type VAT, were put forward in 1919 by a German businessman and government consultant, Dr Wilhelm von Siemens, while Thomas Adams, an American Professor at Yale, had made similar proposals for a business tax a year earlier. Neither of these proposals was adopted at the time, but several countries used value added techniques in some form before World War II, including Argentina, The Netherlands and Finland.

The State of Michigan in the United States also implemented Thomas Adams' Business Activities Tax (an additive-type income-based tax). The first modern consumption type VAT was introduced in France in 1954, but at first it applied only to the transactions of manufacturers and wholesalers and was revised and developed in 1968 and again in 1978. According to Tait (1984), several developing countries in former French colonial territories in Africa introduced VAT in the early 1960s. At least 38 countries now have valued added taxes or firm plans to introduce them, the latest being New Zealand and, with their accession to the EC, Spain and Portugal.[1]

From 1987, all EC countries including Greece (where introduction was twice temporarily delayed) had value-added taxes. Of the three countries which joined the enlarged EC in 1973 and which did not participate in the decision to make VAT mandatory, all had single-stage wholesale taxes prior to the introduction of VAT. Denmark had already introduced VAT in 1967. Ireland's VAT became effective from 1972.

The history of the introduction of VAT in the United Kingdom, where the tax was considered and rejected more than a decade before Britain became a member of the EC, is of interest. From 1940 onwards the UK had a single-stage wholesale tax called Purchase Tax, charged on manufactured consumer goods at multiple rates as a percentage of the wholesale price. In 1963, the government set up the Committee on Turnover Taxation (Richardson Committee, 1964) to consider the possible replacement of the existing wholesale tax (and profits tax) by VAT. The Committee decisively rejected VAT on the grounds that there was no logic in replacing a well-established single-stage tax, which the UK had at the time, with a cumbersome multi-stage tax requiring elaborate and extensive administrative machinery, when the object of the tax was simply to tax consumer expenditure. The difficulties arising from differentiating between basic necessities and other types of goods under a value added tax were also pointed out.

The government did recognize the desirability of broadening the base of the system of indirect taxes, which also included excise duties, but which did not cover services. In 1963, as Robinson and Sandford (1983) record, however, the UK's Conservative Chancellor (Finance Minister) had little enthusiasm for VAT and, with the dismissal of that tax by the Richardson Committee, nothing more was done. The next (Labour) government in 1966 introduced a per capita payroll tax, the Selective Employment Tax (SET), paid by all employers but refunded with a premium in manufacturing, refunded without a premium in the primary sector and transport, and borne in full by the construction, distribution and service sectors. SET was not costly to administer and raised substantial revenue, but was very unpopular among those employers who paid the tax and among trades unions.

The Conservatives who returned to power in 1970 were pledged to abolish SET and in 1973 replaced both SET and Purchase Tax with VAT. This was made necessary by the accession of the UK to the EC on 1 January 1973, though the government claimed that it would have introduced the tax even had Britain decided to stay out of the Community. Much use was made of the now familiar arguments for the neutrality of VAT, its value as a flexible regulator of demand and its favourable effect on the balance of payments. (A report from the National Economic Development Office (NEDO, 1969) had been much more favourable to VAT than had the Richardson Report.)

Exemptions and Rates

Although the broad shape of the VAT systems in the EC are similar and determined by adherence to the directives of the EC Commission (see Appendix 7.5, p.175), there are major differences in administration (see p.123), the treatment of small firms (see p.156), exemptions and rates. In these and many minor points of detail there are extensive differences and we could find no previous attempt to give an overview of variations in the system between member states.

The main features of the EC VAT system are of course that it is of the consumption type with exports free of tax and imports taxed (for the most part) at national borders. According to the 6th Directive, banking, insurance and most other financial services are exempt from VAT and so are real estate, including lettings, educational and medical services, contributions to charitable organizations, works of art and a few other categories of consumption. In some cases, zero-rating (see below) rather than exemption is used for a few of these categories. Government services, such as postal services, generally are also exempt from VAT except where they compete with taxed services from the private sector.

Adherence to the 6th Directive is general but not absolute. For example, telecommunications are not subject to VAT in France and The Netherlands, nor are telegraph services in Italy. France also allows the liberal professions exemption from VAT with the choice of opting in. Some countries exempt authors and other cultural activities and the tax treatment of charitable organizations is not uniform. The European countries with VAT which are not members of the EC, generally operate similar systems, for example the Austrian system is similar to that for West Germany. There are a few important differences, for example, Norway allows input credits for investment goods but taxes registered traders at a special rate (50 per cent of the VAT rate) on these goods.

Most countries give favourable tax treatment to most foods, public transport and other basic necessities to reduce regressivity as well as to certain 'desirable' goods such as books and newspapers. Which goods are included in these favoured categories varies from country to country and the treatment may be either zero rating, exemption or, more commonly, a reduced rate of tax.

As explained in Appendix 7.1 (p.158), supplies of exempted goods (exempted without credit) and services are not allowed to reclaim input taxes, but suppliers of zero-rated (exempted with credit) goods and services are. Most European countries, including non-EC members with VAT systems, restrict zero-rating to exports and the transportation of exports, but three countries, the UK, Ireland and Portugal, make extensive use of zero-rating for the favoured categories of expenditure.

It will also be recalled that zero-rating actually results in a negative tax or subsidy for the domestic consumption of goods and services to which it applies. This complicates analysis of the rates used in VAT systems, but if we restrict our analysis to nominal positive rates rather than the effective rates discussed in Appendix 7.1, we can see that there is little uniformity in the numbers of rates levied (Table 7.5). Only four countries out of the 14 in Europe with VAT have a single standard rate, though the UK's extensive use of zero-rating for favoured goods distinguishes it from the three Scandinavian countries where, apart from exports, only newspapers (and in Sweden, fuels and medicines also) are significant consumption items to be zero-rated. Four countries have three rates and four have four rates.

Table 7.5 presents the picture as it was at the end of March 1985. It can be seen from Appendix 7.3 that several governments have experimented both with more and fewer rates, though most countries have the same number they started with. Only Ireland has fewer rates than when VAT was first introduced. The UK had two positive rates from 1974 to 1976, for example, while for a brief period in 1980 Italy had no fewer than ten rates.

Table 7.5 also shows that there are wide variations in the levels of rates which, for standard rates (the general rate from which exceptions are made), range from 12 per cent for Luxembourg to 23.5 per cent for Sweden. Other rates range from 2 to 38 per cent, both these extremes being in Italy. Standard rates have generally moved upwards and in all EC countries (other than Spain and Portugal where introduction is so recent) these rates are higher than when VAT was first introduced (see Appendix 7.3). Reductions in the standard rate have taken place in five of the nine EC countries on one or more occasions, but in most cases these reductions have been accompanied by changes in the base of the tax or in other rates so that the reductions have been more apparent than real. Certainly, as we saw at the beginning of this chapter, VAT has yielded an increasing proportion of rising total tax revenues in seven out of nine EC states. Only in Denmark where the VAT base is exceptionally wide and the single rate exceptionally high and in Italy, has there been any significant downward movement in the VAT/total tax revenue ratio since 1980. In the past decade the trend has been upward in all countries except France.

Table 7.5: Numbers and range of positive VAT rates levied in European countries, March 1985

Country	No. of VAT rates	Standard rate	Other rates 2	3	4
United Kingdom	1	15.0			
Denmark	1	22.0			
Norway*	1	20.0			
Sweden*	1	23.5			
West Germany	2	14.0	7.0		
Ireland	2	23.0	10.0		
Netherlands	2	19.0	5.0		
Luxembourg	3	12.0	6.0	3.0	
Portugal	3	16.0	30.0	8.0	
Spain	3	12.0	8.0	6.0	
Austria*	3	20.0	32.0	10.0	
Belgium	4	19.0	25.0	17.0	6.0
France	4	18.6	33.3	7.0	5.5
Italy	4	18.0	38.0	9.0	2.0

Source: Appendix 7.3.

* Non-member states of the EC.

Some Measures of Coverage and Distortion

No comprehensive published estimates of the coverage of the VAT bases in relation to consumer expenditure in the EC seem to be available and we have been obliged to construct our own. Table 7.6 presents two alternative estimates of the VAT tax base as a percentage of total consumer expenditure. The first column uses the Commission of the European Communities notional tax base and expresses it as a percentage of total consumer expenditure from the national accounts. (The EC Commission takes an interest in the VAT tax base not only because it needs to monitor adherence to the 6th Directive, but also because a major part of the EC budget is derived from a levy of 1 percentage point of the VAT yield in member states. It does not, however, publish data on coverage.) The second column in Table 7.6 isolates and totals those elements in consumer expenditure which are subject to VAT and expresses them as a percentage of total consumer expenditure.

There are large problems in measurement and definition that affect the construction of these estimates. One factor is that there are wide variations in the extent to which certain services are provided by the public sector. Where this is so and the provision remunerated but not taxed, the percentage coverage is lower; where these services are provided free, then consumer expenditure is lower and coverage higher. In West Germany, for example, medical expenditure accounts for 13.5 per cent of consumer spending; in the UK it accounts for only 1.1 per cent.

Table 7.6: Estimates of the VAT base as a percentage of total consumer expenditure, EC member states, 1983

	EC Basis* (1)	National accounts basis (2)
Denmark	80	75
Italy	75	84
Belgium	77	74
West Germany	89	71
Netherlands	84	72
France	81	70
Ireland	n.a.	58
United Kingdom	95	52
Unweighted average	84	70

Sources: Total consumer expenditure: estimates by Graham Bannock & Partners from Eurostat.

*EC Notional Tax Base: written answer by the Commission to a question in the European Parliament.

The UK figure is also high in column 1 (Table 7.6) because the notional base includes the extensive range of zero-rated items. Our own estimates of coverage in column 2 are lower for the UK (and low for Ireland) because we have included in the tax base only taxed items of expenditure and both these countries make extensive use of zero-rating. Our estimates of coverage are usually lower than those in column 1. This is partly because the national accounts consumer expenditure data are insufficiently detailed to allow for the intricacies of exempted expenditures from the tax base; we were, for example, obliged to include all construction and letting expenditure, only some of which is untaxed in most countries. Moreover, exempt small producers are ignored in this analysis, but in fact they both pay some unreclaimable VAT and absorb some consumer spending on which VAT is not levied.

Despite all these qualifications it is clear that the notional VAT tax base is a very high percentage of total consumer expenditure in the EC, at least 75 per cent excluding the British Isles. If the tax were to be neutral it would have to cover 100 per cent of consumption. Seventy-five per cent, nevertheless, is very high when compared with the coverage of other indirect taxes. The Canadian authorities estimate that the Federal Manufacturers' Sales Tax covers 32 per cent of consumers' expenditure while, we believe, general state sales taxes in the United States cover less than two-thirds of consumer expenditure on average.

In their efforts to lighten the burden of such a widely based tax by the use of multiple rates of tax, however, much of the notional tax base is, as we have seen, taxed only lightly or not at all. One crude way of illustrating this is to calculate effective tax rates and to compare them with standard rates. Table 7.7 shows that the average standard rate of VAT is about 17 per cent in the EC. (Of course the standard rate of tax is only a very rough indicator of the level of VAT actually charged since the proportion of goods and services taxed at the standard rate varies from one country to another, as does the number and spread of lower and higher rates in those countries with more than one rate.) The gross effective rate (we use the term 'gross' to distinguish this rate from the effective rate on production value added used in Appendix 7.1), which is total VAT revenue as a percentage of total consumer expenditure, is only 65 per cent of the average standard rate. If the tax were to be neutral, then one uniform standard rate would be 100 per cent of the effective rate. Only in Denmark, France and West Germany are both the coverage of the tax base and the effective rate as a percentage of the standard rate 75 per cent or more.

Table 7.7: Gross effective and standard VAT rates in eight EC member states, 1983

	Gross Effective Rate (%) (1)	Standard Rate (%) (2)	Effective as % of standard (3)
Denmark	17.8	22.0	81
Italy	9.5	18.0	53
Belgium	11.0	19.0	58
West Germany	10.3	13.5	76
Netherlands	11.8	19.0	62
France	13.9	18.6	75
Ireland	11.8	33.8	35
United Kingdom	8.9	15.0	59
Weighted average	10.9	16.8	65

Sources: (1) Total VAT revenue OECD (1985a) as percentage of total consumer expenditure from Eurostat. (2) Appendix 7.3 adjusted to calendar year.

Disallowed Expenditure

So far, for simplicity, we have assumed that unless a business enterprise is exempt (in which case it neither charges VAT nor reclaims VAT on inputs), it can reclaim all input taxes. However, in the interests of minimizing the acquisition of certain goods free of VAT for personal use through a business, part or all of input taxes on certain goods are disallowed in most EC states even though they may be wholly and properly incurred in the course of business. Thus France does not allow businesses to reclaim input taxes on hotel or restaurant expenses, even for subsistence purposes, on business travel or for motor fuels or passenger cars. The UK and Ireland do not allow any reclaims of input tax on cars (except for car dealers) while Belgium and other countries allow only partial relief for cars. Other common disallowances are expenditure on business gifts, business entertainment and company aircraft.

Exemptions without credits for banking and insurance, medical care and other activities, together with exemptions for small businesses below the threshold and disallowed expenditures, mean that credit for input taxes is not permitted for a significant proportion of business expenditures. The French authorities have estimated that only 71.4 per cent of net VAT revenues are collected from final consumers, 18.3 per cent from business enterprises and 10.3 per cent from general government (Table 7.8). As shown, the extent of exemptions and disallowed expenditure varies between member states and the proportion of the tax collected from consumers is probably higher in other EC countries, certainly in West Germany and perhaps Denmark, where exemptions and disallowances are least important. This is not necessarily true in the UK and Ireland where, although the treatment of business expenses is more liberal, the threshold and therefore the number of small firms exempted are exceptionally high. The estimates in Table 7.8 suggest that even were the 6th Directive strictly adhered to in France, less than 80 per cent of VAT would be collected from households.

Table 7.8: Percentage distribution of VAT collection by economic sector, France 1978, under 1980 legislation and under the full application of the 6th Directive

	Firms	Households	Financial institutions	General government	Total
1980 legislation	16.5	71.4	1.8	10.3	100.0
6th Directive	8.6	78.3	2.1	11.0	100.0

Source: *Conseil des Impôts* (1983).

Note: These estimates were prepared using a VAT simulation model based on input-output analysis.

It will be noted that although a significant proportion of VAT revenue is collected from firms and therefore enters into their costs, this does not necessarily mean that tax is not fully shifted forward to consumers. It does mean, however, that the distortions to the pattern of production and consumption arising from the differences in rates and coverage discussed above are further magnified, and also that at least some of VAT paid enters into export prices.

Regressivity

We have shown that the motive for departing from the application of VAT at a single rate over the whole of consumer expenditure is to avoid placing a heavier burden on the less well off. The poor spend a larger proportion of their income than the more affluent and suffer if all commodities, including basic necessities, are taxed at the same rate. In fact, the use of zero-rating or lower rates of tax for goods which weigh large in the budgets of lower income groups has been largely effective in offsetting the regressivity of VAT.

Table 7.9 summarizes the results of studies co-ordinated by the OECD in which VAT liabilities were calculated for the patterns of expenditure of households in different income groups based on family expenditure surveys and expressed as percentages of household expenditure in each group. It should be noted that differences in coverage and method mean that inter-country comparisons are not valid, but it is clear that within each country, the VAT burden is a constant or rising proportion of consumption as incomes increase (i.e. it is progressive). The exception is Norway, only one of the six European countries in Table 7.9 which has a single rate of tax and makes no use of zero-rating for necessities. In Norway VAT declines as a proportion of consumption as household income rises (i.e. it is regressive).

If the VAT burden is expressed as a percentage of income rather than of consumption, the pattern becomes less clear with the tax remaining progressive in Belgium and the UK but regressive in The Netherlands. In either measure the differences in the proportional burden of the tax are, however, quite small, usually less than one percentage point. Other studies give similar results. In Sweden, for example, another country with a uniform rate, VAT is clearly regressive, while in Italy the tax is progressive whether related to either income or consumption (Aaron, 1981). In France an official study concluded that VAT was progressive with respect to consumption but regressive with respect to income (*Conseil de Impöts*,1983).

THE OPERATION OF VAT

Preparation

VAT is not a tax which can be introduced quickly. The process of study, consultation, legislation, education and installation of the necessary administrative machinery takes a considerable time. How long depends primarily on the strength of the political forces generated and the effectiveness of the planning. It is common for writers on VAT to point out that introducation in Europe was facilitated by the existence of the administrative systems for cascade taxes and the familiarity of the business community with turnover taxes. The EC directives of April 1967 called for the introduction of VAT in all (at the time) six member states by January 1970, a lead time of 2 years and 8 months, though of course the deliberations leading up to the decision gave ample warning. The actual dates of introduction and the time taken from April 1967 were as follows:

France	1 January 1968	8 months
West Germany	1 January 1968	8 months
The Netherlands	1 January 1969	1 year
Luxembourg	1 January 1970	2 years 8 months
Belgium	1 January 1971	3 years 8 months
Italy	1 January 1973	5 years 8 months

In all cases some preparation had been done before the publication of the EC Directive. This was certainly true for the two largest countries in the Community who were the driving forces behind the decision to opt for VAT and the first to get it in operation. France had had a VAT in the industrial sector

Table 7.9: VAT as a percentage of household consumption expenditure by category of disposable income

			Low (first decile) consumption	Intermediate (fifth decile) consumption	High (tenth decile) consumption
Belgium	1973	(1)	9.16	9.36	9.58
France	1969	(2)	10.10	10.70	10.60
West Germany	1975	(3)	6.03	7.00	7.01
Netherlands	1974	(4)	7.00	7.30	7.50
Norway	1975	(5)	14.90	14.60	14.00
United Kingdom	1977	(6)	2.90	4.42	4.95

Source: Organisation for Economic Co-operation and Development (1981). The data are not internationally comparable. Only some of the differences in coverage are listed below.

Notes:
(1) Employees. 1st, 2nd and 4th quartiles.
(2) Couple with 3 children. 1969 consumption pattern, 1975 tax rate. Low = F3,000–10,000, intermediate = F15,000–20,000; high = over F50,000.
(3) Low = 2 persons: pensioners and recipients of welfare. Intermediate = 4 persons: employees of average income. High = 4 persons: employees of higher income.
(4) Two person households. Low = under Fl.16,000; intermediate = Fl.16,000–19,000; high = over Fl.44,000.
(5) Couple with 2 children.
(6) Four-person household.

since 1954 and a law to extend the tax to nearly all economic activities had been passed in 1966; the real lead time, therefore, was well over two years and actually led back to the preparations for the industrial VAT 15 years earlier. In 1963 West Germany had introduced legislation, which was not passed, to replace its turnover tax with a VAT of the income type, using the invoice method. The final law introducing VAT was not passed until May 1967.

The length of the delay in implementing the EC directives in Italy seems to have been caused mainly by political problems. According to Antonio Pedone (in Aaron, 1981), tax officials were concerned about the difficulties of extending a turnover tax system to the highly fragmented retailing system, trades unions were concerned about the impact of VAT on prices and its regressive effect on lower paid workers, exporters were concerned that the exemption of input taxes on exports would result in lower rebates than those enjoyed under the existing turnover tax, while small businesses feared that VAT records would be used in the assessment of income taxes. At the same time, the capacity of the authorities to cope with the changes was limited by other contemporary reforms in direct taxation and in the finance of local government. Three postponements of the date of introduction were authorized by the EC.

Difficulties of a similar kind are being experienced in Greece today, which has twice been granted postponement of the introduction of VAT, though things seem to have moved more rapidly in Spain and Portugal which have just introduced the tax. European countries which introduced VAT after the pioneers in the original six EEC member states have, of course, been able to draw on earlier experience.

The introduction of VAT in the UK, against the background set out earlier (p.113–4), was conducted like a well planned and successful military operation (see Johnstone, 1975), though the Chancellor's announced intention that it would be 'the simplest VAT in Europe' was frustrated. Serious planning began in 1969 and a Green Paper was published in March 1971 committing the government to introduce VAT. The White Paper was published a year later and the enabling legislation became law in the Finance Act of July 1972. VAT was introduced on 1 April 1973, two years from the date of the Green Paper. Somewhat more additional administrative staff were required than expected, some 6,440 in total, but revenue at £1,425 million was 24 per cent more than expected.

Initial Economic Effects

We have already shown that fears about the distributional effects of the introduction of VAT have not, on the whole, been borne out in practice — although they would have been had not the theoretical neutrality of VAT been emasculated by exemptions and multiple rates of taxation. In those countries which have applied a single rate with few exemptions, VAT has proved mildly regressive with respect to consumption and more so with respect to income; however, in Sweden and elsewhere the progressivity of the income tax system was increased to compensate for this.

The effects of the introduction of VAT on the price level have generally been unfavourable — prices rose. However, the extent of this effect has been impossible to determine with any precision because, as always with econometric analysis, all other factors affecting prices did not remain constant. The effects of the introduction of VAT on prices (or changes in VAT on prices) depends on the extent to which the tax is shifted forward, the degree to which monetary policy is accommodating, the effect on wage settlements, the stage reached in the business cycle, the extent to which changes in other taxes compensate, changes in the pattern of consumption and other factors. Some of these factors will have immediate effects, for example, each 1 per cent on a uniform rate of VAT will immediately raise consumer prices by the extent to which the tax base covers consumer expenditure — generally by less than about 0.8 per cent assuming that no other taxes are reduced or eliminated. In practice, VAT replaced other taxes and the initial impact has never been great.

A number of econometric studies have been carried out (for some see Aaron, 1981) and although we have not reviewed them in detail, the general conclusion seems to be that VAT has been only mildly inflationary, particularly through its subsequent effects on the wage price spiral in some countries. These studies lend little support to the view that VAT contributed to the upsurge of inflation in the early 1970s which would, in our view, have happened anyway, even without the 1973 oil price shock.

There is even less evidence of other short-term macro-economic damage from the introduction of VAT. In those countries where VAT replaced turnover taxes which bore on investment goods, there was concern that businesses would defer investment during the transition period. This potential problem was avoided in some countries either by introducing reliefs for investments under the turnover tax (for example in Italy) or by the imposition of a temporary tax on investment after the introduction of VAT (West Germany, Belgium). Some countries, (for example The Netherlands) had no transitional measures for investment goods.

One of the arguments in favour of VAT that we have not previously dealt with is that, because it is widely based and the rate easily altered, it can be used as an effective regulator of demand. The UK Treasury, for example, has powers to alter VAT rates by order without recourse to Parliament for just this purpose. However, it is difficult to find cases where VAT has been used for purposes of macro-economic demand management. One exception was in Britain in 1974 when the standard rate of VAT was reduced to 8 per cent in an attempt to stimulate the economy and check the rise in prices following the oil price shock. However, as we have seen, most changes in VAT have been in an upward direction and to increase revenue.

Administration

It is a fair characterization of VAT in its pure form that it provides economic efficiency at the expense of administrative complexity. We have seen how the economic efficiency of the tax has been undermined in virtually all countries in which it is imposed, but this has done nothing to alleviate the administrative burden; indeed, it has significantly worsened it. There can be no doubt that it is in administration that VAT looks least attractive, and it is to this subject that we now turn.

VAT administrations need to perform four functions: first, to arrange the registration of eligible traders (and their deregistration if they cease to be eligible for any reason), and to distribute explanatory material; second, to despatch and receive tax returns, refund input taxes and receive tax payments; third, to deal with the many queries (and disputes) that arise from new and established traders; and fourth, to carry out audits and enforce compliance with the tax.

These functions have some similarities with those for the administration of incomes and profits taxes, but are, in some respects, more onerous because of the frequency of the tax returns and the scale and regularity of tax refunds. About one-third of VAT received by the authorities is repaid to registered traders. The proportion varies from country to country according to the foreign trade ratio, the extent of zero-rating and other factors. In 1979 the percentage of tax repaid was: Italy, 25 per cent, The Netherlands, 33 per cent, Sweden, 38 per cent; UK, 35 per cent. In France, where arrangements for the repayment of tax are much less favourable than elsewhere, the equivalent figure seems to have been only 7 per cent (see below).

Moreover, while the annual assessment of business income taxes involves the review of accounts prepared in the majority of cases by qualified accountants, VAT accounts are prepared in most cases by in-house staff who may find the complexities of tax difficult to handle, at least until several years' experience has been gained. These complexities, which arise mainly from exemptions and multiple rates and changes in the rates, require the availability of large numbers of officials to deal with queries on a daily basis and to visit premises to ensure that VAT regulations are being properly complied with.

The size of the VAT administrative machine is not of course necessarily greater than with the cascade turnover taxes operated by the original members of the EC, but it would be very much greater than that required for a manufacturers' wholesale tax or a retail sales tax. Value added taxes involve all or virtually all significant business units. In the UK, for example, Purchase Tax (a single stage wholesale tax) involved 74,000 traders. The VAT which replaced it now involves over 1.4 million traders. (VAT also replaced SET (see p.114) but that was collected through the social security contributions system.)

The volume of administrative work for VAT is not simply a function of the number of registered traders. There are very large movements on and off the register each year as new firms start trading or pass the eligibility threshold, or go out of business or contract below the threshold. In 1983 in the UK, for example, 176,549 firms registered and 134,549 deregistered (Ganguly, 1985). There are also a large number of other changes, for example of address and legal status.

Administrative arrangements for VAT are not the same in all countries in Europe. Some countries have quite separate organizations as in Italy, others combine the administration of VAT and income tax as in West Germany and Ireland though the VAT on imports is collected by Customs and Excise. In the

UK, Customs and Excise are responsible for all VAT administration (they were also responsible for Purchase Tax) through a system of 90 main local offices, some with sub offices and central data processing. All countries have local offices, some have decentralized data processing. In some countries the post office giro system is used for tax payments, in others bank giros (electronic funds transfer) or cheques are used. In West Germany, the proceeds of the tax are shared between the Federal Government and the *Länder* (states). This is done on the basis of population not revenue and, since it is used to redistribute revenue between rich and poor states, causes considerable friction.

The Costs of Administration

Since there are major differences in the size distribution of businesses and industrial structures between countries and the turnover threshold is much higher in some countries than in others, the number of registered traders is not necessarily proportionate to the human population. The UK, for example, with a higher threshold and a more concentrated business structure, has only 40 per cent of the number of registered traders as Italy even though the human population is about the same. Table 7.10 shows the number of registered traders in selected countries together with the number of man-years which national administrations say are solely concerned with VAT. (Particularly in countries where the administration of VAT is combined with that of other taxes and where overhead facilities are shared, these numbers will be to some extent estimated. Even where VAT administration is separate, customs staff are involved in import taxation and the numbers should be treated with caution.) It can be seen that in the UK each official deals with 115 traders and in Italy with 267 traders.

Table 7.10: Number of registered traders, VAT officials and traders per official, selected countries

	Belgium	France	West Germany	Italy	The Netherlands	Sweden	United Kingdom
Number of registered traders	565,555 1984	1,711,000 1983	1,752,358 1982	3,600,000 1980	455,000 1984	400,000 1979	1,433,100 1983-4
Number of VAT officials	4,000	11,500	n.a.	13,500	2,400	1,705	12,451
Traders per official	141	149		267	190	235	115

Source: MIA Interviews with national tax administrations.

The differences in numbers of traders per official do not necessarily reflect differences in productivity. Sweden handles more traders per official than Belgium or The Netherlands, which could result from the simpler form of the tax in Sweden, while Italy, which has a more complex system, handles even more, which could, with its greater number of traders, reflect either economies of scale, laxer standards of enforcement or less concentrated industrial structure.

In the UK the average size of trader is very much larger than in the rest of Europe and each trader requires more attention (Small firms which, as is shown in the next section (p.148–9), account for the majority of traders in all countries, contribute relatively little revenue and receive less attention than large traders.) The UK also probably allows more scope for questioning decisions of the administration and has a system of VAT tribunals to arbitrate disputes; in other countries this is left to the judicial system.

A large proportion of VAT staff in all countries are concerned with field audits and other enforcement work. In the UK, 22 per cent of VAT staff are engaged in general administration and fraud work; in Italy, 37 per cent of the total are described as 'financial police'; and in The Netherlands, 63 per cent are engaged in checking and audit. In Sweden, auditing units account for 60 per cent of total staff in the total number shown in Table 7.10 but they also deal with other taxes. On a rough ratio basis to population, there are probably well over 70,000 officials engaged in inland VAT work in those EC member states with VAT.

Even though VAT is a self-assessed tax it is quite labour intensive for the administration, as mentioned, particularly because of the the large numbers of returns, payments and refunds and the requirement for audits on business premises. The Inland Revenue in the UK is able to deal with 387 individual income tax assessments per official employed, well over three times the number of registered traders per VAT official. (The UK does not use a self-assessment system and the Inland Revenue has a relatively low level of computerization; North American productivity levels are much higher — see p.155). High levels of staffing are associated with high levels of other costs, but high as these costs are in absolute terms, they are low compared with the revenue raised.

In the EC, total government costs for VAT probably average about 1 per cent of the revenue collected. Table 7.11 provides figures for the UK; similar ratios of cost to revenue were mentioned by national tax authorities in Belgium, Ireland and The Netherlands. West Germany has no data at federal level on the collection costs of VAT, but we were told that they were 'very substantially less' than the total costs for all taxes as a percentage of revenue (around 2 per cent). In the UK, the cost-revenue percentage for income tax is 2.2, about twice that for VAT, though collection costs for Excise duties are estimated at only 0.3 per cent. Not only are the collection costs of VAT relatively low in relation to revenue, but they have fallen by about 50 per cent since 1977–8 as tax officials and businesses alike have become more proficient at operating the tax and as tax revenues have risen with economic growth and higher rates of tax. It should be noted that even if cost-revenue data were available on a comparable basis, differences in these ratios would not necessarily reflect differences in the efficiency with which the tax is collected. The relatively low nominal and effective rate and the extensive use of zero-rating in the UK should tend to raise the cost-revenue ratio compared with that of other countries. That it seems to be about the same suggests that the UK system is relatively efficient.

Table 7.11: Numbers of VAT staff, registered traders and total administration costs and revenues, United Kingdom 1978–9 to 1983–4

	No. of staff	No. of registered traders	Ratio of traders to staff	Total cost of administration (£ m)	Total revenue (£ m)	Cost as % of revenue
1978-9	12,914	1,286,200	100	99.4	5,218.1	1.9
1979-80	12,243	1,327,200	108	111.8	8,706.2	1.3
1980-1	12,302	1,338,000	109	137.8	11,450.4	1.2
1981-2	12,219	1,379,500	113	154.4	12,363.2	1.2
1982-3	12,255	1,398,300	114	165.7	14,413.3	1.2
1983-4	12,451	1,433,100	115	176.3	15,920.8	1.1
1984-5	12,656	1,458,900	115	193.1	19,280.0	1.0

Source: Commissioners of H M Customs and Excise (1985).

Note: Includes car tax, an additional tax yielding about £750 million.

Compliance Costs

The government's tax administration or collection costs are only part of the total social cost of operating the tax system, however, and are in fact for VAT only a small part of those total costs. First of all, value added taxes, as we have shown, are not neutral; they alter relative prices and by doing so distort the structure of production and consumption in ways which will reduce welfare (in the technical, economic sense of the word). There are also other ways in which value added taxes reduce welfare, for example by discouraging firms to grow beyond the threshold. VAT may also stimulate tax evasion. Finally, as shown, VAT tends to work against the progressiveness built into the rest of the tax system and may promote inequality. We do not attempt to measure social costs which, though very important, are common to a greater or lesser extent to all forms of indirect taxation and are difficult, if not impossible, to quantify.

What are probably most important, although there have been few attempts to measure them, are the costs incurred by businesses in collecting the tax. (Among the few exceptions is the work of Cedric Sandford and his colleagues at the University of Bath Centre for Fiscal Studies, on which we draw heavily in this section and later (p.138 et seq)). These compliance costs are large in aggregate and much larger than the government's administration costs and moreover, as is shown later (p.166), introduce further distortions into the structure of production. Compliance costs consist mainly of the value of the time spent on keeping records, making tax returns and other matters solely for the purpose of meeting the requirements of the tax authorities. This time will be spent by proprietors and directors of businesses, their staff and their professional advisers. There may also be other costs, (stationery, telephone calls and possibly capital costs for equipment), but these will be a relatively small part of the total.

In 1978 the Bath Centre arranged for the mailing of 10,000 postal questionnaires to a stratified random sample drawn, with the co-operation of the authorities, from the VAT register. In addition to classification data on size and type of registration, questions were asked about the time spent on VAT, numbers of invoices processed, terms of credit, the nature of any benefits gained from complying with VAT regulations, sources of advice and visits from VAT officials. The response rate was 31.4 per cent, resulting in some 2,800 usable replies. The response rate was higher for larger businesses but quite adequate in all size ranges. Data were available from Customs and Excise to allow reweighting of the response by size and sector to ensure that the results were representative of the population of registered traders as a whole. A large number of personal interviews with traders and their professional advisers were also carried out.

Respondents were asked to value the time spent on VAT compliance and to record related paid-out costs such as fees paid to professional accountants. The grossed up results are summarized in Table 7.12. Total compliance costs for all registered traders were estimated at £392 million, which amounted to 9.3 per cent of VAT revenue in 1977–8 or over 4.5 times the government's administration costs in that year (which were 2.0 per cent of revenue). The question immediately arises: were traders exaggerating the time spent on VAT or overvaluing that time on the fees paid out to professional advisers? It seems not. Objective analysis does not suggest that the time estimates were excessive and the average hourly rates used are in line with earnings in the sectors covered. It was possible to cross-check professional fees questioning accountants in the personal interviews. Moreover, two specialist firms were found that would handle all invoices and purchase vouchers and complete returns, in other words carried out VAT administration for a fee. Their charges were 12–17 per cent less than the reported values, which is corroborative, allowing for the economies of scale and specialization enjoyed by such firms and the fact that businesses using them would still need to spend some time on VAT affairs.

Were it not for the fact that we have frequently found in the past that many matters of vital importance to small business remain unresearched, we should have been surprised to find that there are very few other studies of the compliance costs of VAT and none carried out on the same scale and with the same rigour as the Bath study. Sandford *et al.*, (1981) review the limited earlier work (one study in West Germany and a number of studies of sales taxes in the United States, including a hypothetical study on VAT by P.A. Barker (1972)) and finds them consistent with their own work. They also review the more general literature on tax compliance, which is also very limited.

In the course of this study we have found three further relevant pieces of research. One study of the compliance costs for VAT in a sample of Dutch firms (Snijder, 1981) and another of sales taxes (Peat Marwick, 1985) are reviewed later (p.145–6). Another in West Germany (Hamer, 1979) found that businesses' administration costs rose by 16 per cent on average following the introduction of VAT.

Table 7.12: Measurable and compliance costs of VAT, United Kingdom, 1977–8

Nature of compliance cost	Normal costs (£m)	Special problems (£m)	Total (£m)	Per cent
Value of time spent on tax compliance by:				
Proprietors and partners	155	7	162	41.3
Directors	59	3	62	15.8
Qualified accounting staff	29	9	38	9.7
Other staff	103	5	108	27.6
Fees to professional advisers	17	3	20	5.1
Other costs	Negligible	2	2	0.5
Total measurable compliance costs	363	29	392	100.0
Per cent	92.6	7.4	100.0	

Source: Sandford *et al.* (1981).

Managerial Benefits of VAT

'It is an ill wind that blows nobody any good', and there are some benefits of VAT. One, an improvement in accounting records, is mentioned later (p164–5). In order to claim input taxes, registered traders need to keep meticulous records of purchases, certainly more detailed and better supported in a small firm than would normally be necessary. They also need records of sales and output tax charged, though the benefits to sales records is likely to be less marked. In fact, the Bath survey found that 32 per cent of respondents agreed with the statement that 'my purchase records are better kept since VAT came in', and 26 per cent agreed that their sales records were better kept. The proportion agreeing that there was an improvement was significantly higher in smaller firms, but large firms also recognized an improvement. However, of all firms agreeing that their records were better, relatively few volunteered a positive value to the benefit. A few claimed that better records had resulted in lower accounting fees and others mentioned improved stock control. In the personal interviews with accountants, most took the view that the standard of bookkeeping of their clients had improved, 'but most qualified their judgement with expressions such as 'initially', 'a little', 'for some firms', 'for small traders' ', and said that there would be no reduction in their fee for accounting work. We can conclude that the benefits to firms of better accounting records are marginal, though the requirement for purchase records and supporting vouchers would benefit income tax audits by the tax authorities.

Payment Periods and Cash Flow

A much more important benefit for many registered traders lies in the improved cash flow resulting from output taxes received from customers and held pending payment to the tax authorities. Some traders, however, experience a deterioration in cash flow where their input taxes exceed their output taxes. A firm which exports 100 per cent of its output, or exclusively supplies other goods and services which are zero-rated, will charge no VAT to its customers but will be entitled to reclaim the VAT on its purchases. In the UK, where zero-rating is more extensive than in other EC countries, about 30 per cent of registered traders (400,000 or so) qualify for regular repayment of tax. Traders will also find themselves in credit with the tax authorities on an occasional basis in periods when they have exceptionally large inputs (for example when purchasing major investment goods) or exceptionally low sales. The Bath survey found that 48 per cent of respondents were clear net payment traders as against 37 per cent who were clear net repayment traders, so very large numbers of small firms suffer a cash flow disbenefit from VAT.

Assessing the scale and incidence of these cash flow benefits or disbenefits is far from being a simple matter since. These are affected not only by the extent to which traders are supplying zero-rated goods and the phasing of their inputs and outputs, but also by the regulations about the frequency of returns and the timing of tax liability and the delays in payments to and from suppliers, customers and the tax authorities.

Regulations about the timing of liability for VAT are not the same in all countries. The 6th Directive requires that VAT is due on delivery of goods or on invoicing of services (the tax points, in VAT jargon). In other words, VAT liability is incurred on an accruals rather than on a payments basis (see Appendix 7.5, p.175). However, member states may, for certain categories of supply, determine tax liability on the date of payment rather than on the date of invoicing or the date of supply of the goods or services (France and Italy operate in that way). The purpose of these rules, which we will not elaborate in detail, is to prevent traders from deferring liability for the tax. The rules for imports may be different again. The formal tax point is the date at which the goods pass the frontier, though some countries require payments of VAT on entry, others allow a delay. (The UK Exchequer recently gained a useful windfall by changing the rules to payment at the frontier.)

In principle, deduction of input taxes is immediate; that is, traders may deduct from the VAT liable on their sales at any given date the full amount of input tax, whether actually paid or not. France is the only exception to this; there, input taxes are deductable only one month after the date at which they are due to the supplier.

The date at which traders actually have to pay their net VAT liability (or receive a refund) will depend on the frequency with which they have to make returns to the authorities and the 'period of grace' allowed for settlement after the date to which the accounts made in the return relate. Nine of the 14 European countries listed in Table 7.5 (p.116) require monthly returns, Ireland,

Norway and Sweden require bimonthly returns; in the UK and Denmark, returns are made quarterly. However, most of those countries with the more frequent returns allow small firms to opt for less frequent returns. The UK allows regular repayment traders to make monthly returns.

The period of grace allowed for the filing of returns after the date to which the return is made up is 30 days in The Netherlands and the UK and 15–25 days in most other countries. West Germany allows only 10 days, while France has different periods for different legal forms of business: sole proprietors are allowed the least time (15–17 days), public limited companies the longest (23 or 24 days). The French system is supposed to reflect the differential times required to prepare accounts in the various types of business, but it also has the advantage of spreading the arrival of returns at the processing centres. The UK requires returns from different sectors of the economy at different three-month periods to spread the load on the tax authorities, though more recently it has allowed firms in any sector to opt for quarters which coincide with the traders' financial year.

In all cases, payments to the tax authorities are made with the return and where this is by cheque there will be several days' further delay until the trader's bank account is debited. Repayment traders are expected to receive refunds of input taxes within 14 days in the UK; in Belgium it is about one month, provided there are no queries. The French authorities say that repayment 'should not in principle exceed two months' (*Conseil des Impôts*, 1983), but admit that delays are often greater than that in the Paris region. Neither in France, nor in any other country that we are aware of, is interest payable to the trader on overdue refunds from the tax authorities, although there are penalties for late payments of tax. In 1980, over 80 per cent of VAT payments were received by the UK authorities after the due date and heavy penalties have now been introduced to correct this. Late payment is, of course, a further possible source of cash flow benefit to the trader.

The final set of factors affecting the cash flow benefit or disbenefit of VAT to traders are the credit terms given to and received from their customers and suppliers. If sales are made for cash and spread evenly throughout the month, and traders make monthly returns, then they will have the use of the VAT they collect for 15 days, plus the period of grace (say 20 days) and the time taken to cash their cheque (say 5 days), a total of 40 days. If suppliers require payment of their invoice and of traders' input tax on these amounts and which the traders will have deducted from their VAT liability after 40 days, then traders will have the use of the whole of the VAT they have collected for that period. If traders have to pay cash to their suppliers or pay within 40 days, then the cash flow benefit will be reduced. If their customers are given lengthy credit, then they may have no cash flow benefit at all and may have to pay VAT before they have collected it.

There are obviously many permutations of these different circumstances, but for those traders who are making net payments of VAT to the authorities, the value of their sales will be greater than the value of their purchases (they will be adding value to their purchases) and their output tax will exceed their input tax.

If they give the same credit period for sales as they are allowed on their purchases, then they ought to be somewhat better off in cash terms with VAT than without it. This will still be true even if they buy inputs some time before they sell their own output, because the input tax is deductible from output tax as soon as the liability is incurred.

Some traders will, as mentioned, have to pay tax before they have received it from their customers. In France and Italy the tax authorities will make loans to traders for the purpose of meeting VAT liabilities, that is, delayed payment is allowed but charged for. In France, the period of these loans is normally up to four months and the interest rate is only 0.5 per cent over the bank base rate. The large minority of repayment traders whose input taxes actually paid exceed their output taxes are, of course, making a loan to the tax authorities until payment is received. However, if repayment traders make major purchases at the end of a tax period they may well receive refund of the input tax before they have paid their suppliers.

Detailed calculations have been made of the benefits and disbenefits of VAT for the cash flow of registered traders in France and the UK and the results are summarized in Tables 7.13 and 7.14. In both countries, the overall effect of VAT on the cash flow of business is favourable, after allowance for commercial credit terms, though the absolute size of the 'loan' from the tax authorities to traders is very much greater in the UK than in France. This is because, as shown above, VAT arrangements are less favourable to the trader in France (and were especially so in 1978 when VAT on UK imports was not required to be paid immediately), returns are made frequently and input taxes are not immediately deductible. Repayments also take longer in France than in the UK, but there are fewer repayment traders because there is less zero-rating. It will be noticed that there are considerable differences between the sectors which benefit from VAT 'loans' in the two countries. Retail distribution, where sales are to a large extent for cash, benefit heavily in the UK from quarterly tax payment periods, but suffer in France from the inability of retailers to deduct input tax immediately, and more frequent tax payments.

We are not able to explain all the differences between the two countries, which are complicated by differences in sector classification and may arise partly from differences in the methods of calculation and (at the time) treatment of imports. However, we can conclude that overall cash flow benefits are less favourable in France than in the UK. These benefits may be less favourable still in West Germany, so that they will differ not only according to traders' individual positions and the sectors they are in, but also according to the country we are looking at.

Net Compliance Costs

The net overall cash flow benefit (it will be remembered that many firms will experience a disbenefit) is most appropriately valued by applying an interest rate to the amount of the 'loan' from the tax authorities to registered traders. For the UK in 1977–8, Sandford *et al.*, (1981) calculated that the cash flow benefits were

Table 7.13: Average VAT cash balances (+) or deficits (−) held or borne by registered traders, by sector, France 1980

		Billion FF
Distribution	-	0.1
Intermediate manufacturing	-	2.0
Capital goods	-	3.1
Agro-industry	-	1.0
Energy	+	0.8
Consumer goods	+	0.1
Transport and telecommunications	+	2.7
Construction	+	3.6
Services	+	0.9
Total	+	1.9

Source: *Conseil des Impôts* (1983).

Table 7.14: Average VAT cash (+) or deficit (−) balances held or borne by registered traders, by sector, United Kingdom 1977–8

		£ million
Primary	-	8.0
Construction	-	11.9
Miscellaneous and public services	+	114.7
Transport and communications	+	2.6
Financial and business services	+	7.2
Professional and scientific services	+	24.8
Wholesale and dealers	+	0.2
Retail distribution	+	434.2
Manufacturing and utilities	+	468.8
Total	+	1033.0

Source: Sandford *et al.* (1981).

worth £56 million at average bank minimum lending rates and this can be deducted from the compliance cost figure of £392 million in Table 7.12 (p.129) to give an estimate of net compliance costs. The resulting figure of £336 million is 7.6 per cent of total VAT revenue in that year, below the gross figure of 9.3 per cent but nearly four times the administrative costs of government.

Sandford has recently updated his estimates to the year 1983–4 (Sandford,

1985). The UK government's administrative costs, as we have seen (in Table 7.11, p.127), had fallen to 1.1 per cent of revenue. Net compliance costs had also fallen because higher interest rates in this later period have boosted the value of the cash flow benefit to traders. Net compliance costs were, on the revised basis, 4.4 per cent, still four times the government's administration costs.

Evasion

Much of the claimed superiority of VAT over sales taxes (and other taxes) depends on assertions that it is more evasion proof. The extent to which VAT is evaded in those countries which operate the tax is difficult to substantiate, but before looking at the evidence available we examine the logic of these assertions.

When it is said that VAT is self-policing it is usually meant that the retailer will ensure that they have a proper invoice from their suppliers so that they may offset their input taxes against the tax charged to their customers; suppliers will have the same incentive to ensure that their suppliers invoice them correctly. In the same way, it is argued, each firm in the chain of production and distribution will ensure that it collects output tax from its customers because the act of supply creates a liability to pay that tax to the authorities.

The VAT system, then, helps reduce evasion in two ways. First, the incentive to underdeclare output is tempered by the risk that the ratio of declared outputs to claimed inputs is low enough to arouse suspicion, or by the fact that the benefit of underdeclaration is only a proportion of value added, not final turnover. Second, it is felt that once a tax invoice is issued by a trader, it takes a greater effort of will to deny the tax due than if cash passes hands without any accompanying documentation.

However, in the absence of comprehensive cross-checking, the multi-stage system does not alter the incentive that exists under any form of sales tax to underdeclare supply. Retailers who sell to customers at tax-inclusive prices and do not record the fact will still be better off by the amount of output tax due, even if they still pay input taxes. If they can find suppliers who will do the same then they have a better chance of escaping detection. If their inputs are relatively low and they are selling mainly to private individuals, as in the case of plumbers for example, they have an incentive to purchase those inputs retail at a tax-inclusive price and not to charge VAT at all. They can do this legally by not registering for VAT if their sales are below the threshold, and they will still be able to quote keener prices than their registered competitors. The temptation not to register and to conceal the true level of their sales will be high and may encourage them to opt out of the legitimate trading system and into the 'black economy'. If retailers are concealing their sales for VAT registration purposes, they are more likely to escape detection if they underdeclare or do not declare their income at all for income tax purposes. Since marginal income tax rates in Europe will, on average, be 30 per cent or more and VAT around 20 per cent, the benefits of evasion are very high. In this way VAT has probably done much to stimulate the growth of the 'black economy', which is causing concern to authorities in all European countries.

If any benefits do result from the incentives for customers to obtain receipts with purchases, they are restricted to transactions between registered traders. Those supplying directly to the public have no more reason to issue an invoice or receipt than they would under a sales tax. Where the authorities have reason to suspect fraud by a retailer, they can check with the supplier to compare the retailer's purchases with the supplier's sales; if the retailer is purchasing more than he/she is selling then there is evidence of fraud if the stock position is inconsistent with the declared sales. If the supplier is in collusion with the seller then the fraud will only be detected by carrying out further inquiries. According to John F Due (1973), checks with suppliers, when there is doubt about the sales of a retailer, are a routine feature of the administration of sales taxes in the United States. The strength of the VAT system is that it allows routine computer checks to be carried out of the ratio of input taxes to output taxes, which can pinpoint cases where these ratios are out of line and where there is a possibility of fraud. What it does not do is to allow the detection of fraud itself; this can only be done by a physical audit.

Automatic detection would only be possible if all traders recorded every purchase and sale on their returns with the VAT numbers of their suppliers so that the computer could cross-check that the claims tallied with one another. For obvious reasons the returns made to the tax authorities are not made in that detail and the more complex the structure of multiple rates and exemptions, the greater the normal range of variations in ratios will be and the less reliable guide they will give to the existence of fraud.

Another claim made for the strength of the VAT system's defences against fraud over a sales tax is that, because collection of the tax is multi-stage, then only part of the proceeds of the tax is lost if it is evaded at any point in the system. This is, of course, true but the corollary is that there are many more points in the economy at which scope for fraud exists. In a minor way it becomes easier for registered traders and their staff to acquire goods and services for personal consumption free of tax than under a retail tax system. More important, because registered traders can reclaim input taxes under VAT, there is benefit to be gained from false invoices covering fictitious purchases which, if supported by fictitious invoices for zero-rated sales (especially exports of invisible services to associated overseas companies), are less likely to arouse suspicion under routine computer ratio checks. These and other possibilities for fraud do not exist at all under a sales tax system.

Reliable estimates of the extent of evasion are obviously difficult to make. One method is to compare the estimated yield of VAT from the national accounts with actual VAT revenue. This is not easily done because the breakdowns of consumption in the national accounts are difficult to reclassify on a basis to which multiple rates of tax and exemptions can be applied. A further difficulty is that the national accounts understate value added because of the existence of the 'black economy'. Estimates based on comparisons between expenditure-based and output-based national accounts indicate that output is typically understated, but since expenditure is also understated, calculations of this sort are unreliable. The circulation of large denomination banknotes and other indicators suggest that the 'black economy' has grown substantially in Europe, and estimates of its extent range from 3 to 30 per cent of GDP. According to Pedone (in Aaron, 1981) in Italy:

> Under any plausible interpretation, however, evasion is pervasive and large, reducing value added tax collections by as much as two thirds in some broad sectors and by two fifths overall. Only in the production of energy, which is a quasi-public enterprise, and in manufacturing, which is dominated by large firms that require modern accounting procedures and complete records to do business, is evasion below 40 per cent.

The problem of VAT evasion (and evasion of other taxes) is undoubtedly greater in Italy than in other European countries, but there is no doubt that it exists everywhere on a significant scale. Some indication of the extent of evasion can be gained from the results of control visits which are published in several countries. Control visits are made continually in Britain for all newly registered traders to ensure that the tax is being administered properly. Thereafter visits are apparently concentrated on large firms where yield is greatest and on those businesses where there may be reason (for example from computer checks) to suspect irregularities. In 1983–4, 350,000 visits were made, amounting to 24 per cent of the total number of registered traders, but a large proportion of these visits, perhaps half, were to newly registered firms. The total number of visits to established businesses has been declining. Tax assessments are issued following about one-third of all audit visits. VAT is so complicated that innocent errors are easily possible, and the assessments relate both to under-and overdeclarations of tax. In 1983–4, overdeclarations, however, at £6 million, were overshadowed by underdeclarations of tax or overdeclarations of repayment claims at £320 million, amounting to a net 2.0 per cent of total revenue (Commissioners of HM Customs and Excise, 1984a). Given that only one-third of traders are audited, we see that true evasion is probably nearer 6 per cent of revenue, and this is without taking into consideration those who fail to register at all, or undetected fraud by those audited.

According to the papers in Aaron (1981), the position was very similar in The Netherlands. In 1976, 20 per cent of registered underdeclared tax. Recovery of tax underdeclared amounted to 1.2 per cent of VAT revenue in The Netherlands, while in West Germany the corresponding figure was 1.4 per cent. The French authorities estimate that losses of VAT revenue detectable by audit and investigation amount to 2.2 per cent of revenue (0.8 per cent of this is attributed to the work of the Customs authorities). A further 0.3 per cent could be attributed to detectable fraud in the 'black economy'. Undetected fraud is estimated however, to raise total losses to between 6 and 10 per cent of total VAT revenue in France (Conseil des impöts, 1983). In a few countries, quite spectacular VAT frauds have been reported. In Belgium, for example, there have been cases where fraudulent input tax repayment claims amounting to many millions of francs have been met from firms which had gone out of business some time previously (Wauters, 1984). Total evasion in Belgium is estimated at 8 per cent.

It seems to be the general experience that losses of revenue are relatively greater in small firms than in large, among service industries more than other sectors, and more in retailing than in manufacturing. Revenue authorities are understandably reticent about the methods of evasion used, particularly the more sophisticated devices. The French authorities, however, state that of detectable fraud, 43 per cent is accounted for by the omission of taxable transactions, 11 per cent by irregular deductions of input tax, 10 per cent by false exports, 5 per cent by early input claims (a problem largely peculiar to France) and 5 per cent by failure to pay tax on goods and services for personal use.

A government report on tax fraud in The Netherlands (Sijbren Cnossen, in Aaron 1981) revealed that 'although VAT fraud was slightly more frequent at the retail stage than at other stages of production . . . less revenue was involved than at the other stages'. Forty-four per cent of all reassessments 'for tax evasion involved deliberately incorrect applications of the law, such as rules regarding deductions for prior stage taxes. Sixteen per cent had tried to postpone payments improperly. Thirty-eight per cent had failed to enter sales in their books or had kept incomplete accounts. Seven out of ten violations were committed by former offenders, perhaps because the penalties for violation tend to be rather low.'

Enforcement Measures

The principal instrument of enforcement is the audit visit and one of the disadvantages of VAT is that it requires giving power to large additional numbers of officials to enter virtually all significant business premises in the country. In the UK, VAT officials have the right to gain access to business premises at any reasonable time and without a search warrant although, except in some cases where fraud is suspected, appointments are made in advance. When in the premises, these officials have the right to examine all VAT bookkeeping records and any correspondence or material relating to specific transactions.

Since delay in making VAT returns can be a useful source of finance for businesses, penalties are necessary for late returns as well as for failure to keep proper records or for fraudulent returns. Penalties for late returns are generally imposed administratively in EC countries, usually as a percentage of the tax due, although those for other offences are left to the judicial system. There has been a distinct tendency for administrative powers and penalties to be increased over time (for the UK see Committee on Enforcement Powers, 1983 and Commissioners of Customs and Excise, 1978, 1984a).

In some countries, the methods used to enforce VAT compliance go far beyond audits on business premises. In several countries, inspections of goods in warehouses are regularly carried out and vehicles transporting goods are required to carry documents listing the buyers and sellers of the goods carried, with their VAT registration numbers. In Italy, since 1980, hotels and restaurants must issue VAT receipts, a copy of which must by law be taken off the premises by the customer who may be asked to produce it in the street.

VAT AND SMALL FIRMS IN THE EC

Small Business Attitudes

In his 1978 UK survey, Sandford, (1981) asked respondents to agree or disagree with matched pairs of statements, one set pro-VAT and the other anti-VAT. For example:

'VAT is a simple method of collecting tax.'
'As it stands, VAT is unreasonably complicated.'

Pro-VAT responses were scored positively, anti-VAT responses negatively, while agreement or disagreement received a score of one and strong agreement or disagreement received a score of two. The responses of those who were indifferent (neither agreed nor disagreed) received a zero score. Had every score been very anti-VAT for any respondent, the score would have been −16; had every response been very pro-VAT, the score would have been +16.

The average result was −2 (slightly anti-VAT) and there were few large deviations. The least well disposed towards the tax were small and medium-sized retailers, and the sectors where the strongest anti-VAT views were expressed were retailing (though not among the largest firms), construction and professional and scientific services. Overall, the respondents broke down as follows, according to their attitude to VAT (per cent):

Very pro	0.6
Pro	15.9
Indifferent	47.0
Anti	27.1
Very anti	9.5
Overall	100.0

It is, at first sight, surprising that 47 per cent should be indifferent though 36.6 per cent were anti compared with 16.5 per cent pro. However, very few indeed can be expected to actually like taxes and one might expect to find that VAT compares unfavourably with other taxes.

Overall, there was evidence in the survey that in response to the statement 'Most other taxes work more efficiently than VAT', there is a marginal preference for other taxes over VAT. However, at an average result of barely −0.1, this anti-VAT response was actually less pronounced than for attitudes to VAT in isolation. When these average responses were calculated by size of firm, however, there was a very clear tendency for the rating of VAT, compared with other taxes, to improve with size of firm. In fact, the two largest categories of traders actually favoured VAT over other taxes (Table 7.15).

It is well known that small firms complain more than large firms about the burden of government taxation, regulation and paperwork. The reasons are simple ones: there are economies of scale in dealing with government; the proprietors of small firms have less administrative support (little or none in some cases) and are therefore bearing much of the paperwork burden personally.

Attitudes to taxation itself (as distinct from the compliance costs of taxation) are also less favourable among small firms because taxes bear not only on personal income, but on the sources of capital for investment and expansion. Large firms have easier access to the capital markets for both loan and equity capital than do small firms, and therefore this aspect of taxation is of less concern to them (see Bannock, 1981). VAT is largely neutral to capital investment and is not borne to a major extent by the registered traders themselves. We saw earlier (p.119) that a proportion of VAT is in fact borne by business. Insofar as this results from the inability of exempt traders to reclaim input taxes, small businesses are discriminated against since virtually all exempt traders are small firms, except in financial services and real estate (though of course they can register voluntarily). However, the compliance costs do fall on all registered businesses and particularly heavily, as will be demonstrated, on small businesses.

Table 7.15: Responses to 'Most other taxes work more effectively than VAT'

Annual taxable turnover category (£000s)	Mean of scores
0 - 9.9	-0.24
10 - 19.9	-0.14
20 - 49.9	-0.17
50 - 99.9	-0.05
100 - 499.9	-0.02
500 - 999.9	0.25
1000 & over	0.12
Overall	-0.06

Source: Sandford *et al.* (1981).

An international survey among small firms carried out in a number of countries in 1984 showed that, except in Japan, the combined problem of government taxes and paperwork received more mentions in response to the question 'What is the most important problem facing your business today' than any other single set of problems (Table 7.16). Only in Japan was the basic problem of realizing sales not overshadowed by the burden of government. This survey threw no light on individual taxes or regulations but certainly there is ample evidence in the UK that, of all aspects of the compliance burden of government activity, VAT is regarded as the most onerous.

Table 7.16: Most important problems faced by small business

	Japan	USA	UK	West Germany	The Netherlands	Canada
Government regulation and paperwork	2.5	18.3	20.8	14.0	24.8	16.4
Taxes	9.2	12.5	15.8	8.6	10.2	9.2
Subtotal	11.7	30.8	36.6	22.6	35.0	25.6
Interest rates and financing	7.2	11.0	17.5	19.7	5.8	20.8
Realizing sales	37.8	8.4	9.7	4.6	11.8	8.6
Competition from large business	11.9	9.7	10.8	13.7	11.8	8.9
Other	31.4	40.1	25.4	39.4	35.6	36.1
Subtotal	88.3	69.2	63.4	77.4	65.0	74.4
Total mentions	100.0	100.0	100.0	100.0	100.0	100.0

Source: SKIM (1984).

The UK Forum of Private Business carries out regular surveys (brought together in Bannock, 1984) among its members and asks 'Which act has the most adverse effect on your business?' and 'Which act would you like to see changed?' As to the first of these questions, VAT came top of the list on every occasion in surveys carried out between March 1979 and March 1982, with percentage mentions running from 35 to 57 per cent. In six out of the seven surveys in which these questions were included, VAT also came top of the list as the Act which respondents would most like to see changed (14–43 per cent).

In both cases, the trend of mentions has been broadly upwards over the period 1979–82 (i.e. subsequent to the Sandford survey), even though the UK abolished multiple positive rates of VAT within that period.

Similar results were obtained in a more recent independent survey carried out for the UK Department of Industry (Table 7.17). Professor Bryan Carsberg carried out a survey of small firms and their auditors for the UK Institute of Chartered Accountants in 1984. He found that small business proprietors ranked VAT well above all other administrative requirements in terms of the cost, time and effort involved, including tax administration for employees, the preparation of annual accounts and social security administration (Carsberg *et al.*, 1985). The auditors took a similar view and ranked VAT above the annual accounts and the provision of information for banks.

VAT Administration in Business

Before we go on to review the more detailed evidence on compliance costs by size of registered trader, it will be helpful to the reader unfamiliar with VAT if we give a picture of the practicalities of administration of the tax in a small firm.

The process starts with the routine bookkeeping and sales administration of the firm. Most small businesses, whether registered for VAT or not, will keep a record of major purchases with a file of purchase invoices. The purchase ledger

Table 7.17: Government burdens on small business: per cent of mentions and seriousness rating

	Per cent mentions	Rating (1 = least serious, 10 = most serious)
VAT	39.0	4.7
Employment protection	29.0	4.7
Statistics	21.0	2.9
Local authority planning regulations	20.5	5.6
Employed/self employed tax treatment	13.5	4.5
Sick pay	13.5	3.4
PAYE income tax administration	12.5	4.1
Health and safety	11.0	3.5
Local authority building regulations	7.5	4.1
Environmental regulations	6.5	4.1

Source: Research Associates Survey in *Burdens on Business*, March 1985, HMSO, London.

or cash book will need an extra column for VAT, however, and if proprietors wish to reclaim all the input taxes they pay, they will need to ensure that every entry is supported by an invoice or tax receipt giving the VAT number of their supplier. Credit card counterfoils and till receipts will not be sufficient for this purpose unless they bear the VAT number and, where appropriate, the rate of VAT charged. (This means for most cash purchases that proprietors and their staff will need to remember to ask for a VAT receipt.) In entering the input VAT in the ledger, the proprietor or bookkeeper will need to distinguish between disallowed input taxes, including items for personal consumption (which may require an additional calculation if they are part only of the total on the voucher) if additional work is to be avoided when the VAT is totalled for the purposes of the regular return.

For sales, the firm will need to ensure that VAT is charged at the appropriate rate and that all the necessary information (date of supply, VAT number, name and address of customer) is on the invoice. The amount and the VAT charged will also need to be entered separately in the books so that output tax can be totalled for the return to the tax authorities. Note that the tax to be paid is not just the VAT rate times sales because the tax is expressed on the net price. A 10 per cent VAT is 9.09 per cent of the tax inclusive price, and this calculation will need to be made frequently for both purchases and sales where the tax is not shown separately on receipts. For cash sales, a retailer may have to write out by hand a special tax invoice on a pre-printed form if requested. The more invoices a firm issues or receives, and the more complex the VAT rate structure, the greater the administrative burden will be.

At the end of the month or longer period, depending on the regulations, the firm will have to make a return showing its input tax, output tax and net tax payable or repayable. At its simplest, this may be a one-page form with just a few boxes to insert the numbers, and at its most complex it may be a forbidding document of several pages. Complexity in the return is largely a function of the regulations — the more rates and special rules there are governing payments, the longer the form will need to be. As in other aspects of VAT, simplicity and fairness often conflict. Until recently no relief was allowed on bad debts in the UK for example. Since output VAT becomes liable on invoicing, subsequent refusal or inability to pay creates administrative hassle as well as financial loss. Where traders subsequently agree on different terms from those invoiced, credit notes may be issued. A similar procedure can be used (illegally) to circumvent the bad debt rule. For payment traders, the form will need to be accompanied by a cheque which requires further bookkeeping entries, although in Sweden the tax return also acts as the instrument for the transfer of funds via the post office giro system.

Who in the firm does all this will vary. According to surveys by the Forum of Private Business (Bannock, 1984), in some 60 per cent of small firms the proprietor completes the form, and in most cases he or she will need to check and sign it. According to the SKIM (1984) survey, 43 per cent of respondents also kept the books themselves and in a further 19 per cent of cases the books were kept by their spouses. In only 22 per cent of firms were the books kept by an employee, although this proportion was much lower than in other advanced countries. In Britain, about 30 per cent of small businesses have computers (Small Business Research Trust, 1985) (somewhat lower than in the United States). Even where bookkeeping is done electronically, the verification and inputting requirements for VAT are not lightened and we know of no small firm that prepares its VAT returns on the computer.

There are, however, several other elements in the burden of VAT administration which have not yet been described. The first of these are errors, queries and disputes. As a general rule, in a small firm only the proprietor and the bookkeeper will understand VAT. Customers and other employees may get things wrong (as they themselves will, too, on occasion). Failure to specify that a price quotation to an exempt trader does not include VAT will result in a query and possibly the loss of a sale when an invoice is issued. Incorrect rates may be applied — this is very common under multiple rate systems — and in some cases the distinctions between manufactured and non-manufactured foods, repairs and new construction, new and used goods and other borderline cases will require arcane knowledge of the regulations. (For example, frozen yoghurt and a hot sandwich may be subject to VAT, fresh yoghurt and a cold sandwich may not be subject to VAT.) Other instances which create difficulties include the distinction between the purchase of a good or service when acting as a principal or as an agent (VAT will be liable in the former but not in the latter case), the supply of a service from overseas by telephone or other electronic means and its supply in person, trading between exempt and non-exempt organizations under common ownership and the special VAT documentation requirement for exports and imports. In West Germany, VAT is applied to sales to East

Germany, which in other respects would be treated as exports. Some of the misunderstandings, disputes and problems will be dealt with at the time, others will not be brought to light until months or years later when the VAT inspector calls to make an audit.

Second, dealing with the audits themselves is another element in the VAT burden, although it will be relatively infrequent, perhaps once every few years for a small firm. An audit will inevitably take up some of the proprietor's or bookkeeper's time, and, to the innocent and guilty alike, will create some anxiety. VAT is a self-assessed tax where the rules are so complex that in many cases VAT inspectors will need to seek higher authority for their interpretations, but where the small firm will pay a penalty, even if only in underpaid tax, if it gets it wrong. Although the tax is supposed to be borne by the end customer, the firm has no recourse to that customer if tax is incorrectly applied.

Third, there is the necessity of keeping records of past transactions. In Europe, firms are required to maintain invoices and receipts for an average of seven years.

Anxiety about these matters is a part of the 'psychic cost' of VAT which is not measurable but is nonetheless real. Sandford *et al.* (1981) point out that income tax officials are normally happy, and indeed prefer, to deal with the taxpayer's accountant, but with VAT, the professional adviser cannot stand between the tax authorities and the client in the same way, although the adviser may, of course, be present at audits where advance warning is given. There is also an obvious difference between the position of a senior employee in a large firm dealing with the VAT authorities and the proprietor of a small business whose personal pocket is at stake.

Another area of difficulty for some traders is 'partial exemption'. Firms, some of whose output is exempt and some of whose output is taxable (including zero-rated items), for example construction companies, are not allowed to claim tax back on all their inputs (for example the timbers they buy), but only on those that contributed to taxable outputs. Tax experts all agree that apportioning input tax between taxable and exempt outputs is the worst aspect of VAT administration, leading to many disputes between traders and authorities. Other areas of difficulty exist too. Sale or return items may be treated in a special way and bad debts need to be written off if permitted.

Finally, there is the whole question of VAT policy for the proprietors of small firms and, for that matter, the finance directors of large firms, to worry about. In all firms, the completion of VAT returns is not necessarily a simple matter of routine; it requires the attention of a senior person and in a small firm this is normally the proprietor. Since the date of the return is fixed and penalties for late returns significant, proprietors need to ensure that they and the necessary cash are available on the appropriate date. As we have shown, however, the maximization of the cash flow benefit (or the minimization of the disbenefit) requires conscious management decision. Bringing forward the delivery of a major capital item or postponing a major sale for a few days either side of a VAT account period can make a very considerable difference to the cash flow in that period.

It should be added that what we have been describing here are the ongoing costs of VAT administration. When small traders first register for VAT (and the vast majority of new registrations are of small firms), they will have to invest a considerable amount of time in understanding the VAT system and then in training their staff, if appropriate, to maintain the new records and apply the tax (Mendham, 1983). As a start, they will need to read (in the UK) the *VAT Guide*, some 44,000 words, and a number of other leaflets and booklets depending on their trade. There are a considerable number of official VAT leaflets and publications in Britain to choose from — over 100 in all — and even a regular publication, *VAT Notes*. These publications are, to say the least, not easily understood and some questions will probably have to be put to the local VAT office.

The Regressivity of Net Compliance Costs

All registered traders will bear the compliance costs of VAT, though not all will enjoy the cash flow benefits discussed earlier (p.130–2). As far as compliance costs are concerned, these may be expected to decline in relation to turnover for the following reasons given by Sandford *et al.* (1981).

1 The larger the firm, the greater the scope for the use of specialist staff whose costs can be spread over a larger volume of sales — in a small firm the proprietor has to do much of the work and the cost of the proprietor's time is normally greater than for specialist staff.
2 The larger the firm, the greater the scope for computers, programmed point of sale registers, etc.
3 'The number of invoices to be dealt with will not rise in proportion to size. Large firms are likely to buy in bulk and often to sell in larger quantities than small firms.'

The Bath survey, described earlier (p.128), found in fact that compliance costs fell sharply with the size of firm, from 1.64 per cent of turnover for the smallest category of trader down to an average of only 0.04 per cent for firms with a turnover of £1 million and over (Table 7.18).

What this means is that compliance costs are 40 times higher, *as a proportion* of turnover for the smallest category of firms in Table 7.18 than for the largest. (Strictly speaking, the compliance costs discussed in this section are marginal costs since they do not include any allowance for overheads (office space, heat and light, etc.); were we to use average costs, then the regressivity might be greater still.)

Moreover, the threshold for the largest category at £1 million ($1.438 million) was not high, even for 1978. There were 22,000 VAT registered firms with a turnover in excess of £2 million in 1983 (the equivalent threshold at 1978 prices would have been about £1.4 million) and for the very largest firms with sales of hundreds of millions of pounds, we can safely assume that compliance costs of VAT were well under 0.01 per cent of turnover. Checks on the influence of factors not related to size indicate that the mix of VAT rates (the number of

Table 7.18: Compliance costs and net compliance costs as a percentage of taxable turnover by turnover size category, United Kingdom, 1977–8

Annual Taxable turnover (£ 000s)	Compliance costs (%)	Net compliance cost (%)
0 - 9.9	1.64	1.69
10 - 19.9	1.23	1.13
20 - 49.9	0.74	0.68
50 - 99.9	0.54	0.50
100 - 999.9	0.24	0.22
1000 & over	0.04	0.03
Weighted overall mean	0.92	0.88

Source: Sandford *et al.* (1981).

positive rates) is a determinant of compliance costs. Repayment traders had lower costs than payment traders, partly because of the special schemes for farmers, but also because zero-rated or exempt outputs involve less work. A number of large firms, particularly in retailing, undoubtedly make a large profit out of VAT when the cash benefit is allowed for. Incremental compliance costs for a highly computerized firm in this category are negligible.

A study on the compliance costs of taxation was also carried out in The Netherlands and the results were published at about the same time as those of Sandford *et al.* Snijder (1981) surveyed 286 firms and asked his respondents to value the time spent on VAT administration, fees to accountants and other associated costs. Recalculating his results onto a similar basis to those of Sandford *et al.*, we find that although as a percentage of turnover they are lower, they show a similar reduction with increasing size of firm: 0.59 per cent for traders with a turnover of DG 250,000–499,000; 0.43 per cent (DG500,000–999,999); 0.23 per cent (DG 1,000,000–1,999,999) and 0.19 per cent (DG 2,000,000–3,999,999). These calculations were made by assuming turnover was at the midpoint of turnover size categories and by omitting the open-ended lower and upper categories. We presume Snijder's costs are lower for smaller firms than those of Sandford *et al.*, partly at least because he nets out the allowance for these costs given by the Dutch authorities (see Appendix 7.4, p.170).

It is now well established that the compliance costs of all forms of taxation are highly regressive and a recent study of the compliance costs of state sales taxes in the USA gives a similar, though less steeply regressive, picture. Peat Marwick

(1985), in a study of some 200 retailers, for 80 of which on-site measurement was carried out, found that net compliance costs (that is, after allowing for cash flow benefits) were more than three times higher for small retailers than for large retailers (Table 7.19). Overall, Sandford *et al.* (1981) estimated the total value of the 'loan' from the tax authorities to UK registered traders at £56 million, about 14 per cent of the estimated total compliance costs borne by these traders.

Table 7.19: Net compliance costs as a percentage of tax collected by compliance element and total sales by size of firms, representative US states

	Total sales turnover category		
Compliance Element	Small ($1m & under)	Medium ($1m-$10m)	Large (Over $10m)
As % of tax collected			
Collection	2.996	2.382	1.637
Reporting	1.306	0.258	0.160
Payments	-0.401	-0.585	-0.599
Auditing	0.009	0.020	0.025
Miscellaneous	0.115	0.020	0.025
Total	4.025	2.095	1.256
As % of taxable sales			
Total	0.161	0.084	0.050

Source: Peat Marwick (1985).

This benefit does not seem to vary systematically with size. The main determinant of the cash flow benefit in proportional terms seems to be the economic sector, not the size of firm. The different pattern of commercial credit experienced by small and large firms seems to have little effect; although large firms are slower to pay their debtors, they also experience longer delays in receiving payment from creditors. Sandford *et al.* did observe that the cash benefit of VAT was more appreciated by large than by small firms. Many small firms (and some large) did not perceive the benefit at all (or did not acknowledge it). Peat Marwick (1985) also found that the value of the use of sales tax funds was neutral to size. (This is not borne out by Table 7.19 because the payments item includes not only interest on tax held, but bank charges and other costs related to the handling of tax payments which do diminish proportionately to the volume of funds involved.)

It is clear from Table 7.18 that the pattern of distribution of net compliance costs after subtraction (or addition) of the cash benefit (disbenefit) by size of firm is little different from that in the gross figures. What is striking about the US sales tax compliance figures in Table 7.19 is that they exhibit a very similar pattern but are about one tenth of the size of the corresponding data for the UK. Peat Marwick's data are based on a computer model using parameters derived from the survey and reflecting the conditions in a representative state where the sales tax rate is 4 per cent. Since this rate is much lower than the UK VAT rate, which would tend to push up costs as a percentage of taxable sales, the magnitude of the difference is surprising.

We should expect the compliance costs to be lower for a sales tax than for VAT because retailers tend to benefit more than the average from the cash flow advantages and under a sales tax do not have the additional work of recording inputs or of dealing with multiple tax rates. The difference is greater than we should expect, however, and is clearly mainly attributable to the fact that in the US data, the turnover categories are at a higher level. 'Small' US firms are bracketed under $1 million and have net compliance costs of 0.16 per cent of sales. This corresponds more nearly to the second highest bracket in the Sandford *et al* data ($144,000–1.44 million) where compliance costs were 0.22 per cent of sales. This is 70 per cent higher.

Administration Costs by Size of Firm

Not only are the compliance costs of VAT regressive in terms of firm size, but so are the government's collection or administration costs. The vast majority of all firms in all countries are small firms, and this is also true of the number of traders registered for VAT. An extreme case is France, where there is no minimum threshold and where 73.2 per cent of registered traders had a turnover in 1983 of less than FF 1 m ($ 132,400) (Table 7.20). Even in the UK, where the threshold is relatively high, over 18 per cent of traders (some 262,000 firms) were below that threshold in 1983 – 4 (£18,000) ($ 25,880), but had voluntarily opted into the VAT system (Table 7.21).

The threshold (which has subsequently been increased) in fact only applied to newly registered traders whose actual turnover or expected turnover was £18,000 or more per annum. Existing registered traders had to remain on the register if their expected turnover was £17,000 or more. There are, therefore, different thresholds for registration and for deregistration. The limits refer to taxable turnover including goods and services which are zero-rated. A person whose taxable supplies are all zero-rated, however, may apply for exemption from registration even if those supplies exceed the limit. Firms whose taxable turnover is below the registration limit may apply for voluntary registration.

The net revenue yielded by these large numbers of small firms is a small proportion of total revenue. In the UK, the smallest 1.08 million firms (75.6 per cent of the total) together account for only 6.7 per cent of the VAT revenue, while the largest 6,000 firms (0.4 per cent of the total) accounted for 61.5 per cent of revenue (Table 7.20). In France, the largest 4.1 per cent of firms account for 77 per cent of gross VAT revenue.

The total costs of administering VAT in the UK in 1983 – 4 were £176.3 million ($201 million), which works out at £123 ($ 180) per registered trader. If we assume for a moment that the cost per trader is similarly distributed by size of compliance costs, then the administration costs for the 125,000 traders with a turnover of under £10,000 could be £7 million, compared with £10 million of

Table 7.20: Numbers of VAT registered traders and net tax receipts by taxable turnover category, United Kingdom, 1983–4

Annual Taxable Turnover (£000s)	Number of registered traders ('000s)	Cum. %	Net tax receipts £ m	Net tax receipts Cum. %
Up to 8.5	82	5.7	-5	-
8.6 - 10	43	8.7	15	0.1
10.1 - 12.5	39	11.4	20	0.2
12.6 - 15	64	15.9	35	0.4
15.1 - 17.5	34	18.3	25	0.6
17.6 - 20	142	28.2	80	1.1
20.1 - 50	424	57.8	380	3.6
50.1 - 100	256	75.6	465	6.7
100.1 - 500	260	93.8	1465	16.3
500.1 - 1000	41	96.7	710	21.0
1000.1 - 10000	42	99.6	2670	38.5
10000.1 and over	6	100.0	9360	100.0
Total	1433	100.0	15220	100.0

Source: Commissioners of HM Customs and Excise (1984b).

Table 7.21: Numbers of VAT registered traders and gross VAT charged by turnover category, France, 1983

Annual turnover (FF 000s)	Number of registered traders (000s)	Cum. %	VAT charged	Cum. %
Under 1,000	1253	73.2	43	5.7
1,000-1,999	188	84.2	31	9.9
2,000-4,999	143	92.5	52	16.8
5,000-9,999	56	95.9	47	23.0
10,000 & over	69	100.0	578	100.0
Total	1711	100.0	751	100.0

Source: Ministère des Finances.

revenue obtained from them. These figures are affected by the fact that small traders are often voluntarily registered and are thus likely to be claiming money back from the authorities rather than handing it over.

The same is true of some sectors, for example construction and primary (agriculture, forestry, fishing and mining), from which no net revenue is obtained at all (because output in these sectors is largely zero-rated). Substantial net refunds of tax are made at considerable administrative cost (see Appendix 7.5. p.175).

In fact, the cost of collecting VAT from a small firm is, on average, probably somewhat less than for all firms, largely because fewer and shorter visits are made by tax officials, but this does not affect the general conclusion that the administration cost of VAT is regressive with respect to size of firm. In fact, Sandford *et al.* (1981), on the basis of more detailed estimates on the costs of administration derived from the Bath survey, show that administration costs are actually even more regressive than compliance costs. Their overall estimates of operating costs (administration plus compliance costs) for 1977–8 are shown in Table 7.22. It can be seen from this table that for the first three size categories, covering 881,100 firms or 69.1 per cent of all traders, the total cost of operating the tax exceeded the net revenue by over 13 per cent. Incredibly, even for 96 per cent of the traders, operating costs accounted for nearly half of the revenue. It is only for the 4 per cent of larger traders that total costs fell to 15 per cent of revenue.

As pointed out earlier (p.115), since 1977–8 a higher standard rate of VAT had been applied in the UK while higher interest rates will have increased the value of the cash benefit. These changes reduced estimated overall operating costs as a percentage of revenue from 11.7 in 1977–8 to 7.9 per cent in 1983–4, but the disproportion between large and small firms remains (Sandford, 1985).

Table 7.22: Number of registered traders, net VAT revenue, and net operating costs in total and by turnover category, United Kingdom, 1977–8

Annual taxable turnover (£000s)	Number of registered traders (000s)	Cum. %	Net tax paid (£m)	Net operating costs (£m)	Net operating costs as % of net tax collected %	Cum. %
0 - 9.9	270.7	21.2	15	42	280.0	280.0
10 - 19.9	269.5	42.4	55	64	116.4	151.4
20 - 49.9	340.9	69.1	120	109	90.8	113.2
50 - 99.9	177.7	83.1	140	82	58.6	90.0
100 -999.9	185.4	96.1	600	129	21.5	45.8
1000 & over	30.0	100.0	3305	69	2.1	15.0
Total	1274.2	100.0	4235	495	11.7	11.7

Source: Adapted from Sandford *et al.* (1981).

Are Small Firms a Problem?

Despite the known regressivity of compliance costs and the inefficiency of administration of VAT for small firms, authorities are apt to forget why it is that these are undesirable features of a tax. There are, in fact, three important reasons why they should be dealt with.

The first is that economic efficiency is enhanced by the removal of all distortions on production methods and form. Imposing a relatively heavy burden on small firms distorts production away from what might, in some cases, be its natural and most efficient unit. Distortions against small firms can impair not only present economic performance but also growth, given the important role of small business in innovation and change.

The second consideration is equity: it simply is not fair to impose differing burdens on different groups in society indiscriminately.

The third consideration is that all taxes involve compliance and administration costs. These costs are a net loss to society. When resources are poured into merely administering or complying with a tax, those paying them still suffer the loss but there is no offsetting social gain. It is as though, in our determination to distribute a bottle of champagne between ourselves fairly, we spilt much of it on the floor. When administrative costs are a significant proportion of revenue, it is difficult to believe that the value of the spending exceeds the cost of the tax.

The inequity of indiscriminately applying a social burden, the value of the costs of administering a tax and the distortions caused by an unequal application of the full tax burden are the reasons for concentrating on simplifying VAT for smaller traders.

Special Schemes for Small Business

All European countries recognize that VAT administration for the very smallest firms is an unfruitful burden for business and government alike, and this concern is reflected in a variety of forms of special treatment (see Appendix 7.4, p.170).

The simplest solution is to allow firms with a turnover below a certain level (threshold) to opt out of the system altogether. For firms which opt out, however, the compliance burden is exchanged for a tax burden since they are still obliged to pay VAT but are unable to reclaim input taxes while their registered customers cannot reclaim any of the tax element in the cost of supplies from them (except in Sweden where special arrangements apply). Unless the saving in compliance costs is greater than the tax burden, small firms below the threshold selling to registered traders will therefore suffer a competitive disadvantage unless they opt into the VAT system and, as mentioned earlier, many do so.

According to the Commissioners of HM Customs and Excise (1978), following increases in thresholds in 1977 and 1978, only about one fifth of payment traders eligible to deregister did so. Some small firms opt into the system because they do not wish their customers to know how small their sales are, others may not appreciate the extent of the compliance burden.

Small exempt firms which have very low taxable inputs and sell directly to end consumers, as in many service industries, in contrast will gain a competitive advantage by remaining unregistered. Firms which are unregistered may find it easier to evade income taxes but it is interesting that the UK, which has the highest threshold in the EC, has kept the administration of income and value added taxes more independent of each other than in other member states. This may not last; experiments in exchanging information betwen the VAT and income tax administrations have already been carried out in one part of the UK. To avoid these distortions and to keep as many businesses as possible within the VAT surveillance net, other European countries have other ways of treating small firms. There is a variety of flat rate schemes which involve setting VAT liability as a fixed percentage of sales or relating it to inputs. These schemes also result in distortions since they normally require the use of crude industry-wide margins, while attempts to tailor fixed rates for individual firms seem to result in higher administrative burdens for both government and business.

Another method widely used in the EC for farmers is to exempt them from VAT registration and from charging the tax, but to allow their customers to deduct the farmers' notional input taxes from their VAT liability. In this way, the burden of administration is passed from farmers to their customers, but this is only effective where all the farmers' sales are to registered traders. 'Farm gate' and other direct sales thus become free of tax and this tends to encourage inefficient methods of distribution. A variant of this approach is to transfer the burden of administering VAT to the suppliers rather than to the customers of small firms. This method works like a tax levied at the wholesale stage, but since it involves discriminating between different types of wholesale customer it greatly complicates administration for registered firms. The other systems used to ease the burden of VAT on small firms involve compensating them for part at least of the compliance burden by allowing them to retain part of the tax collected. (Some US states and Canadian provinces allow the retention of a percentage of sales taxes, up to a ceiling, to compensate for compliance costs.) This relief usually takes the form either of a VAT liability threshold below which tax need not be handed over to the authorities, or a tapered percentage relief varying with turnover size bands. All of these compensatory schemes involve some increase in the complexity of the system and therefore in the operating costs for both government and business.

Other alternatives exist. One method would be to allow small firms the option of being assessed for VAT on an annual basis, calculated from the annual accounts which have to be prepared anyway for business income tax purposes. The disadvantage of this approach is that, unless these accounts were to become more elaborate, the use of more or less arbitrary ratios of inputs and outputs would be necessary and some form of regular payment would also be required, which would still leave some of the administrative burden.

Another alternative which has its attractions would be to eliminate all VAT payments between registered traders. Traders would be able to purchase tax free by quoting an exemption certificate number. Retailers would continue to charge VAT and their business customers would be entitled to reclaim taxes paid on retail purchases. This is the 'ring system' of VAT operated in some Latin-American countries. Since VAT payments between registered traders do not contribute to net revenue collected there would, in theory, be no loss of revenue. At the same time, since the vast majority of all individually recorded VAT transactions are between registered traders, there would be a massive reduction in business record keeping and in the self-cancelling flows of tax revenues to and from the tax authorities.

Proposals to this effect were made by the Consultative Committee of Accountancy Bodies (CCAB) in the UK in 1978, but not adopted on the recommendation of an investigative committee which included representatives of the CCAB, the Confederation of British Industry (CBI), retailing and wholesaling bodies and Customs and Excise, but not small business as such (Commissioners of HM Customs and Excise, 1979). The tax authorities argued against the change on the grounds that only 28 per cent of registered traders predominantly supplied registered customers, while about 50 per cent sold regularly to both registered and non-registered traders, and their compliance costs would be worsened. The task of enforcement would also become more difficult so that neither most firms nor the tax authorities would find the administrative burden easier.

The tax authorities were mainly worried about the risk of increased evasion in the retail sector where 'a disproportionate amount of VAT errors, underdeclarations and fraud occurs'. It has been argued that under the CCAB proposals one major source of fraud (false input tax reclaims) would be eliminated (see National Federation of Self-Employed and Small Businesses Ltd, 1982). Not mentioned in the official report was the fact that by cutting input tax returns, a major tool in policing the system (through computer ratio checks) would be removed from the hands of the authorities.

Retailers, including small retailers, were against the change because it would increase their administrative burden (mainly because the special simplifying schemes operating in the retail sector depend on input tax invoices). The CBI and wholesale interests did not feel that the advantages of the CCAB proposals would offset the adverse effect on cash flow that would result. It was also doubtful if the proposals were consistent with either the letter or the spirit of the EC 6th Directive.

The debate over the CCAB proposals has been summarized at some length because it illustrates how, once a VAT system is in place, it is likely to remain. The arguments and investigation were certainly not exhaustive; for example, no serious attempt was made to measure the effect of the proposed changes on the compliance costs of business as a whole, nor was the following question faced: once VAT between registered traders is eliminated, what are the advantages of that system over other indirect tax systems? A VAT without tax between registered traders is, in essence, identical to a comprehensive sales tax.

All schemes for lightening the burden of VAT on smaller registered traders inevitably introduce further complexity and economic distortions or increase the opportunities for evasion or all three. The fact is that although better schemes might be devised, small business and VAT do not go well together.

VAT IN NORTH AMERICA

Towards Greater Realism in Tax Policy

Our review of experience of VAT in Europe has shown that, although on the surface it works smoothly enough, it is in practice far from the economically neutral and evasion-free tax dreamed of by so many economists and tax administrators 25 years ago when it first began to spread around the world. The same conclusion was reached at the conference of fiscal specialists held by the Brookings Institution in Washington DC in 1980 (Aaron, 1981). This demonstrated that differentiated VAT rates, operated in order to reduce regressivity among final consumers, 'inevitably complicate administration and compliance and destroy both neutrality and the advantages that uniformity may bring'.

The present study, looking at VAT from a different perspective, presents an even more unfavourable picture of this tax by bringing out the fact that both the compliance and administration costs of VAT are highly regressive with respect to size of firm. In other words, VAT is bad for small business, and collecting the tax from small business is costly for government.

It has, of course, always been recognized by economists that taxes of all kinds can have profound effects on economic structure and performance, and indeed the development of VAT systems owes much to the desire to minimize economic distortions. The conflict between economic efficiency and the design of a VAT system which will not bear more heavily on the less advantaged members of society has, as mentioned, in most European countries resulted in the loss of much of the theoretical neutrality of VAT. But there are other dimensions to the economic neutrality of a tax system than its effect on relative prices. Income taxes, for example, are generally believed to discourage risk-taking and effort and discourage saving more than taxes on expenditure (either type of tax can be made progressive in terms of income or expenditure). Income taxes, both corporate and personal, also, as mentioned earlier (p.98–101), tend to discriminate against small businesses, which are more dependent on personal savings for investment than are large firms, which have greater access to capital markets. Payroll taxes, in general, also discriminate against labour-intensive small businesses. For these reasons, a shift from taxation of incomes and payrolls to the taxation of consumer expenditure would be less detrimental to small business, but there is a danger that the removal of one set of distortions will be replaced by another.

Complexity in any kind of tax system always discriminates against small firms because their administrative resources are so limited and they can rarely afford the best advice. Expenditure can be taxed at source by means of an expenditure tax which relieves all forms of saving from income tax — there is growing support for income tax reform along these lines in the UK — or expenditure outlays can be taxed, as they are through VAT and excise taxes in Europe and sales and other taxes in North America.

Figure 7.3 shows lists the available forms of outlay taxes in two groups. The first group, single stage taxes, are listed roughly in order of the magnitude of the total compliance and administrative burden they impose on government and business. A single stage tax is one which is imposed only at one point in the chain of production and distribution. The nearer that point is to the final consumer, the more business units there are involved in collecting the tax and, generally speaking, the greater the national cost of operating the tax. However, the nearer the tax point to the end consumer, the more nearly the tax comes (or can come) to approximate to a tax on total value added with minimum distortion to the pattern of production and consumption (provided the taxes are designed so as not to enter into business costs, which is possible with any form of single stage tax).

The second group, multiple stage taxes, are levied at all stages in the chain of production and, in some cases, also of distribution. These taxes are also listed roughly in order of total operating cost and are more costly to administer than single-stage taxes. The turnover or cascade tax, as we showed in Appendix 7.1 (p.163), cannot be prevented from cumulating at every stage in production, nor can it be at all accurately excluded from exports. Even if it is not levied at the retail stage, it has to be operated by very large numbers of businesses, though it is quite a simple tax to operate. VAT, which in its comprehensive form creates the minimum of distortion to the pattern of production and consumption, is, in absolute terms, very costly to administer and has an even higher compliance cost. Variants of the comprehensive VAT, the ring system and the business

Figure 7.3 Types of outlay taxes.

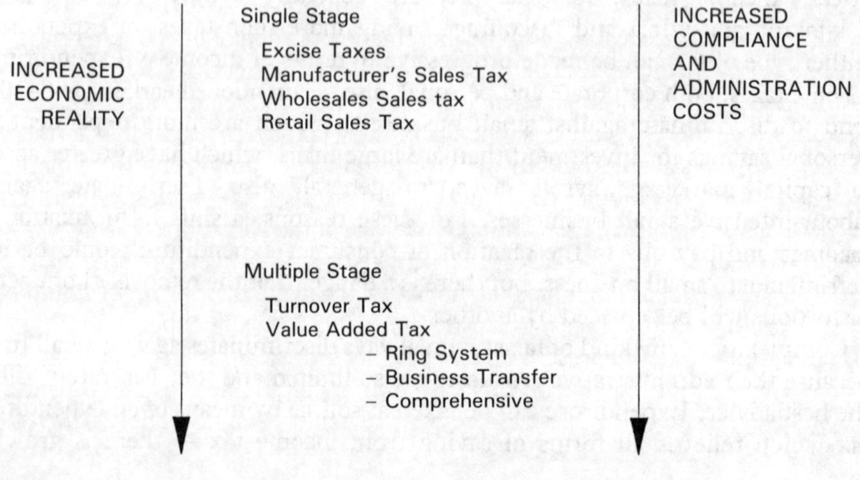

transfer system, each have somewhat lower total operating costs than the full VAT, but suffer from other disadvantages.

In the ring system, VAT registered traders charge tax only to traders or end consumers so that economic neutrality is unaffected with somewhat lower compliance costs, but it has more problems in policing than the full VAT. The business transfer tax (BTT) is the opposite of the ring system in that only transactions between registered traders are taxed. In the BTT, the compliance burden is lifted from retailers at the expense of failing to tax value added at the retail stage. Even if state sales taxes remained in force, a federal BTT would, in the United States, probably favour retailers in terms of compliance burden at the expense of other businesses, while the ring system would do the opposite, as compared with a full VAT.

European experience can throw little light on the special difficulties of introducing a value added tax into the federal systems in North America. While West Germany is a federal state with VAT, the two North American countries face different conditions in the relationships between the levels of government than did West Germany when it introduced VAT. Both federal constitutions, traditions of Canadian federal/provincial tax integration and state/provincial dependence on sales tax revenues, create a quite different set of circumstances.

VAT Versus a Sales Tax

Both the United States and Canada have state sales taxes; if new federal indirect taxes are to be raised, the alternatives available include a sales tax piggybacked onto, or integrated with the existing state taxes or a VAT. As shown in Appendix 7.1 (p.167), and at lower rates of tax at least, the choice between a comprehensive sales tax and VAT should be determined by administrative and compliance cost considerations alone. For any given coverage of consumer expenditure, the sales bases of the two types of tax and the economic effects on the pattern of production and expenditure are, in principle, the same, provided arrangements are made to allow traders to reclaim sales taxes paid on inputs.

From the point of view of both government and business, however, VAT is very different from a sales tax, and the incremental burden of introducing the tax would be very considerable. The US Internal Revenue Service (IRS) (Treasury Department, 1984) has published an estimate of the cost of administering VAT. It assumes that there would be some 20 million taxpayers (excluding farmers) and that IRS costs would amount to $700 million per annum by the time the system was fully operational. An additional 20,700 IRS staff would be required. The yield of VAT would depend on the coverage of the consumption base. At 77 per cent of the base, which is about the average coverage in Europe, the yield of an effective 10 per cent rate of tax (again below the average in Europe) would be over $240 billion at the Treasury's estimated 1988 levels of expenditure (more than enough to cover the present budget deficit). Administration costs would be about 0.3 per cent of revenue on this basis. If net compliance costs for business were at the same 4.4 percentage of revenue that Sandford (private communication to the author) estimated for the UK for 1983–4, then the incremental compliance burden on business in the United States would amount annually to over $10 billion in 1988, much, if not most, of it borne by small business.

These figures are subject to wide margins of error since even if the VAT system adopted in the USA were identical, productivity levels, interest rates, differences in the industry mix and size structure and other factors would lead to different compliance cost ratios. All the figures are intended to demonstrate is that the numbers are very large. The IRS costs given above are not the whole costs since they exclude the costs of the US Customs Service, which would administer import VAT. The IRS costs, at 0.3 per cent of revenue, also seem a little on the low side compared with European levels of around 1 per cent at a higher tax rate, even allowing for much higher productivity. The IRS estimates assume that there would be about 1,000 registered traders for each official, compared with 100–250 or so in Europe, i.e. four to ten times more. The IRS has a somewhat larger staff manpower than the UK Inland Revenue, which has similar functions but does not operate a self-assessed tax system and is hardly computerized. The ratio of the US to UK population is about four to one.

Canada has not yet published estimates for the cost of VAT administration, but the number of registered traders there could hardly be less than 700,000 and could, depending on coverage, exceed 1 million. Costs for government and business should not be proportionately less than for the USA.

We have seen no comparable estimates for the cost of introducing federal sales taxes in North America, but they would be a small fraction of the costs of a VAT system. Retailers in most states in the USA and provinces in Canada are already handling sales taxes and both business and state governments have had up to 50 years' experience of sales taxes. Federal and state sales taxes could be collected on the basis of a single tax return (as is done with state and local taxes) and by reliance on audits at only one level of government for both sets of taxes (as is done with corporate income tax). Some states already have arrangements to allow registered traders in some sectors to purchase goods free of sales tax, and these could be extended (Due, 1973). The incremental compliance costs for retailers would be very small (and could be compensated for), while other businesses would remain relatively unaffected. There would, no doubt, be political and administrative problems but they would, as far as we can see, be dwarfed by those of a full value added tax.

The only real practical objection to the introduction of federal sales taxes instead of VAT is that, at the sort of effective rates we are talking about, the incentive for evading sales taxes would be greater and the scope for controlling this more limited. There may be some force in this objection, but it seems inconceivable that the public costs of enforcing higher rates of sales tax would be greater than those of a VAT system, while the enormous saving in compliance costs would remain. In fact, there is no way of knowing what the consequences of generally higher rates of sales taxes would be, but since some US states and Canadian provinces seem able to cope with much higher than average rates of sales tax there is no reason to suppose that such rates are impracticable. The *average* nominal rate of sales tax in Canada is already nearly 8 per cent, while the highest rate as 12 per cent (Newfoundland). In the USA, the average rate is 4.5 per cent but Connecticut has a rate of 7.5 per cent.

The Sea Change

Whether an increase in the total level of taxation is desirable at all is a political issue although some economists, including ourselves, would argue that tax ratios in most European countries have long since passed the point at which they began to impair economic growth and flexibility.

Europe's relatively slow recovery from the 1973–81 recession and its sluggishness in adapting to new technologies and sources of competition compared with Japan and the United States (Canada, in economic performance, is somewhere between these two groups of countries), are leading to a reassessment of the role of high taxation, industrial regulation and employee protection in inhibiting economic change. At the same time, there has been a reaction against the simple-minded notions of 'bigger is better', which characterized industrial policy in Europe in the 1960s. It is now accepted that but for the jobs created by small business, unemployment in Europe would be very much higher, while the dynamic role of small firms in American and Japanese economic development is being more widely understood (Organisation for Economic Co-operation and Development, 1985b). There are also signs, both in Europe and North America, of a desire to simplify tax systems and to reduce reliefs and allowances (tax expenditures) in order, among other objectives, to improve the functioning of capital markets. These changes were precipitated by the end of the long post-war boom which ended in the early 1970s and the difficulties encountered subsequently in maintaining the growth of public expenditure in the face of inflationary pressures and stagnant economic growth. They are of profound importance, and amount to a sea-change in economic and social affairs, which can be seen reflected everywhere, for example in a revaluation of the role of the entrepreneur and in ideas and values in architecture and urban redevelopment.

At a time when the general current of change in all the advanced industrialized countries is in the direction of reducing the burden of government on business and, in particular, promoting small business, proposals to introduce value added taxation in North America need very careful consideration. The tide may already be turning. Though New Zealand has just introduced VAT, Australia has recently decided against this form of taxation. Norway has set up a committee to re-examine the administrative burdens of VAT, and in Britain there is an active debate on how these burdens on small business might be lightened.[2] Although the general tendency in modern tax theory is to favour some shift towards taxes on expenditure, practical experience of VAT suggests that it is an unnecessarily complex and burdensome tax for business. There is a risk, to put it mildly, that by the late 1980s VAT would, in North America, look as old-fashioned and unsatisfactory as the cascade taxes that it began to replace in the older bureaucratic traditions of Europe a quarter of a century ago.

APPENDIX 7.1: VAT IN THEORY AND PRACTICE

The Nature of VAT

VAT is a tax on final consumption which is collected at every stage of production and distribution rather than at the retail stage alone, as with the sales taxes that are familiar in North America. VAT is levied on the difference between the sales of each firm and its purchases, that is, on the value it adds to these purchases. Traders who are registered for VAT are entitled to credit the tax they pay on their inputs against the tax they collect on their outputs and remit only the difference to the tax authorities. (If the input tax is greater than the output tax, they receive a refund.)

Since traders do not bear the tax on their inputs and charge the output tax on their sales to their customers, the formal incidence of the tax largely falls on the consumer. The effective incidence may be shared, however, by other stages in the chain of production and distribution. For example, the imposition of VAT may stimulate shifts in the pattern of consumption away from taxed goods and towards untaxed goods. Producers and retailers may attempt to arrest these shifts by reducing margins, which may force some out of business. The incidence of taxation is a complex subject, and while most economists would agree that VAT is fully shifted forwards to the consumer in the long term, it is possible that business bears some of it in the short term. This is especially likely to be the case when the tax is not applied uniformly on all consumer spending. In a recent Forum of Private Business survey (Bannock, 1984) 93 per cent of small businesses claimed to pass on the whole of VAT to their customers.

Although VAT is described as a multi-stage tax, these considerations indicate that it is only really the collection which is multi-stage. A main purpose of the additional complexity of the multi-stage collection over a single-stage retail sales tax is to make evasion of the tax more difficult, although there are other advantages. To understand fully how VAT works and its appeal to economists and governments, it is necessary first to understand the relationship between value added and national output and expenditure.

Value Added and the National Accounts

Value added is a useful concept in economics because it enables us to distinguish the unique contribution which individual firms or whole industries or sectors make to the national output. It is a necessary concept because these contributions are not measured by gross output or the value of sales or turnover. If we added up the sales of all firms in the economy, we should come to a figure which is several times greater than the value of the wages and salaries, rent, interest and profits paid by these firms; that cannot be right because for the economy as a whole or a sector of it, the value of output cannot be greater than the value of incomes or, for that matter, the value of expenditure plus savings. (We ignore the complications of investment and foreign trade which do not affect the point we are making.)

The reason why the addition of the sales of all firms gives a larger total than their contribution to national output, income or expenditure, is simply that the sales of each individual firm include the value of the inputs from its suppliers. The sales turnover of General Motors (GM), for example, if added to the sales of its suppliers, would double count the value of the steel in its products several times over. First, a steel company digs iron ore out of the ground and produces ingots and, after further processing, finally sells coils of sheet steel to, say, stockists or wholesalers. Then a small stamping company buys steel strip from the wholesaler and produces blanks for an electrical company which assembles these blanks into an alternator which it then sells to GM which installs it in a car. The car is sold to a dealer who, in turn, sells to the final consumer. The steel has been sold six times: once by the producer, once by the wholesaler, once by the stamper, once by the alternator manufacturer, once by GM and finally by the dealer.

At each stage in this process, value is added to steel, either by a manufacturing process as in the slitting of the coil into strip and the stamping of the metal blanks, or by the provision of a service, such as the stocking of the steel sheet by a wholesaler or the car by the dealer. The steel company is at the beginning of the chain as far as the steel is concerned, but it too will need to buy fuel for its blast furnace, electricity and lubricating oils for its strip-mill, and so on. The difference between the value of these purchases and the value of its sales is the value the steel company adds to its inputs, and the sum of the added values of all the firms contributing to the manufacture and distribution of passenger cars is equal to the total value of the new passenger cars bought by consumers.

The gross national product (GNP) is the sum of all values added in the economy and (if we ignore overseas trade and payments) is equal to consumer expenditure and saving and also to the total of what economists call 'factor incomes'.

Values added in:	*Disposal of incomes:*	*Factor incomes:*
Output of consumption goods and services	Expenditure	Wages and salaries
+ Output of investment goods (capital goods and inventories)	+ Saving	+ Rent + Interest + Profit
= Gross National Product	= Gross National Product	= Gross National Product. Product.

A 10 per cent tax on the value added at each point in the chain of production and distribution, and including the public sector, would produce a yield of 10 per cent of the GNP.

Value Added and VAT

When we refer to a value added tax, we can actually be thinking of one of three types of tax. The type of VAT just described is what is called a *gross product*

VAT. In fact, this kind of tax is not used anywhere and is not under consideration for North America. The reason for this is that under a gross product VAT, value added would be calculated by deducting only purchases of raw materials and not machinery or other investment goods or the depreciation on those goods. This would mean that capital goods would effectively be taxed twice, once when they were purchased and again in the depreciation element embodied in the products they were used to produce. An alternative type of VAT would be to allow the deduction of depreciation (an *income type of VAT*) but this would still involve the taxation of net investment and could lead to distortions in the choice of production methods.

Both the gross product and income types of VAT would also create administrative difficulties. In practice the VAT system used in Europe and under consideration in North America is of the *consumption type*, which means that value added is defined as sales minus purchases of energy, materials, semi-finished products, machinery and equipment and services (but not direct labour services).

The consumption type of VAT at a comprehensive and uniform rate of 10 per cent would produce a yield of 10 per cent of the total of personal consumption, which is equivalent to GNP minus saving. In theory it would, therefore, yield the same as a sales tax levied at the same rate on all final expenditure.

So far we have not considered transactions across national boundaries. Usually, VAT is not charged on exports because the consumer is outside that boundary. This means that the exporter claims back the input tax but charges no output tax. Imports are subject to VAT at the border on their landed value, that is including CIF charges (cost, insurance and freight) and customs duty, if any. The jargon for this type of tax treatment of foreign trade is that VAT is applied on the *destination principle*. It maintains domestic consumption as the tax base. If the tax were applied to exports but not imports then this would be the *origin principle*. Domestic production is the tax base under this system.

VAT does not cover all value added in an economy even on the chosen base. Certain industries are always exempted from the tax. There are two ways of treating the exemption of particular classes of expenditure from VAT. One is to grant exemption with credit for input tax, which is invariably done for exports, and the other is to grant exemption without credit for input tax. In both cases, the trader does not add the tax to the selling price. The trader is also entitled to reclaim the tax on the purchases made in connection with the sale in the first case but not in the second. In some countries, the term '*exempt*' is reserved for those instances where input tax is not credited; those where it is credited are referred to in these countries as '*zero-rated*'. A zero-rated trader is as much part of the VAT system as a standard rated one, filing tax returns and registered with the authorities. Exempt traders are completely outside of it and in the same position as final consumers. Very small traders whose turnover is below a defined limit or *threshold*, and for whom the administrative costs would greatly exceed the revenue, are usually exempted. So, too, is housing, where both new construction and rented accommodation are normally exempted because of the difficulty of otherwise taxing owner-occupiers and tenants on the same basis.

The services of certain financial institutions, for which the calculation of value added presents special difficulties, are also usually exempted. There are many problems in applying VAT to the services of financial institutions. One difficulty is that some services (for example 'free' checking accounts) are not explicitly charged for and therefore the straightforward credit system is not operable. Insurance companies, to give another example, do not make a net charge for risk protection: in any individual case, value added cannot be calculated until claims made are subtracted from premiums paid. Other instances of exemption are discussed in Chapter 7 (p.114–5).

How VAT is Calculated

Just as, in theory, there are several types of VAT, there are also several ways in which the liability for the tax of each type may be calculated. So far we have simply described value added as sales minus purchases; this *subtraction method* is one way of calculating the VAT base to which the rate may be applied. Since, as we have shown, value added is the pool out of which all factor payments are drawn, it can also be calculated by adding up wages, interest, rent and profit made by firms. The *addition method*, as this is called, would, under a consumption VAT, require that profits be defined after writing off capital expenditure as it is incurred. It would, in effect, be a payroll and cash flow tax.

Tax liability in the VAT adopted in Europe and under consideration in North America, however, is assessed by a third alternative: the *invoice method*. What this means is that each firm invoices its customer for the value of its sale to that customer plus VAT (output tax) and receives an immediate credit against the amount of VAT it is due to pay to the government for the VAT paid on its own purchases (input tax). At the end of the accounting period (which may be monthly, quarterly, or even annually as we explained earlier (p.130–1) it pays the difference between the output tax and the input tax, if positive, or applies for a refund if its output tax is less than its input tax. Since value added is defined as the difference between purchases and sales, then the same rate of value added tax applied to purchases and sales will, if credits are given for the tax on purchases, yield the same net tax as if the same rate were applied to value added.

In fact, the VAT system in practice does not tax the true value actually added in any period at a particular rate, not only because depreciation is not allowed for but also because the tax has to be paid even if the producers are making a heavy loss and not adding value at all. Moreover, since, in practice, input tax is not reclaimable on all inputs, value added is not accurately calculated by the invoice method.

Table A.1.1 illustrates how VAT liability is calculated by the invoice method and how this reconciles with value added at various stages in the chain of production and distribution. For simplicity we assume that the first firm in the chain, as primary producer, has no purchases and therefore no input tax. It sells, say, wild fruit to a manufacturer for $20 plus output tax at 10 per cent = $22. The manufacturer processes the fruit and cans it and sells it to a retailer for $100 plus 10 per cent output tax = $110. The retailer sells the canned fruit to a consumer for \$130 plus 10 per cent output tax = \$143. The consumer has paid \$13 in VAT. The primary producer has remitted \$2 of this total to the tax authorities, the manufacturer \$8 and the retailer \$3. In each case the tax remitted is the output tax charged minus the input tax paid. The manufacturer, for example, paid \$2 tax to the primary producer and collected \$10 in tax from the retailer, the difference of \$8 is equal to 10 per cent of the difference between the manufacturer's sales (before tax) of \$100 and his purchases (before tax) of \$20.

Table A1.1: Simplified example of VAT input and output tax liabilities at various stages of production and distribution

			VAT rate 10 per cent
	Primary producer sells to manufacturer (\$)	Manufacturer sells to retailer (\$)	Retailer sells to consumer(\$)
(1) Purchases	-	20	100
(2) Input tax	-	2	10
(3) Tax-inclusive purchases: (1) + (2)	-	22	110
(4) Sales	20	100	130
(5) Output tax: (4) x 10%	2	10	13
(6) Tax-inclusive sales price	22	110	143
(7) Value added: (4) - (1)	20	80	20
(8) Net tax remitted: (5) - (2)	2	8	3

This example is highly simplified since the primary producer in practice would have had some purchases – if only baskets to carry the fruit. VAT on these baskets would have been fully deductible from the output tax on sales to the manufacturer and the cost of purchasing them would have reduced the producer's 'value added' in proportion. 'Value added' would be reduced immediately by the full capital cost of the baskets, even though they will be used many times. Next time the primary producer sells fruit to the manufacturer, the value added would, in this case, be higher because the baskets will already be paid for, even though true value added would be the same. This brings out the fact that VAT levied in any period will not be strictly proportional to the value added in that period because of the way capital goods are treated in the consumption type of VAT.

It should be pointed out that the remittances of tax to the tax authorities indicated in Table A1.1 will only all be made in any single tax accounting period if all the transactions take place within that period. In practice, the retailer will purchase the canned fruit from the manufacturer sometime before selling it to the consumer, and will pay for the goods some time after receiving them. The manufacturer will be liable to remit the VAT on the sale to the tax office when it becomes due, whether the retailer has paid the manufacturer or not. The manufacturer will also be able to deduct the input tax from the output tax whether he or she has paid his supplier, the primary producer, or not. These features of VAT mean that the collection and remittance of the tax benefit the cash flow of some registered traders and have a negative impact for others. The precise cash flow impact of VAT on individual traders will depend on the frequency with which they have to make returns to the tax authorities, their timing in relation to the collection period to which they relate, and the length of the credit periods they give to their customers and receive from their suppliers. The cash flow impact will also crucially depend on the rate of tax charged on inputs which, in practice, will necessarily be the same as the rate on outputs.

The Advantages of the VAT System

It is only possible to discuss the advantages of a tax system in relation to other alternative systems and in this section we compare VAT as adopted in the EC with other alternative taxes, notably turnover taxes, excise taxes and general single-stage wholesale and retail taxes.

Turnover taxes are taxes levied as a proportion of the price of goods on each sale in the chain of production and distribution. These taxes were common in Europe before the advent of VAT in the 1950s and were adopted at a federal level in Canada between 1920 and 1924 (Gillis, 1985). *Excise duties* are taxes levied on specific goods consumed in the domestic market, invariably 'non-essential' goods, the demand for which is not very sensitive to price (those for which demand is inelastic), for example alcohol and cigarettes. *Wholesale taxes* are single stage taxes levied on sales by manufacturers or importers like the Purchase Tax levied in the UK prior to 1973 and the Federal Manufacturers' Sales Tax in Canada. *Sales taxes* are levied on retail sales and are applied by provincial governments in Canada and the states of the United States.

The theoretical advantage of VAT over these other forms of *indirect taxation* (indirect taxes are levied on expenditure, direct taxes on the income or wealth of individuals or companies) is that it can be completely neutral with respect to producers and consumers. Because purchases of firms including capital goods are not taxed, VAT does not spill over into the costs of firms and distort decisions on methods of production in the way that turnover taxes do. These are also called 'cascade taxes' because they cumulate at each stage of the chain of production and distribution. Manufacturers pay turnover tax on their purchases from suppliers and charge tax on their gross sales to their customers so that some elements of their costs are taxed twice. By acquiring their suppliers they can save tax by eliminating a point in the chain at which the tax is levied. These taxes encourage vertical integration and negate the efficiencies of subcontracting.

VAT is also neutral between exports and imports. Turnover taxes cannot be easily and precisely eliminated from export prices and in Europe, deductions of turnover tax provided a convenient means for hidden subsidiaries to exports. Although wholesale taxes are not levied on exports, some tax element enters into the costs of exporters which cannot be reclaimed by them. Wholesale taxes do not treat imported and domestically produced goods uniformly either, since, among many other things, they are applied at the time of importation and thus do not tax some distribution costs, such as delivery to the retailer and advertising costs, which may be included in the taxed wholesale price of domestically produced goods. Other problems with imports arise which, like this one, are neatly avoided by VAT (see Gillis, 1985, for a discussion of the problems of the Canadian Manufacturers' Sales Tax).

Another advantage of VAT is that it can be applied virtually across the board, thus it need not distort consumer spending towards any untaxed items.

While turnover taxes, which can be applied to services, result in double taxation and other distortions, wholesale taxes cannot be applied to many services where there is no wholesale stage — most services, such as dry cleaning or business consultancy, are produced and distributed at the retail stage. VAT can apply to the value added in services after allowing deduction of input tax on the purchases of cleaning fluids or electronic calculators used by service firms. This means that VAT at a uniform rate applied over the whole range of consumption will not introduce distortions into the pattern of either production or consumption, which some other forms of indirect taxation seem inevitably to do. Moreover, there are problems under a wholesale tax of defining the wholesale stage and the wholesale price. Under modern systems of distribution where producers may sell to very large retailers at lower prices than they sell to wholesalers, similar goods may end up being taxed at different rates.

It will be noted that while the advantages of VAT over turnover and wholesale taxes are very clear, the advantages over a general retail sales tax are less clear cut. A sales tax is not levied on exports and is applied equally to the retail price of goods irrespective of their origin. Sales taxes can also be applied equally to goods and services and they do not enter into producer costs except to the extent that some producers and distributors purchase inputs, including services, at the retail level.

There are, however, advantages to VAT other than its neutrality. One desirable feature of the tax is that it treats all firms identically, irrespective of their industry, production stage or type of customer. Complex problems of classifying firms as retailers or wholesalers do not arise; under modern methods of distribution where sales to final consumers are often made at early stages of the production chain, this is an important advantage of VAT. Moreover, firms themselves do not have to distinguish between their business and non-business customers. They levy the same tax on all those to whom they supply.

It is commonly said that VAT is self-policing because all traders will have a strong incentive to register so that they may receive credit for their input taxes. For the same reason, they will also want to ensure that they receive proper invoices from their suppliers and that they collect their output tax from their own customers. In this way, each trader keeps an eye on the firm above and below in the chain of production and distribution. Because the collection of the tax is multi-stage, it is also said, evasion at one point in the chain can only affect part of the tax-take, though this patently does not apply to service industries. In practice, VAT is far from evasion proof. It may offer less scope for evasion than a sales tax in some respects but opens up new opportunities for the fraudulent reclaim of input taxes (see p.135).

A further aspect of the appeal of VAT to government is that it forces smaller registered traders to keep more elaborate records than most of them would in the absence of the tax, and allows cross-checking of business income tax and VAT declarations, which should lead to improved compliance with this and other taxes. It is clear that these advantages have been appreciated at least by the Canadian tax policy-makers, who have pointed out that VAT 'provides an opportunity for one-stop audit, i.e. both income tax and VAT audits could be carried out simultaneously' (Weyman, 1985). Like all indirect taxes, VAT imposes some taxation on the expenditure of those who have evaded assessment for income taxes and on non-residents visiting the country. This is considered to be an important advantage in a period when the 'black economy' and international tourism and business travel are expanding activities.

It has also been asserted in Europe that the more elaborate records required for VAT lead to improved efficiency in small businesses. Although many accountants would agree with this, we consider it more likely that most registrable small business proprietors are able to decide which accounting systems are most cost-effective. At best, the additional benefits of VAT records will be marginal and they will not, for example, tell businesspeople whether their business is profitable or not or which activities are profitable and which are not.

Disadvantages of VAT

It is, of course, widely recognized that, like all taxes, VAT does present problems to both the taxpayer and the tax authorities. The most common objection to the introduction of VAT is that a broadly based tax on consumers' expenditure will bear disproportionately heavily on those with lower incomes, that is to say it is *regressive* with respect to income. Since people with high incomes on average spend a smaller proportion of their income (they save more, either before or after income tax), then a given rate of VAT on total consumer spending will tax a higher proportion of income of the poor than of the rich.

It is because of concern about regressivity that most VAT systems charge lower or zero rates of tax on expenditure on basic necessities such as food and housing. Some countries have more than two VAT rates; three European countries have four. Of 32 countries with VAT, only nine had a single-rate system in 1984 (Tait, 1984), but none of these actually levied its single rate on all consumer expenditure.

The items which are VAT exempt because they present intractable problems to the designers of VAT systems account for a relatively small proportion of consumer expenditure — perhaps around 10 per cent on average in EC countries. Items of expenditure, lower rated or exempt to offset regressivity, however, typically account for a somewhat greater proportion of consumer expenditure, usually nearer 30 per cent. Together, these special categories, however, are so important that all the theoretical advantages of the VAT in terms of neutrality towards production and consumption and its clear superiority over single-stage wholesale or retail taxes go out of the window.

It is easy to understand why this should be so for neutrality of consumption since different rates of tax clearly distort consumer choice and the operation of market forces. The effects of differential rates on production, however, are more complicated. Producers who do not charge VAT on their output of exempted goods but are allowed credit for their inputs, for example, are receiving a subsidy from taxpayers while other producers who are not entitled either to charge VAT or reclaim it are paying a tax which is intended to apply only to final consumers. In a few cases, exempt (as distinct from zero-rated) exporters will be paying a tax in this way on their exports.

More serious are the effects of multiple rates on the taxation of value added. Exemptions can give rise to either positive or negative effective rates of tax, which are widely dispersed about the nominal rate. Where half of the costs of a restaurant meal is food and half value added and food is zero-rated, for example, then a 10 per cent rate of VAT on the whole cost of the meal is 20 per cent of value added, twice the nominal rate (Kay and Warren, 1981).

Kay and Warren (1981) calculated that effective rates of VAT in Britain are, for these reasons, different in virtually every sector of the economy and range from minus 27.5 per cent on the output of certain manufactured food products to 37 per cent on leather and leather goods. These particular extremes are not troubling from the point of view of regressivity, but it hardly makes sense to subsidize shipbuilding at minus 7.9 per cent and tax electronics and communications at 19.2 per cent through the VAT system.

Virtually all economists are agreed that multiple rates and exemptions should be kept to a minimum in the interests of avoiding distortions of these kinds. The regressivity of VAT systems in most countries is, in practice, mitigated or made more progressive by exemptions (Organisation for Economic Co-operation and Development, 1981), but at the cost of considerable distortions. These distortions are not inevitable with a VAT system: the effects of uniform rates on the distribution of income can be dealt with more efficiently by other means – for example by adjustments to income tax thresholds and social security benefits (Davis and Kay, 1985), but their avoidance in practice has been a rare occurrence.

There is, however, an even more intractable shortcoming of VAT: that it imposes heavy compliance costs on small firms and requires an entirely new and expensive administrative machine in government.

The acquisition of the necessary knowledge and machinery to impose, record and remit VAT is largely a fixed cost and it inevitably follows that there are economies of scale in tax compliance as in other spheres of business-government relations (Faucett Associates, 1984). Because the administrative resources of small businesses are limited, the burden tends to fall to a significant extent on the proprietor, whose time is the most precious resource in most small firms. Small businesses are also unable to spread the cost of in-house professional advisers over a wide range of activities and their data-processing activities are computerized to a lesser extent. All this means that the compliance costs of taxation and VAT in particular are highly regressive with respect to size of firm. VAT is also expensive to collect from small firms so that government administrative costs as well as business compliance costs are relatively higher for small firms.

As we saw earlier (p.145–6), other indirect taxes are also regressive by size of firm, but because VAT involves the participation of all businesses, not just retailers as with a sales tax or manufacturers and importers as with a wholesale tax, and because it requires records of inputs as well as outputs, the total social costs and distortions of a VAT system are very much greater at the national level than with, say, a retail sales tax. For the same reason, the costs of administering VAT for government are also absolutely much greater than for other indirect taxes: more returns have to be processed, refunds have to be made as well as remittances received, and a major system of local offices staffed to audit traders' records and deal with queries as well as to perform the other functions of tax administration is necessary.

It has been shown (p.126) that the government's administration costs probably average around 1 per cent of VAT revenues in the EC at nominal standard rates of tax, which range from 12 to 23 per cent. (Private compliance costs as a percentage of revenue are many times higher but neither compliance nor administration costs can be measured with precision.) Where costs are effectively fixed, a doubling of the rate halves the administration costs as a proportion of revenue. Thus, fixed costs of 1 per cent of revenue would rise to 20 per cent of the total if the VAT rate were reduced from 20 to 5 per cent, prohibitively high compared with a sales tax at a similar rate. This mechanism helps to explain why VAT, initially introduced at low rates in most countries, has been swiftly increased and has, so far at least, tended to climb more or less inexorably upwards (see p.111).

There are also major start-up costs for a VAT system both for government and taxpayer and, as we saw earlier (p.122), troublesome, though containable, transitional macro-economic problems to do with the level of investment and inflation.

We have been able to show in this appendix that, theoretically, VAT is a good tax because it does not enter into the costs of producers of goods and services; if levied at a uniform rate on all consumption it will not distort the pattern of production and consumption; it is neutral with respect to imports and exports; and it is perhaps less easily evaded than a retail sales tax. In practice, however, against these advantages have to be set the disadvantages that arise from the regressivity of VAT with respect to size of firm and the income and expenditure of consumers. In almost all countries, political pressures to minimize the burden of VAT on the less advantaged sections of the community have proved irresistible. With the multiplication of rates and exemptions, not only are compliance costs pushed up still further but the neutrality of the tax towards the pattern of production and consumption has gone by the board.

As we saw earlier (p.150–3), measures to lessen the impact of VAT on the smaller firm have introduced further distortions without significantly affecting the distortions in the size structure of economic organization that VAT creates.

Finally, the inherent complexity of VAT and the way this complexity is multiplied by attempts to lessen regressivity of the two kinds identified mean that the administration costs for government are excessive at lower rates of tax.

We have shown that there are economies of scale in compliance by taxpayers, there are also obviously economies of scale in administration of the tax. Once the heavy infrastructure of VAT has been laid down, major increases in tax revenue can be achieved by government at negligible incremental administrative cost.

Appendix 7.2: Chronology of countries adopting VAT

1960 (1) Ivory Coast	**1970** (15) Ecuador Luxembourg Norway	**1977** (29) Korea
1961 (2) Senegal	**1971** (16) Belgium	**1978** (30) Nicaragua
1962 (3) Morocco	**1972** (17) Ireland	**1980** (31) Mexico
1965 (4) Colombia	**1973** (22) Austria Bolivia Italy Peru UK	**1983** (32) Dominican Republic Guatemala
1967 (6) Brazil Denmark	**1975** (25) Argentina Chile Costa Rica	**1985** (33) Indonesia
1968 (9) France West Germany Uruguay	**1976** (28) Honduras Israel Panama	**1986** (36) New Zealand Portugal Spain
1969 (12) Madagascar Netherlands Sweden		**1987** (38) Greece Turkey
		1989 (39) Japan

Source: *Tait* (1984); updated by Graham Bannock & Partners Ltd.

Appendix 7.3: VAT rates applicable in the member states of the European Community

		Rate				
Country	Date	Standard	Intermediate	Increased	Reduced	Zero
West Germany	1.01.1968	10	-	-	5	-
	1.07.1968	11	-	-	5;5	-
	1.01.1978	12	-	-	6	-
	1.07.1979	13	-	-	6;5	-
	1.07.1983	14	-	-	7	-
Belgium	1.01.1971	18	14	25	6	Yes
	1.01.1978	16	-	25	6	
	1.07.1981	17	-	25	6	
	1.01.1983	19	17	25(1)(2)	6	
Denmark	3.07.1967	10	-	-	-	
	1.04.1968	12;5	-	-	-	
	29.06.1970	15	-	-	-	
	29.09.1975	15	-	-	9;25 (3)	Yes
	1.03.1976	15	-	-	-	
	3.10.1977	18	-	-	-	
	1.10.1978	20;25	-	-	-	
	30.06.1980	22	-	-	-	
France	1.01.1968	16 2/3 (4)	13	20	6	-
	1.12.1968	19 (4)	15	25	7	-
	1.01.1970	23	17;60	33 1/3	7;5	-
	1.01.1973	20	17;60	33 1/3	7	-
	1.01.1977	17;60	-	33 1/3	7	-
	1.07.1982	18;60	-	33 1/3	7 & 5;5 (5)	-
Ireland	1.11.1972	16;37	11;11	30,26	5;26	
	3.09.1973	19;50	11;11	36,75	6;75	Yes
	1.03.1976	20	-	35}	10	
				}(6)		
	1.03.1979	20	-	40}	10	
	1.05.1980	25	-	-	10	
	1.09.1981	25	-	-	15	
	1.05.1982	30	-	-	18 (7)	
	1.03.1983	35	-	-	23 (7)	
	1.03.1984	35	-	-	5/18/23 (7)	
	1.03.1985	23	-	-	10	
Italy	1.01.1973	12	-	18	6	
	1.01.1975	12	18	30	6	
	18.03.1976	12	18	30	6	
	10.05.1976	12	18	30	6 and 9	
	23.12.1976	12	18	30	1/3/6/9	
	8.02.1977	14	18	35	1/3/6/9/12	Yes
	3.07.1980	15	18	35	2 and 8	
	1.11.1980	14	15 and 18	35		
	1.01.1981	15	18	35	1/2/3/6/9/12	Yes
	5.08.1982	18	20 (8)	38 (8)	2/8/10/15(8)	
	19.04.1984	18	20 (8)	30/38 (8)	2/8/10/15(8)	
	20.12.1984	18	-	38	2 and 9	
The Netherlands	1.01.1969	12	-	-	4	
	1.01.1971	14	-	-	4	
	1.01.1973	16	-	-	4	Yes
	1.10.1976	18	-	-	4	
	1.01.1984	19	-	-	5	
United Kingdom	1.04.1973	10	-	-	-	
	29.07.1974	8	-	-	-	
	18.11.1974	8	-	25	-	Yes
	1.05.1975	8	-	25	-	
	12.04.1976	8	-	12,5	-	
	18.06.1979	15	-	-	-	
Greece	1.01.1986	-	-	-	-	

Source: EC Commission, DG XV

Appendix 7.4 Special schemes for small business

Introduction

All the countries of Europe which have a value added tax in operation make some administrative recognition of the heavy compliance burden of the tax on small businesses. The forms this recognition takes are summarized in Table A4.1. Broadly, we may put them into two categories: schemes which attempt to compensate the small firm for bearing a disproportionately large compliance burden, and schemes which attempt to actually cut that burden by simplifying the administration of the tax.

Exemption

Exemption cuts both the tax burden on small firms and the compliance burden. Exempt traders have no need to fill out returns, keep receipts, claim back input tax or charge output tax. Exemption also reduces the administration costs of the tax without, as shown earlier (p.147), sacrificing much revenue. The registration thresholds currently in force throughout Europe are shown in Table A4.2.

However, although exemption helps some firms, there are many for whom it will pay to register despite the administrative cost of so doing. These are traders who

- sell output to other registered traders who can claim back the VAT they are charged;
- have high input VAT liabilities which under exemption are unrefundable;
- sell output at a lower rate than they buy inputs.

For traders who opt in, the exemption system neither compensates them for the compliance burden nor relieves them of it. It is not, therefore, a solution to the compliance problem. Moreover, exemption causes distortions in patterns of trade in favour of very small firms against small and medium sized firms. However, even if just to obviate the need for casual self-employed workers to enter the VAT system, some cut off point is desirable.

A distinction should be drawn between VAT systems which allow traders below the exemption threshold to opt for registration if they wish, and those that do not. It can never fail to benefit general dislike having to cope with the administrative burden of this permission. The EC countries all allow voluntary registration for small firms, but many do insist that once they enter the system, they stay within it for a minimum number of years; in West Germany, for example, the minimum is five years.

Table A4.1: Special schemes for small business

		Information required of small business to participate in scheme	Countries in which scheme applies	Information required of small business in order for it to know whether to be in scheme
A.	Designed to simplify administration of the tax for small firms at the expense of accuracy of assessment			
I.	Exemption of small businesses, defined by turnover	None	All but France, Sweden and The Netherlands	Turnover
II.	Exemption of small businesses, defined by turnover, though allowing them to issue tax invoices	None	Sweden	Turnover
III.	Flat-rate schemes by which value added is deduced from inputs	Value of inputs	Belgium	Turnover Industry margins relative to rest of industry
IV.	Flat-rate schemes by which input tax is deduced from turnover	Value of turnover	West Germany, Italy	Turnover Industry margins relative to rest of industry
V.	Flat-rate schemes which apply to individual firms as opposed to individual industries	Full information	France, Belgium	Turnover
B.	Designed to compensate small firms for regressivity of compliance burden			
VI.	Deductions in tax payable by small firms	Full information	Austria, France, The Netherlands, West Germany, Italy	Full VAT accounts
C.	Designed to pass compliance burden on to others			
VII.	Tax compliance burden passed on to suppliers of small business (where all sales of small business are to non-registered sector)	None	Belgium	Turnover Industry margins relative to rest of industry
VIII.	Tax compliance burden passed on to customers of small business (where all sales of small business are to registered sector)	None	Many countries with respect to farmers	Turnover Industry margins relative to rest of industry

Exemption with Power to Issue Tax Invoices

In Sweden exempt traders are allowed to issue tax invoices, thus allowing their customers to reclaim VAT even though their supplier does not have to account to the authorities for the tax. This creates less distortion because exempt traders receive compensation for the VAT they pay on their inputs in the form of the output tax charged, while registered firms trading with them can reclaim input taxes in the normal way.

Table A4.2: European exemption thresholds

	Turnover below which VAT registration is not compulsory, 1985	
	Local currency	US $
Austria	AS 40,000	2,350
Belgium	None	-
Denmark	Dkr 10,000	1,120
France	None	-
West Germany*	DM 20,000	8,090
Ireland	IP 25,000	32,630
Italy	None	-
Luxembourg+	LFr 200,000	4,030
The Netherlands	None	-
Norway	NFr 12,000	1,600
Portugal	Esc 8 million	52,600
Spain	None	-
Sweden	Skr 10,000	1,330
United Kingdom	£ 19,500	28,040

* Tax-inclusive turnover.
\+ 1982.

Flat Rate Schemes

Value added derived from input data

The need for full VAT bookkeeping can be reduced by the use of industry-wide data on profit margins. Normally, traders must keep information on both their purchases and their sales. Under this scheme, traders keep records of their inputs alone. To calculate output and total tax due, inputs are grossed up by some industry-wide coefficient which should be equal to the average ratio of output to inputs for the industry. Clearly, those with smaller than average margins will benefit from registering in the normal way for they will be allowed to claim back more input tax than the average firm and this is only possible in the normal VAT scheme. In a country where all traders in an industry had exactly the same margins, the system would exactly match a full VAT system.

Input tax derived from turnover

As an alternative to deriving output tax from actual inputs, input tax can be derived from actual output. This saves traders the need to keep receipts of invoices paid although they must now keep records of their sales. Again, those who run on low margins will benefit from registering in the normal way. The

EC Commission favours this as a method of helping small firms. As both this and the other flat rate schemes involve making the same simplifying assumption, the choice as to which is preferable should depend on whether it is easier for businesses to keep a record of sales or a record of purchases. This scheme is to be preferred on administrative grounds by the authorities, as it allows them to cross-check that the customers of small firms have purchased all that they say they have.

Flat rate schemes provide a sensible balance between the interests of simplicity and accuracy, though their applicability is limited to narrow industries of homogeneous products.

Separate coefficients for individual firms

The French run a flat rate scheme which does not use industry-wide data to calculate inputs or outputs, but past behaviour of individual firms. In essence, a careful study of each firm is conducted in which its ratio of outputs to inputs is calculated. That ratio is then used for all future tax calculations. The scheme swaps the distortion caused by divergent margins within industries for distortions caused by divergent margins across time. The scheme as operated in France actually requires firms to keep full VAT records anyway, and the fact that many traders choose to adopt it all the same is an indication that proprieters believe they can manipulate the assessment period to their advantage.

It is not even clear that if assessments are made frequently enough to be accurate, the burden on small firms is any less than it would be if the tax were administered normally, for the cost of an assessment is high to both a firm and the authorities.

Tax compliance burden passed on to suppliers

One way of alleviating the problems of small firms is to tax them at 'source' — to levy the tax charge from them without actually requiring them to fill out tax returns. The first approach one might take on this path is to get the suppliers of small firms to levy a VAT charge in excess of the normal rate. For example, suppose all the small firms in a certain industry used $1 of flour for every $2 of output; if the standard rate of VAT is 10 per cent, under a normal system a small firm would buy, say, $100 of flour (paying tax of $10) and would sell $200 of output (obtaining $20 of tax) and would remit $10 of tax to the authorities, who would also receive $10 from the supplier. Under this scheme, the supplier would charge a special high rate of VAT – 20 per cent – and the small firm would do nothing other than pay it on purchase of flour. The state would be equally well off, the supplier has a worse compliance task, the small firm has a better one.

Belgium operates such a scheme for a small number of retailers; however, it carries so many flaws within it, it could not be widely adopted. First, it discourages suppliers from dealing with small firms at all. Second, it is extremely hard in practice to set premium rates of VAT that would reasonably approximately tax small firms by the right amount. Third, it is administratively extremely complex. Multitudes of firms are all required to distinguish between their small firm or non-small firm customers. One of the administrative advantages of VAT is that all customers are treated alike and no separate accounts need be kept for different types. Finally, the scheme is only suitable for industries where all sales are to the non-registered sector, for otherwise unrefundable tax charges are passed up the production chain.

Tax Compliance Burden Passed on to Customers

In contrast to passing the burden of administration on to the suppliers of small firms, it is possible to pass it on to their customers. This can only work when all sales are to the registered sector, for the non-registered customers cannot be expected to pass tax on to the authorities. This is the basic method used in six of the EC states with respect to small farmers. Under the normal scheme, farmers charge tax and their customers (being registered) reclaim it. Under the special scheme, farmers do not charge tax and their buyers do not reclaim it. But their customers are allowed to claim a deduction against their tax bill for the input tax paid by farmers on their purchases. Farmers are thus saved the bother of reclaiming it themselves as they would under the normal scheme.

Graduated Relief Schemes

In the absence of measures to simplify the administration of VAT in small firms, some of the distortions created by the regressive compliance burden can be removed by compensating those worst affected by it. Many EC countries have a form of graduated relief from the tax. As the tax liability has to be calculated in order that entitlement to relief can be established, this approach does nothing to lower the cost of administration. Relief can take one of several forms.

First, there can be a VAT liability cut-off point below which VAT collected need not be handed over to the authorities. This is very similar to the Swedish 'exemption with power to issue tax invoices' system, and is adopted in France in place of a turnover exemption threshold.

A second form is the deduction of a percentage of the total VAT bill. This is in force in Austria, for example, where there are three turnover bands, each with a certain discount — the discount for smaller firms is bigger (20 per cent for the smallest above the exemption threshold). West Germany has a maximum 80 per cent rebate falling by 1 per cent for every DM 500 of turnover in excess of the exemption threshold.

The Netherlands have a form of VAT allowance, withdrawn as VAT liability increases — the first DG 2,300 of VAT is ignored. Up to DG 2,500, tax liability is merely calculated tax minus DG 2,300. With liabilities above that, there is an allowance of DG 1,650, withdrawn by DG 1 for every extra tax liability of DG 1. This involves putting firms under the scheme on a marginal VAT rate twice that of other taxable units. When they make an extra sale, they must hand over output VAT on that sale and also hand over some tax that was previously being discounted from their liability. Whatever allowance remains is taxable under business income taxes.

It can be seen that no clear favourite system has emerged. Some countries cut the marginal rates of small firms, others compensate them but raise their marginal rate. Given the desirability of having constant marginal rates for all firms, it may be that the optimum scheme is a combination of withdrawable allowance and percentage rebate, or perhaps a flat rate payment by government to all small firms in the VAT system. A graduated relief scheme does not benefit those who are net reclaimers any more than an a rise in income tax allowances benefits people who pay no tax anyway.

Retail Schemes

Mention should be made of the special schemes specific to retailers and which exist in each EC member state. These schemes aim to cope with the special problems of retailers, who often sell a range of items taxed at different rates, and who cannot practically be expected to issue VAT invoices with all purchases. Generally, these special schemes apply to all retailers, but Ireland, Italy and the UK operate exceptional regimes for small traders.

In Ireland and Italy, smaller retailers are allowed to apportion output tax payable on a range of items at several rates on the basis of the proportion of costs that each item represents. If two items are traded, therefore, and each accounts for half total input costs irrespective of the margins marked-up on each item, half of total sales turnover will be taxable at the rate of one item and the other half at the rate of the other. It will not pay retailers with low margins on highly rated goods to enter these schemes.

The UK runs nine retail schemes. Despite criticism of the complexity of the choice facing retailers, each does serve a distinct purpose. Scheme 'C' is specially designed for retailers with a turnover below £75,000 at 1983 prices. Under this scheme, sales turnover does not need to be recorded. Instead, inputs of different rates are all grossed up by a flat rate margin (one for each type of retailer), which leaves an assumed turnover for each rate category of items sold. In effect, the authorities are both assuming that margins are uniform throughout each type of retailer and that purchases of goods each month accurately reflect sales in the same month.

Although the retail schemes do not remove the VAT burden from retailers, they make it a good deal easier than it would otherwise be for a group potentially particularly badly affected by the tax.

APPENDIX 7.5: The EEC 6th Directive on VAT

The primary force behind the drafting of the 6th Directive was a need for nine member states to agree on all its components. It is thus not surprising that the principles for implementing VAT, which it outlined broadly, conformed to existing practice in most states, rather than to an ideal VAT system. Even where practices in individual countries diverged, the Directive usually chose to leave issues open rather than directly opt for one system in preference to another.

The result is a document which, in a rather fluid way, describes the current VAT system in operation in EC countries. A country not bound by the Treaty of Rome, though, may choose not to structure the tax on identical lines to those outlined in the Directive.

1 The first issue the Directive tackles is who shall be taxable. This is not usually a controversial matter. Employees are not required to register for tax purposes (even when earning more than the exemption threshold) but all independent traders engaged in economic activity are required to register.

The Directive leaves open the degree to which businesses linked to each other can register as a single unit. It should not make any difference to tax revenues whether a country is tolerant to groups registering as one or as several traders, though evasion may be easier to detect in cases where firms producing different items submit separate returns.

The Directive specifies that local government and other state authorities shall not be registered for tax, except in certain listed activities or where this would 'lead to a distortion of competition'. In principle, government bodies should be indifferent as to whether they are registered or not, for the pricing and budget policies of these bodies can be adjusted without the tax to match, in every way, the effects of having the tax. However, in practice, it is probably better to put government bodies into the VAT system. This removes any incentive for them to provide services 'in house' which could be contracted out but which would then incur an unreclaimable VAT charge.

2 The second issue the Directive tackles is what shall be taxable. This is taken to include virtually any supply made in return for a consideration.

Goods taken out of a business for consumption purposes, used by the owner or given to the employees, qualify as taxable. The sale of a whole business is not considered a 'supply for consideration'.

3 The next issue considered is the location of supply. This is not important except in the context of exemption of exports. Goods are taken as located at the start point of their delivery while services are positioned at the office of the supplier or where the services are physically carried out. Certain services usually purchased by business users are considered supplied at the location of the receiver, for example advertising.

4 The Directive then defines the 'chargeable event' — the moment that tax officially becomes liable (putting aside delays in payment allowed). The tax rate charged is that in force at the time of the chargeable event.

The point is deemed to be the first of either receipt of payment or delivery of supply. This is not convenient for those selling items on a sale or return basis.

Imports are taxable when they enter the country. Some countries have, however, been running 'postponed accounting' whereby importers are not liable for VAT on imports until their next return is filed. Importers then can both reclaim and declare the tax charge on imported goods simultaneously. This leads to a cash flow loss to the government, but, everybody agrees, simplifies the administration immeasurably.

5 The 'taxable amount' is normally to be taken as the amount of the consideration obtained for the supply. Items consumed out of a business which are not paid for are taxable — at the purchase price (or, in the absence of the purchase price, the cost price).

Taxable amount includes duties, levies and other charges. This will be an important issue in any state with a local sales tax. It does not include the VAT itself — the tax is expressed as an exclusive rate. Discounts offered in return for quick payment are not included in the taxable amount.

States are left free to decide how to treat tax paid on goods returned, bad debts or discounts offered after supply has taken place.

6 Under the Directive, reduced and increased rates of tax are permitted. It is an issue on which virtually all tax experts agree; if you can avoid multiple rates, do so.

7 The Directive lists a set of exemptions from the tax which states are expected to make. Most of these exist for good reason and would be exempt under any VAT in or out of the EC.

Exports of goods are exempt with a refund of input VAT allowed; i.e. the destination principle is in force. It might be logical to introduce a VAT which taxed exports and exempt imports — one would expect exchange rate movements to compensate largely for the trade effects of so-doing and administration would be more straightforward; however, not surprisingly, no country does so.

Exports of services do not enjoy the tax free status of exports of goods, despite the fact that the logic of VAT is that they should do so. Instead, a schedule of listed service supplies made to foreigners is zero-rated so that in practice virtually all service exports would be free of tax. The reason that goods and services do not enjoy the same treatment is that whereas it is thought possible to tax imports of goods it is not as easy to tax services which are, in principle, rather difficult to locate. Zero-rating all exports would probably lead to many service purchases avoiding tax in any country at all, hence the business services are exempt by specific listing, while other services are taxed in country of supply.

There are exemptions relating to some international supplies. Transport, like shipping and aircraft for international use, is exempt – it would be a nuisance to tax and refund tax every time an aeroplane flew into the country. Gold held for central banks, defence equipment and items temporarily imported are also exempt.

Certain difficult areas are excluded from the tax — financial services, insurance, certain charitable institutions and the letting or leasing of land or buildings. The treatment of these items is a complex and widely discussed issue. It is certainly the case that VAT is peculiarly bad at coping with them.

Finally, there is a set of exemptions which is less necessary – postal, health and education services. The reason for the latter two is that they are usually provided in the public sector in EC countries.

8 The refunding of input tax paid is made through the operation of the invoice system. There is no reason why a country introducing a new VAT need adopt this type of administration though it does make multiple rates possible.

EC members are allowed to remove the right to deduct tax on various 'consumption items' such as entertainment allowances or cars.

It is the declared aim of the EC that VAT should be a consumption type tax with a full and immediate refund of tax paid on capital goods. It is permitted to introduce rules for refunding VAT on capital goods which limit the state's liability in the short term, for example the French 'buffer system' in which reclaiming on capital goods is only permitted against positive VAT liability.

9 Partially exempt traders — by far the most difficult to administer — are only allowed to deduct a proportion of VAT paid, set as the proportion of total turnover which is taxable. It seems sensible to introduce a *de minimis* rule so that traders with, say, less than 5 per cent of exempt transactions can reclaim 100 per cent of their input tax.

10 The Directive is flexible on the issue of how often returns have to be submitted. For traders, it is desirable that those who are net reclaimers should be allowed to claim back tax quite frequently. For those paying tax it is important to balance the cash flow advantage of long gaps between returns with the administrative inconvenience of such gaps.

It is possible under the Directive to have an annual tax period, and to demand interim payments.

States are allowed to waive tax charges which are very small.

11 The Directive issues guidance on several special schemes for different groups of traders.

On small firms, the Directive sets limits to the VAT exemption thresholds the states are allowed to impose and forbids members to introduce new graduated relief schemes.

The registration limits are defined in terms of tax exclusive turnover of taxable outputs, not including capital disposals.

It stipulates that small firms must be allowed to opt for normal taxation if they want to — a provision against the interests of the tax authorities but in the interests interests of the tax authorities but in the interests of firms themselves.

The Directive also outlines the flat-rate farmer scheme, which effectively passes the compliance burden of the tax on to the buyers of farm products.

Travel agents are to be taxed only on the margin they add to the price of holidays they organize. For trips organized outside the EC, the travel agent is taken as an exempt intermediary. These measures ensure that a travel agent paying foreign bodies who do not charge VAT will not be taxed on the full value of the trip organized. This is a measure that could be adopted for any trader with exempt inputs who, when taxed on the full value of output, is effectively paying a very high rate of tax as a proportion of value added.

Second-hand goods are an issue that the Directive raises but leaves unresolved. Traders in second-hand items should, like travel agents, only pay tax on their margin not on the full value of their sales. This is because they tend to buy their inputs from the personal sector and hence cannot reclaim back any input tax on their purchases.

Appendix 7.6: Number of registered persons and net tax paid by sector, United Kingdom, 1983–4

	Approximate number of registered traders at 31 March 1984	Net tax paid or repaid, 1983-4 (£ million)
Primary industries		
Agriculture, forestry and fishing	181,700	-536.3
Mining and quarrying	1,400	-240.6
Manufacturing industries	139,600	7,730.3
Construction	226,200	753.1
Utilities	200	392.7
Transport and Communication	61,600	768.6
Distributive trades		
Retail distribution	267,600	1,125.3
Wholesale distribution	79,300	3,179.0
Dealers	30,700	507.2
Services		
Insurance, banking, and business services	70,900	1,061.8
Professional and scientific services	81,200	877.1
Miscellaneous services	291,500	2,461.9
Public administration and agencies	1,200	-834.7
Total	1,433,100	14,953.8

Source: *Commissioners of HM Customs and Excise* (1984b)

NOTES

1 Greece introduced VAT in January 1987.
2 See Chapter 8 (pp. 000–000) for details of recent changes to the VAT system in the UK.

REFERENCES

Aaron, H.J. (ed.) (1981), *The Value Added Tax, Lessons from Europe*, The Brookings Institution, Washington DC.

Aaron, H.J. (ed.) (1982), *VAT Experiences of Some European Countries*, Kluwer, Deventer.

Bannock, G. (1981), *How to Survive the Slump*, Penguin Books, Harmondsworth.

Bannock, G. (1981), *The Economics of Small Firms*, Basil Blackwell.

Bannock, G. (1984), *Surveys of Forum Members*, The Forum of Private Business.

Barker, P.A. (1972), *Value Added Tax, The Cost to the Businessman, Journal of Accountancy*, September .

Carsberg, B.V. *et al.* (1985), *Small Company Financial Reporting*, Prentice Hall International, Englewood.

Commissioners of HM Customs & Excise (1978), *Review of Value Added Tax*, Cmd. 7415, HMSO, London.

Commissioners of HM Customs & Excise (1979), *Elimination of VAT Between Registered Traders*, HMSO, London.

Commissioners of HM Customs & Excise (1984a), *The Collection of Value Added Tax*, HMSO, London.

Commissioners of HM Customs & Excise (1984b), *75th Report for the Year Ended 31st March 1984*, HMSO, London.

Commissioners of HM Customs & Excise (1985), *76th Report for the Year Ended 31st March 1985*, HMSO, London.

Committee on Enforcement Powers of the Revenue Departments (Keith Committee),Report, Volumes 1 and 2, HMSO, 1983.

Conseil des Impôts (1983), *Sixième Rapport au President de la République Relatif a la T.V.A.*, Journaux Officiels.

Davis, E.H. and Kay, J.A. (1985), *Extending the VAT Base: Problems and Possibilities*, Institute of Fiscal Studies.

Department of Trade and Industry (1985), *Burdens on Business: Report of a Scrutiny of Administrative and Legislative Requirements*, HMSO, London.

Due, John F. (1973), *The case for the use of the retail form of sales tax in preference to value added tax*, in R.A. Musgrave (ed), *Broad Based Taxes*, Johns Hopkins University Press, Baltimore.

Faucett Associates, Jack (1984), *Economies of scale in regulatory compliance: evidence of the differential impacts of regulation by firm size, Small Business Administration* (Mimeo).

Ganguly, Pom (1985), *UK Small Business Statistics and International Comparisons*, Paul Chapman Publishing, London.

Gillis, Malcolm (1985), *Federal sales taxation: a survey of six decades of experience, critiques and reform proposals, Canadian Tax Journal*, January-February.

Hamer, Eberhard (1979), *Burokratieuberwalzung auf die Wirtschaft*, Schluter, Hanover.

International Bank for Reconstruction and Development (1985), *World Bank Development Report*, Oxford University Press.

International Bureau of Fiscal Documentation (1983), *Value Added Taxation in Europe*, (2 Loose Leaf Volumes).

Johnstone, D. (1975), *A Tax Shall be Charged*, HMSO, London.

Kay, J.A. and Warren, N.A. (1981), *Effective Rates of Value Added Tax*, Working Paper no.16, Institute of Fiscal Studies.

Mendham, S. (1983), *Exploiting and Overcoming Government Regulations*, Forum of Private Business.

National Federation of Self-Employed and Small Businesses (1982), *VAT: The Myth and the Reality*,

National Economic Development Office (1969), *Value Added Tax*, National Economic Development Office, (revised 1971).
Organisation for Economic Co-operation and Development (1981), *The Impact of Consumption Taxes at Different Income Levels*, OECD.
Organisation for Economic Co-operation and Development (1984), *National Accounts 1953-1982*, Vol. 1, OECD.
Organisation for Economic Co-operation and Development (1985a), *Revenue Statistics*, OECD.
Organisation for Economic Co-operation and Development (1985b), *Employment Outlook*, OECD.
Peacock, Alan and Forte, Francesco (eds) (1981), *The Political Economy of Taxation*, Basil Blackwell, Oxford.
Peat Marwick (1985), *A comparative analysis of sales tax compliance costs for retail business*, *Small Business Administration* (Mimeo).
Richardson Committee (1964), *Report of the Committee on Turnover Taxation*, HMSO, London.
Robinson, Ann and Sandford, Cedric (1983), *Tax Policy Making in the United Kingdom*, Heinemann, London.
Sandford, Cedric (1984), *Economics of Public Finance*, Pergamon, Oxford.
Sandford, C. *et al.* (1984), *Costs and Benefits of VAT*, Heinemann, London.
Shoup, Carl (1969), *Public Finance*, Aldine Publishing Co., Hawthorne, NY.
SKIM Industrial Market Research, (1984), *International Small Business Survey* (Mimeo). Rotterdam.
Small Business Research Trust (1985), *Quarterly Survey of Small Business in Britain*, Vol.1, no.3.
Snijder, M.A. (1981), *De Invloed van de Fiscus op het Midden-En Kleinbedrijf*, Fed-Oeventer, Amsterdam.
Tait, Alan A. (1984), *The Value Added Tax: Why and How*, Draft Paper for the Canadian Tax Foundation, November (Mimeo).
Treasury Department (1984), *Tax Reform for Fairness, Simplicity and Economic Growth*, Vol. 3, *Value Added Tax*, Department of the Treasury, November.
Wauters, F.J. (1984), *Un nouveau son de cloche les soldes crediteurs en T.V.A.*, *Revue Générale de Fiscalité*, December.
Weyman, C. David (1985), *Federal Sales Tax Reform in Canada*, Address to the Eastern Regional Association of Sales Tax Administrators, Baltimore, August 18–22 (Mimeo).

Chapter 8

THE COMPLIANCE COSTS OF VAT FOR SMALLER FIRMS IN BRITAIN AND WEST GERMANY*

INTRODUCTION

The main purpose of this study was to compare the compliance burden of VAT on small firms in Britain and West Germany and attitudes of business proprietors towards the administration of the tax. It was hoped that the findings would have some relevance for tax policy at both a national and EC level.

These broad terms of reference and the resources available did not allow us to examine exhaustively all the issues raised. Our choice of survey method, a small scale postal questionnaire survey, allowed us to collect quantitative information, but to maximize the response rate we were obliged to restrict the length of the questionnaire and hence the range of information collected. Despite these limitations, the results of what we believe is the first international comparison of compliance costs reveal important differences between the two countries and, we consider, some important implications for tax policy.

Not the least of the difficulties of international economic comparisons is the choice of the exchange rate to use when comparing monetary values. Since considerably less than one-third of marketed goods and services are extensively traded between our two countries and since the exchange rate is affected by capital movements and speculation, market exchange rates are not appropriate for comparing compliance costs. We have used a purchasing power parity (PPP) exchange rate derived from OECD data where our conclusions are particularly sensitive to the exchange rate used. The reader has to bear in mind that even conclusions based on a PPP rate are subject to qualification.

---

* A report of a study completed in June 1987 under finance provided by the Anglo-German Foundation and reproduced here with their permission. The study was carried out by Graham Bannock & Partners Ltd in collaboration with Professor Horst Albach, University of Bonn/Koblenz School of Corporate Management and the Institut für Mittelstandsforschung.

THE VAT SYSTEMS IN BRITAIN AND WEST GERMANY

Introduction

The VAT system now levied in the European Community was affirmed as mandatory for all member states in two Directives in 1967, almost 10 years after the Treaty of Rome agreement to form a customs union. West Germany introduced the tax in January 1968 and the UK in April 1973, following its accession to membership of the EC in January of that year.

Despite the mandatory nature of the tax and a long succession of EC Directives governing its applicability and administration, there remain many differences between the VAT systems in member states in terms of rates and coverage and on points of detail. In some respects the range of differences in VAT rates, and coverage in particular, is so great that averages and generalizations can be misleading. The UK shares with Denmark the distinction of being the only countries in the Community with a single positive VAT rate of tax (several countries have four), but the extent of zero-rating and exemptions is, in compensation, much greater in the UK than in other member states (except for the Republic of Ireland) and this is much lower in Britain than the Community average (Table 8.1).

West Germany is, in fact, much closer to the EC norm in several aspects of VAT than is the UK. Table 8.1 shows that only just over half of UK consumer expenditure is subject to VAT while West Germany, at 71 per cent, is close to the EC average. This difference reflects widespread exclusions from the VAT tax base in the UK where, although the standard rate is 15 per cent, the effective rate is 8.9 per cent. Table 8.1 shows that while in West Germany the consumer pays VAT on postal services, travel over 50 km, most foods, books and periodicals, adult sports, medicines and children's clothing, for example, all these goods and services and more are exempt from tax or zero-rated in the UK.

In West Germany, the impact of VAT on 'essential' goods is limited not by exemption as in the UK, but by the applicability of a lower rate of tax of 7 per cent compared with the standard rate of 14 per cent. From Table 8.1 it can be seen that this results in a much higher effective rate as a percentage of the standard rate as well as a higher overall tax rate.

The use of one positive rate of VAT in the UK compared with two in West Germany simplifies the administration of the tax for business. In practice, however, some of this simplicity is lost for some UK businesses because many more goods and services are deductible for input tax in Britain but do not bear output tax (zero-rated).[1]

Moreover, it appears that the treatment of disallowed items of business expenditure (notably motor car expenses and business entertaining) is less favourable in the UK than in West Germany (especially since the current year).

In Tables A1.1–A1.4 (pp.214–6) we provide comparisons between the total population of registered traders in the two countries and those of our samples. The total number of registered traders in West Germany in 1984 was 1.86 million[2] compared with 1.43 in the UK. We should expect the number of registered traders to be higher in West Germany for several reasons:

Table 8.1: Estimates of the VAT base as a percentage of total consumer expenditure and gross effective and standard VAT rates, UK, West Germany and the EC, 1983

	VAT taxable base as per cent of total consumer expenditure	Gross effective rate*	Effective rate as per cent of standard rate
West Germany	71	10.3	76
UK	52	8.9	59
EC Average	70†	10.9‡	65‡

Source: Bannock (1986).

Notes: *Total VAT revenue as a percentage of consumer expenditure.
†Unweighted average of eight States.
‡Weighted average of the same eight States.

1 The population is 5.5 per cent greater and several studies indicate that the proportion of output and employment accounted for by small firms is greater than in the UK.
2 The registration threshold is much lower and fewer sectors are exempt from VAT in West Germany. A higher proportion of business units may therefore be registered in West Germany than in the UK. However, it should be noted that in 1983–4 over 262,000 UK traders had a taxable turnover below the threshold and were registered voluntarily (H M Customs and Excise, 1984).

In addition to differences in rates and coverage, there are other important differences between the VAT systems in Britain and West Germany as they affect the costs of compliance for business.

Administration

The VAT system appears to be more tightly administered in Britain than in West Germany in some respects. A number of interesting differences emerge from Table 8.2.

More information is required on tax invoices in the UK. Inclusion of the supplier's VAT registration number on the tax invoice is not mandatory in West Germany (although this is under review), nor is it necessary to specify the terms of supply or the rate of any discount offered.

Visits by tax inspectors are less frequent in West Germany than in the UK, perhaps by a factor of three. In West Germany, a special visit is unlikely in the first 10 years of operation of a business, unless there is evidence of irregularity. In Britain a visit is usual in the first year of operation, while subsequent visits depend on the circumstances. A large firm is likely to receive more visits than a smaller one.

Until 1986, there were no special penalties for late payment of VAT in the UK, though offenders could be brought before the courts. In West Germany there is a standard penalty of 1 per cent per month for all outstanding tax liabilities, including VAT, which is similar to the system operated for Schedule D income tax in the UK. Since October 1986, new penalties have been introduced in the UK, however, which are more severe than those in West Germany.

Another advantage of the West German system from the business point of view is that in West Germany all taxes affecting a business are administered from one local office. In the UK, a business proprietor may be dealing with one or more local Inland Revenue offices for income or corporation tax assessments, another Inland Revenue office for matters affecting the collection of taxes and a local VAT office, while VAT returns are submitted to a central office.

In other respects, however, the VAT system in the UK has its comparative advantages. Returns are made quarterly by most businesses in the UK, irrespective of size, whereas in West Germany quarterly returns are only permitted for traders with an annual tax remitted in excess of DM 6,000 (£2,000). Also, UK traders are allowed 30 days' grace after the end of the tax period to file their returns; this is three times longer than in West Germany. Delays in repayments by the authorities are shorter in Britain. The British regular VAT return is considerably simpler than its West German counterpart (see Appendix 8.3, p.220 et seq) while West German traders are also required to complete a more elaborate annual return which is not required in Britain. A further difference is that UK traders receive their regular return blanks through the post at the end of the period with their name, address and registration details printed on them. West German traders receive a supply of blank forms from the authorities in advance. British traders' returns are phased to spread the administrative load on the authorities, but traders can, on request, have the reporting periods aligned with their annual financial account year end. No such flexibility is provided in West Germany where VAT is operated on a strict calendar year basis.

Business VAT records need to be retained for six years in the UK (increased from three years under the 1985 Finance Act). In West Germany, records other than correspondence have to be preserved for ten years.

Finally, in Britain traders have the right of appeal to VAT tribunals in questioning decisions of the VAT authorities. These tribunals with lay members provide a faster, more economical and flexible system for dealing with disputes than in West Germany where appeals have to be made through the courts of justice.

Special Treatment For Small Firms

A major difference between the UK and West German VAT systems lies in the treatment of small firms. The British philosophy has, until very recently, been to rely on a high threshold which removes any necessity for many very small firms, particularly sole proprietors without employees, to register at all. Traders below this limit (presently £21,300) who do not register are, of course, relieved of the paperwork burden of VAT, but are unable to reclaim the tax on their inputs. The UK registration threshold, which is about three times higher than the West German one, is in fact substantially higher than that in any other member state except Ireland. Several member states have no threshold at all. In the 1987 Finance Act, a number of changes to the treatment of small firms in VAT regulations were introduced in the UK:

1 From the 1st of October 1987, traders with a taxable turnover of below £250,000 may, if they wish, incur liability for output taxes only when their customer invoices have been paid and not, as at present, when the invoice is issued. This is called the Cash Accounting Scheme and brings UK practice roughly in line with the West German procedure described below.
2 The same group of traders will also be permitted to make annual, instead of quarterly, returns. Payments of tax, however, will have to be made on account on a regular basis.
3 Modification of the rules for registration and deregistration which lengthen the time limits for notification.
4 Changes to the special retail schemes which are intended to make them simpler to operate and to make them available to more small and medium-sized businesses.

In West Germany, there are four special provisions for non-farm small firms within specified turnover limits. Certain businesses in the primary sector also receive special treatment (see Table 8.2).

1 Enterprises with a turnover which did not exceed DM 20,000 in the previous year may voluntarily opt for exemption from registration in the current year, even if they expect their turnover to be up to DM 100,000 in the current year. Effectively, this provides relief for new enterprise.

2 Registered enterprises with a total (not taxable) turnover of up to DM 60,000 are automatically rebated, with a proportion of the output tax they collect. The percentage of this rebate is 80 per cent where current annual turnover is less than DM 20,500. The rebate is reduced by one percentage point for each additional DM 500 of turnover until DM 60,000 is reached, at which point the rebate is zero. The average rebate for all firms participating in this scheme works out at about £400 per annum at current exchange rates.

3 The professions and enterprises with a turnover of less than DM 250,000 in the preceding year are permitted to account for VAT on a cash basis, rather than the normal accrual basis. Bad debt relief as in Britain is not available to larger enterprises.

Table 8.2: Comparison between VAT systems in the United Kingdom and West Germany, end February 1987

	WEST GERMANY	UNITED KINGDOM
(I) BASIC TAX ORGANIZATION		
Responsible government department	Ministry of Finance (responsible for administration regulations) Ministry of Finance of each provincial state (supervisory authority)	Customs and Excise
Responsible financial office	'<u>Finanzamt</u>' situated in each city (responsible for all taxes of one enterprise)	Local VAT office
Introduction of VAT and major changes	Introduction: 1968 Changes: Tax rates increased from 10 to 14 % in four stages, and from 5 % to 7 % over the period 1968-83	Introduction: 1973 Changes: 01.04.1974 Standard rate extended to cover petrol and diesel oil (derv) and certain food products 29.07.1974 Standard rate reduced to 8 %. 18.11.1974 Higher rate introduced at 25 % to cover petrol (but not derv) 01.05.1975 Higher rate at 25 % extended to cover goods and services

Table 8.2: (cont)

	WEST GERMANY	UNITED KINGDOM
		specified in the Higher Rate Schedule 12.04.1976 Higher rate reduced to 12° % on all goods and services specified in the Higher Rate Schedule, including petrol 18.06.1979 Higher rate abolished and standard rate raised to 15 % (covering all goods and services previously either standard-rated or higher-rated)
	No significant changes in coverage	Changes in coverage include: abolition of zero rating on newspaper advertising, 1985; extension of standard rating to repairs and maintenance of buildings, 1984, etc.
Tax registration number	Only one (eight digits: the first three are the number of the <u>Finanzamt</u>). In the case of an integrated inter-company relationship only the dominant enterprise is taxable. Supplies made between branches are not taxable.	One per VAT collection point. A single enterprise may have more than one number

Table 8.2: (cont)

(2) TAX PROCEEDINGS

Tax rates	Standard rate 14 % Reduced rate 7 %	Standard rate 15 % Zero rate 0 %
Reduced rated goods and services	Reduced rated - agricultural products - forestry - books and newspapers and copying services - goods for handicapped persons - wool (untreated) - artificial fibres - cinemas and private theatres	
Exemptions	Exemptions with credit - exports, cross-frontier transport of goods - travel up to 50km distance	Exemptions with credit - exports, cross-frontier transport of goods - transport of passengers or freight - sewage and water - most foods - books and periodicals (but not advertising) - items for the blind - fuels - construction services (but not repairs or maintenance) - medicines dispensed by pharmacists - charity goods - clothes and footwear for children

Table 8.2: (cont)

	WEST GERMANY	UNITED KINGDOM
	Exemptions without credit - capital transactions - insurance agencies - rental of real property - interest - services of hospitals and medical doctors - supplies made by charities - youth activities	Exemptions without credit - real estate - insurance - postal services - most financial services - education, health - burials and cremations - non-profit trade and professional organizations - sports, competitions and works of art - betting, gaming and lotteries - services of trades unions
Tax refund	Input tax can be reclaimed by organizations of public benefit as defined in §§ 51-68, German Fiscal Code	Charities may reclaim VAT on inputs subject to certain conditions.
Current payment periods	- Monthly if the tax amount probably exceeds DM 60,000 - Quarterly if tax amount probably between DM 600 and 6,000 - Yearly if tax amount probably less than DM 600 - Payment/repayment return must be issued 10 days after	Generally three months. Repayment traders (except those voluntarily registered) are normally allowed to make monthly returns. Returns made within 30 days of end of due period

Table 8.2: (cont)

Tax invoices	Information required on a tax invoice: - name and address of supplier - date of supply - customer's name and address - description, which identifies the goods or services supplied - the total charge made - the total VAT payable Less detailed tax invoices are allowed if the charge for the individual supply is less than DM 200 (incl. VAT) Then only: - name and address - date of supply - description, which identifies the goods or services supplied - the charge made, incl. VAT - the rate of VAT	Information required on a tax invoice: - identifying number - name, address and VAT registration number - date of supply - customer's name and address - type of supply e.g. cash, credit - description, which identifies the goods or services supplied - the total change made - the rate of any cash discount offered - the total VAT payable Less detailed tax invoices are allowed if the charge for the individual supply is less than £50 (incl. VAT) Then only: - name, address and VAT registration number - date of supply - description, which identifies the goods or services supplied - the charge made, incl. VAT - the rate of VAT

Table 8.2: (cont)

	WEST GERMANY	UNITED KINGDOM
Records	The enterprise is obliged to keep commercial books of accounts and to preserve them for 10 years (correspondence: 6 years). § 147 German Fiscal Code	The enterprise is obliged to keep business records for six years unless Customs and Excise have agreed a shorter period
Delay penalty	1 per cent of the delinquent tax each month (as for all taxes) § 240 German Fiscal Code	5 per cent surcharge on amount of tax owed, increasing to 30 per cent with each successive default. Applies to those who make a late return more than once in a 12-month period
Methods of payment	Giro, cheque	Giro, cheque
(3) SPECIAL SCHEMES FOR SMALL BUSINESSES		
Threshold for registration	DM 20,000 taxable turnover in the previous year and DM 100,000 in the current year (waiver of exemption possible) § 19 Abs. 2 UStG	Where taxable turnover exceeds, or is expected to exceed, £ 20,500 p.a. or has exceeded £ 7,000 in the previous quarter. Must notify within 10 days of end of quarter
Rebate of tax liability	Enterprises with a turnover of DM 20,000 up to DM 60,000 are granted automatically an amount of tax they collect. § 19 Abs. 3 UStG	No

Table 8.2: (cont)

Cash instead of accrual basis	Free professions, enterprises with a turnover of less than DM 250,000 in the previous year and enterprises which are not obliged to keep books according to § 138 German Fiscal Code (Abgabenordnung) can calculate their surplus tax amount on in-payment and out-payment. In the case of loss of receivable outstandings no VAT arises. This means an interest gain against regular taxation when there is time allowed for repayment	No	
Average input-tax calculation	For the above-mentioned enterprises the input tax amount can be calculated in agreement with the financial office according to average rates. The average rates differ with regard to profession and are fixed by the Ministry of Finance	No	
Special schemes for retailers	None other than the above	Nine different schemes are available for the calculation of output for retailers	

Table 8.2: (cont)

	WEST GERMANY	UNITED KINGDOM
Special schemes for small agriculture and forestry	Agricultural enterprises with less than 350 animal units receive a tax deduction of 5 % on the turnover until 1 July 1984 to 31 December 1988 and of 3 % of the turnover until 31 December 1991. ╜ 24a UStG Abs. 1	No

4 The enterprises benefiting from the cash accounting basis and certain others (mainly retailers and artisans) are allowed to reclaim input tax on the basis of specified average rates of tax which are applied to turnover. These rates range from 10.9 per cent for fuel retailers to 6.2 per cent for sculptors, 4.2 per cent for journalists and 2.2 per cent for authors.

Stability

The compliance cost (the cost borne by the taxpayer over and above the amount of the tax) of any form of taxation which requires individual assessment is obviously affected by the stability of the system. The time spent by both taxpayers and their advisers on compliance will tend to fall (with the 'learning curve') as administration becomes a matter of routine and systems are refined and developed. Changes in tax regulations interrupt this process, requiring an investment in time to understand the changes, retraining of staff and possibly changes to recording systems and, in some cases, reprogramming of computer operations. In theory, businesses do not bear VAT but simply collect it for the authorities. For firms the only cost of VAT is the compliance cost, except where input taxes cannot be reclaimed (as for some items of disallowed expenditure or where the tax cannot be fully passed on to the consumer).

We have not been able, in the course of this study, to quantify the relative stability of the UK and West German VAT systems, but there can be no doubt that on points of detail the British system has been subject to a very much greater degree of change. This is evident from Table 8.2. These changes in the UK have to a greater extent been the product of changes in borderlines between exempt, zero-rated and taxed goods and services, for example affecting the publishing, construction and catering industries. In addition, there have been administrative changes affecting imports and financial services, clarification of treatment of second-hand goods and antiques, and basic changes to administration such as threshold definitions, treatment of partially exempt traders or bad debt relief. Indeed, the changes have been so continuous that a regular, twice-yearly publication, *VAT Notes*, is issued by the authorities and well over 100 different explanatory booklets on specialized aspects of VAT have been made available.

The West German system, in contrast, has changed little since the early 1970s and the basic law appears to be straightforward enough to be interpreted by the layperson. No explanatory leaflets or booklets are considered necessary or issued by the tax authorities in West Germany and, thanks to a lower inflation rate, only one change in the level of the threshold has been made since 1968. The relative stability of the West German system arises largely from the greater coverage of the tax base and, it might be added, a less accommodating attitude towards special pleading. West Germany has had four changes in the rate of VAT since 1968, the last in July 1983. The UK has had five changes in the rate (though none since June 1979) and nine changes in the thresholds between 1973 and 1986.

THE POSTAL SURVEY

Sample Characteristics and Representativeness

The sampling frame for the postal questionnaire survey used in West Germany was the membership list of the Association of Young Entrepreneurs (*Bundesverband Junger Unternehmer* (BJU)). This body has some 2,500 members, well distributed among all sectors of the economy and among all sizes of firm. Since the organization was founded some 37 years ago and the rate of membership renewals is high, the Association is, as we see below, probably reasonably representative of the population in terms of age of firm. However, we cannot exclude the possibility that active and successful enterprises are over represented and artisanal and professional enterprises under represented.

In Britain, our sampling frame was a list of 4,000 respondents to the Small Business Research Trust (SBRT) annual survey of readers of the *National Westminster Small Business Digest* who had indicated a willingness to participate in other surveys. The NatWest Volunteers, as we refer to them, are, of course, a self-selected sample, but analysis carried out for the SBRT by Graham Bannock & Partners Ltd does not provide any evidence for thinking that the sample is seriously unrepresentative, at least in terms of enterprise characteristics and sectoral spread although, like all comprehensive small-firm surveys, the smallest firms are under-represented (Small Business Research Trust, 1986).

The West German sample of 800 enterprises was selected at random from all BJU members in Nordrhein-Westfalen and Hessen. The UK sample of 600 was selected at random from the NatWest Volunteer list, which covers enterprises located throughout Britain and Northern Ireland. A total of 197 West German and 262 UK usable responses was received, giving response rates of 25 and 44 per cent respectively. No follow-up was carried out in either country and these response rates are high for small-firm postal surveys in the experience of the research teams, and especially so for the UK. A copy of the questionnaire used is included in the Appendix 8.2 (p.218). The surveys were carried out in February 1987 in the UK and in March 1987 in West Germany. The characteristics of the two samples are summarized in Tables 8.3–8.6.

Tables A1.1–A1.4 (pp.214–6) show that manufacturing was over-represented and the primary sector and construction under-represented in the UK sample. In the West German sample, manufacturing was also over-represented while retailing was under-represented. The West German sample enterprises were on average larger and older than those in the British sample: 51 per cent of the West German firms were over 20 years old compared with 17 per cent Table 3.1 and 3.2 of the British, while 80 per cent of the British firms had fewer than 10 employees but only 36 per cent of the West German ones. There is independent evidence that the age distribution of the British sample does reflect that of the population. It also seems that Britain does have relatively fewer medium-sized firms than do West Germany and other developed countries, including the United States, though the West German sample may exaggerate the actual difference. The age structure of the smaller

West German enterprises is quite close to that of the UK sample. If respondents with more than nine employees are excluded from both samples, then 53 per cent of the West German firms were less than six years old, while the corresponding figure for the UK was 51 per cent.

Table 8.3: Number of respondents by turnover size range

Turnover size range	United Kingdom	Per Cent	West Germany	Per Cent
Less than £ 10,000	19	7.3	1	0.5
£ 10,000 - 24,999	30	11.5	1	0.5
£ 25,000 - 49,999	35	13.4	5	2.5
£ 50,000 - 99,999	36	13.7	14	7.1
£ 100,000 - 249,999	72	27.5	26	13.2
£ 250,000 - 999,999	51	19.5	46	23.4
£ 1 million and over	19	7.3	102	51.8
No response	-	-	2	1.0
Total	262	100.0	197	100.0

Source: Anglo-German Foundation VAT Study, Question 5.

Table 8.4: Number of respondents by sector

Sector	United Kingdom	Per Cent	West Germany	Per Cent
Agriculture, forestry, fishing	4	1.5	5	2.5
Construction	13	5.0	19	9.6
Manufacturing and processing	60	22.9	62	31.5
Transportation and public utilities	17	6.5	9	4.6
Wholesale trades	14	5.3	17	8.6
Retail trades	51	19.5	19	9.6
Business services	60	22.9	38	19.3
Personal services (UK) Liberal professions (West Germany)	23	8.8	19	9.6
Hotels and restaurants	8	3.1	9	4.6
No response	12	4.6	-	-
Total	262	100.0	197	100.0

Source: Anglo-German Foundation VAT Study, Question 1.

Table 8.5: Number of respondents by employment size range

Employment size range	United Kingdom	Per Cent	West Germany	Per Cent
1 - 4	150	57.3	47	23.9
5 - 9	60	22.9	24	12.2
10 - 14	20	7.6	22	11.2
15 - 49	20	7.6	47	23.9
50 - 99	6	2.3	20	10.2
100 and over	2	0.8	36	18.3
No response	4	1.5	1	0.5
Total	262	100.0	197	100.0

Source: Anglo-German Foundation VAT Study, Question 6.

Table 8.6: Number of respondents by age of business

Age of business (years)	United Kingdom	Per Cent	West Germany	Per Cent
Less than 1 year	1	0.4	3	1.5
1	18	6.9	4	2.0
2	25	9.5	9	4.6
3	34	13.0	13	6.6
4	19	7.3	6	3.0
5	23	8.8	12	6.1
6 - 10	54	20.6	29	14.7
11 - 20	43	16.4	21	10.7
More than 20	45	17.2	100	50.8
Total	262	100.0	197	100.0

Source: Anglo-German Foundation VAT Study, Question 2.

The vast majority of respondents sold taxed goods and services in both countries, though the proportion was lower in the UK because of the greater range of products which are exempt or zero-rated (Table 8.7). The West German sample included no respondents selling exempt goods and services without credit for inputs, which accounted for 17 per cent of British respondents. There was almost twice as great a proportion of traders selling zero-rated goods and services, where credit is given for inputs, in Britain than in West Germany. In terms of the percentage of traders affected, the proportions of

Table 8.7: Number of respondents by VAT category of sales

VAT category	United Kingdom	Per Cent	West Germany	Per Cent
Standard rated	231	88.2	189	95.9
Lower rated	-	-	44	22.3
Exports	61	22.3	80	40.6
Zero rated (other than exports)	83	31.7	35	17.8
Exempt	45	17.2	-	-
Total	262	100.0	197	100.0
Sum of percentages		160.4		176.6

Source: Anglo-German Foundation VAT Study, Question 4.

Note: Multiple mentions possible.

British and West German respondents operating a multi-rate system were surprisingly close: 60 per cent had more than one rate in the UK (including zero-rated) compared with 77 per cent in West Germany. This difference is almost entirely accounted for by the difference in the percentage of export zero-rated enterprises. The lower proportion of exporters in the UK sample is probably a consequence of size and age differences, at least in part since propensity to export is correlated with size.

Compliance Costs

Respondents were asked to estimate how many man-days per annum within the business were spent exclusively on VAT work. The results are summarized in Table 8.8 and are remarkably similar for the two samples: 53 per cent of the West German and 56 per cent of the British enterprises spent 10 or fewer days a year. However, these figures are distorted by the larger average size of the West German respondents. We should expect the volume of work, and therefore the number of man-days, to be greater the larger the firm. This effect would be reinforced by the greater propensity of small firms to use external accountants for their VAT work. If enterprises with more than nine employees are excluded from both samples, then the percentage of respondents spending 10 or fewer days a year on VAT work rises from 53 per cent to 75 per cent for West German respondents and remains unchanged at 56 per cent for the British respondents. The average number of days spent per firm, excluding three UK respondents with unreasonable replies, which was 16.1 for the West German respondents and 10.1 for the British respondents, falls to 5.3 for West Germany and 9.4 for Britain if larger enterprises are excluded.

Table 8.8: Number of man-days within the business spent on VAT work

No. of man-days	United Kingdom	Per Cent	West Germany	Per Cent
1 - 5	99	37.8	58	29.4
6 - 10	43	16.4	46	23.4
11 - 15	37	14.1	25	12.7
16 - 20	12	4.6	17	8.6
21 - 30	18	6.9	15	7.6
31 - 50	10	3.8	7	3.6
51 - 100	6	2.3	1	0.5
Over 100	3	1.1	3	1.5
No response (or zero days spent)	34	13.0	25	12.7
Total	262	100.0	197	100.0

Source: Anglo-German Foundation VAT Study, Question 7.

It seems, therefore, as if smaller firms on average spend considerably more days on VAT work in Britain than in West Germany, though, as we show below, this difference is, in part, explained by the greater propensity of West German firms to put their VAT work out to external accountants.

In answer to Question 8, only 20.2 per cent of the UK respondents used an accountant or other person in private practice to do any VAT work, compared with 32.5 per cent for the West German respondents. For smaller firms only, these percentages were 21.7 and 33.3 per cent for British and West German respondents respectively.

On average, those firms using outside accountants spent about £360 in the UK and £710 in West Germany (at the PPP exchange rate) (Table 8.9), reflecting both the larger size of enterprises in the West German sample, and, probably, higher daily fees. If amounts spent were calculated only for firms employing nine or fewer persons, then the average expenditures fall to £340 in the UK and £404 in West Germany.

Our postal questionnaire provided no information on the functions performed by external accountants in the two countries. From our telephone inquiries we gained the impression that more West German firms were using accountants to prepare returns while British firms were more likely to be using accountants for advice on specific VAT problems.

Total Compliance Costs

It seems fairly clear that on their own assessments, average compliance costs, at least for smaller firms, are higher in the UK than in West Germany in terms of the numbers of days spent within the firm. In Table 8.10 we have valued these costs at average gross domestic product per head of the working population at current exchange rates. This is not, of course, an entirely satisfactory method of valuation. The correct method would be to value the time spent in terms of its value in the best alternative use (what economists call 'opportunity cost'), which might be the amount by which the total income of the firm would increase had the resources spent on VAT work been devoted to revenue generation or cost reduction. The information to do this is not available, nor is the proxy for it, the salary and overhead costs of the personnel carrying out the work.

Table 8.9: Payments to external accountants for VAT work

Payment	United Kingdom	Per Cent	West Germany	Per Cent
None	212	80.9	135	68.5
£ 1 - 350 (DM 1 - 1,000)	30	11.5	20	10.2
£ 351 - 700 (DM 1,001 - 2,000)	10	3.8	20	10.2
More than £ 750 (DM 2,001)	7	2.7	22	11.2
No response	3	1.1	-	-
Total	262	100.0	197	100.0

Source: Anglo-German Foundation VAT Study, Question 9

Table 8.10: Average number of days spent on VAT work, expenditure on outside accountants, and estimated annual gross compliance costs (£1 at DM 3.28)

	Full sample			Enterprises employing nine persons or fewer		
	Average no. days spent (1)	Expenditure on outside accountants (2)	Total gross costs (3)	Average no. days spent (1)	Expenditure on outside accountants (2)	Total gross costs (3)
United Kingdom	10.1	£ 62.50	£ 715	9.4	£ 66.00	£ 674
West Germany	16.1	£ 72.40	£ 1389	5.3	£ 129.00	£ 512

Notes: Column (2) is the total expenditure recorded divided by the total number of respondents. Column (3) is Column (2) plus Column (1) x GDP per head of the working population per working day.

In Table 8.10 we have added to the valuation of days spent the average expenditure by all firms on external accountants for VAT work to arrive at an average gross compliance cost per respondent. The comparisons need to be interpreted bearing in mind that exchange rates based on purchasing power parities have been used. These value the £ sterling at some 15 per cent higher than conventional market exchange rates and thus increase the gap between the British and West German compliance costs. Total average compliance costs for the businesses in our sample on these calculations at the PPP rate amount to £3 per £1,000 of turnover in the UK and less than 50 pence in West Germany (see Table A1.5, p.217). This difference would be reduced if, as Sandford *et al* did in their 1981 study, we made an allowance for the cashflow benefits to arrive at a net compliance cost figure. As we saw earlier, these benefits are greater in Britain than in West Germany. It should be noted that we have not included the government's own collection and administration costs which are about 1 per cent of revenue in the UK.

Regressivity of Compliance Costs

It is now well established that the compliance costs of VAT and other forms of taxation tend to fall steeply as a proportion of taxable income or turnover as the size of firm increases (see Sandford *et al.*, 1981, for the UK and, for an international survey, Bannock, 1986). The reasons for this are essentially that there are economies of scale in tax compliance, especially since, in the smallest firms, much of the work may have to be carried out by the proprietor, the opportunity cost of whose time will be relatively high.

Our results show the same regressive pattern as earlier studies. Figure 8.1 shows the average total compliance cost per £1,000 of turnover in each country for each turnover size band. Both curves slope downwards to the right, indicating that compliance costs rise from well under 1 per cent for firms with a turnover of £2 million or more to 2.5–8.0 per cent for firms in the £15,000 and under range. Costs are higher in relation to turnover in Britain than in West Germany for all size classes except the lowest. Costs in West Germany in this lowest size band would be lower if the VAT rebate were allowed for, though West German costs would still be higher than those in Britain.

Attitudes

Several surveys in the UK and all of those carried out on the subject have shown that small firms have very critical attitudes towards VAT and consider it to create more work and problems than several other forms of taxation. The attitudes of large firms are, however, favourably influenced by the typically positive cash flow effects of VAT (Sandford *et al.*, 1981; Bannock, 1986). A survey carried out for the Department of Industry put VAT at the top of the list of government burdens on small business (Research Associates, 1985). Although there are studies of the compliance costs of taxation, including VAT, for West Germany, we were unable to trace any attitude surveys on VAT. We know of no

Figure 8.1 VAT compliance costs: cost per £1,000 of turnover.

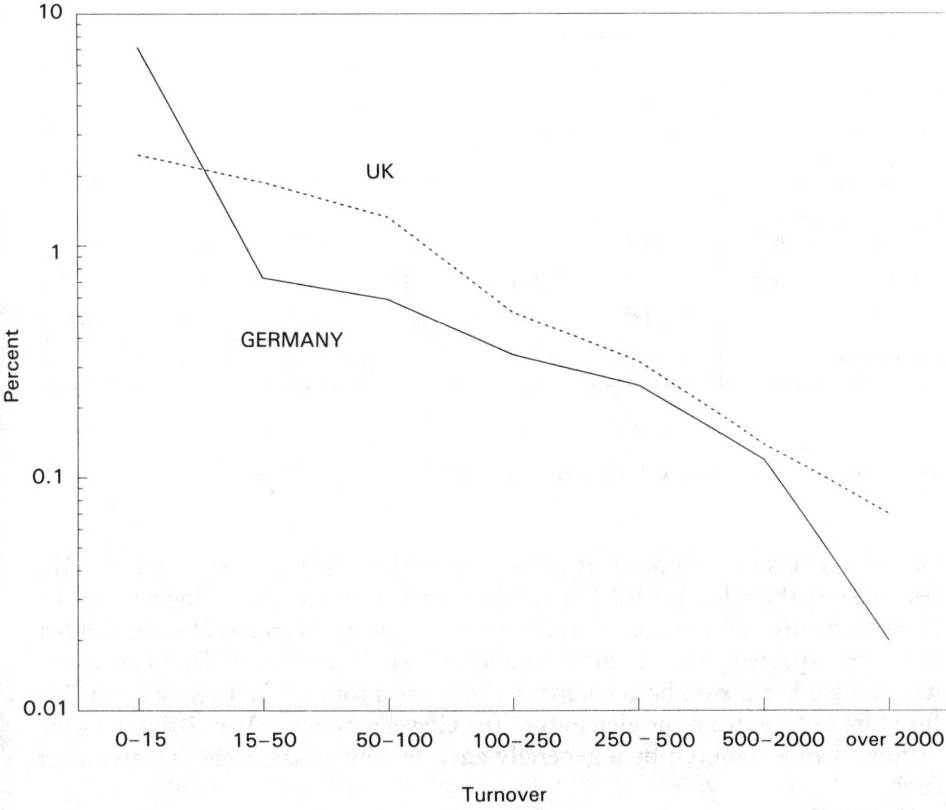

Source: Table A1.5

other international surveys on this subject; our results are, therefore, of particular interest.[3]

Respondents were asked to give their opinion on whether VAT was better, the same or worse compared with three other groups of taxes. Response to this question was good in both countries but somewhat lower in West Germany and this should be borne in mind in interpreting the results in Table 8.11.

Compared with taxes collected by the respondents from employees (PAYE and social security contributions), VAT was clearly regarded as administratively easier and less costly by West German respondents while UK respondents regard it as at least as bad.

West German respondents rated VAT as about the same as business income taxes, while UK respondents regarded VAT as marginally worse, corroborating the somewhat stronger findings of earlier UK studies (Carsberg *et al.*, 1985; Research Associates, 1985).

The UK respondents overwhelmingly believe VAT to be worse than local rates which, once property valuations are agreed, place little administrative

Table 8.11: VAT compared with other taxes in terms of complexity and administrative cost to the firm

	VAT worse		VAT same		VAT better	
	UK	West Germany	UK	West Germany	UK	West Germany
Taxes collected from employees	31.3	12.7	26.0	24.4	27.5	60.4
Income tax and corporation tax	32.4	25.9	27.9	47.2	26.3	25.9
Local taxes (rates)	58.8	31.0	16.8	40.1	11.8	25.4
Base	262	197	262	197	262	197
No response	12.6-15.3	1.0-3.6				

Source: Anglo-German Foundation VAT Study, Question 10.

burden on business. Indeed, it is surprising that almost 29 per cent of UK respondents thought that VAT is the same or better than the rating system. In West Germany, VAT is considered only slightly worse than local taxation. This was to be expected given the greater complexity of local taxes in West Germany, which include a tax on both company assets and profits, although most smaller firms are exempt from the elements of the Gewerbersteuer. As in Britain, views were probably coloured by a generally adverse view of the local tax system as such.

Overall, VAT is clearly regarded as more costly and troublesome than other taxes to a greater extent in Britain than in West Germany. This comes out still more clearly in the responses to Question 13 which asked respondents to select one of two statements first formulated by Professor Sandford (Sandford *et al.*, 1981). While 48.1 per cent of the British respondents agreed that 'VAT is a simple method of collecting tax', 80.2 per cent of West German respondents selected that statement. The same number, (48.1 per cent) of British respondents agreed with 'As it stands, VAT is unreasonably complicated' compared with only 18.8 per cent of the West German respondents. (Non-reponses were 3.8 and 1.0 per cent respectively.) The percentage of UK respondents who were anti-VAT in Sandford's 1978 survey was 36.6 per cent. However, he also allowed his respondents to express indifference between the two statements (47.0 per cent) and those who gave an anti opinion were more than twice as numerous as those who were pro-VAT (36.6 as against 16.5 per cent). These comparisons and the official survey in which 39 per cent of respondents mentioned VAT as a burden on business (Research Associates, 1985) suggest that our sample response might perhaps be biased somewhat towards anti-VAT respondents. However, there is no reason to suppose that the

Anglo-German comparisons are not representative of differences in attitudes between the two countries.

Table 8.12 gives the percentage of respondents agreeing that VAT is 'unreasonably complicated' by size of firm and these figures are shown graphically in Figure 8.2. As we should expect from the regressive nature of compliance costs, the percentage of respondents falls with size of firm in both countries, but the UK percentages are higher throughout. Another interesting feature of the chart is that the UK curve is convex while the West German curve is concave. This may reflect the effect of the special schemes in West Germany for alleviating the burden on smaller firms.

The open-ended Question 14, which asked for further comments on the difficulties experienced with VAT or suggestions on how the tax could be simplified, was answered by only 23.4 per cent of West German respondents, but by 55.7 of the UK respondents. In answer to Question 15, 48.1 per cent of the UK respondents compared with only 23.4 per cent of the West German respondents also gave their telephone numbers for further questioning if

Figure 8.2 Is VAT too complicated? Percentage of respondents agreeing by size of firm.

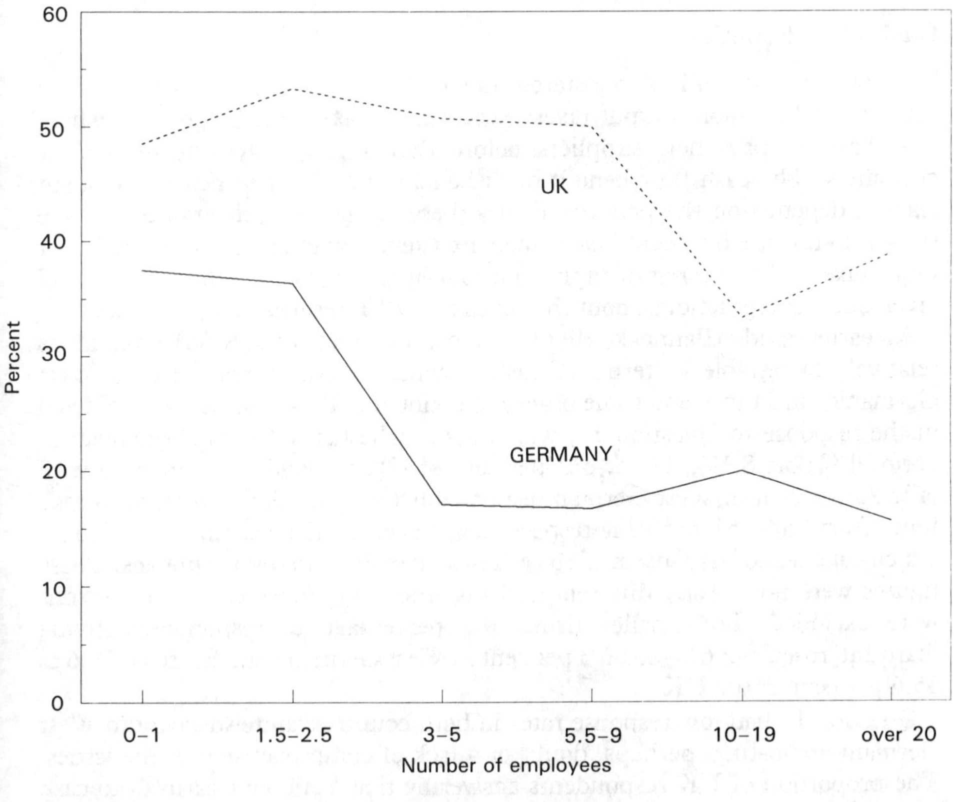

Source: Anglo German Foundation VAT Study. Question 13.

Table 8.12: Number of respondents agreeing that VAT is unreasonably complicated by employment size class

No. of employees	United Kingdom	Per cent of respondents in class	West Germany	Per cent of respondents in class
1 employee or less	33	48.5	8	37.5
1.5 - 2.5	60	53.3	11	36.4
3.0 - 5.0	71	50.7	35	17.1
5.5 - 9.0	50	50.0	18	16.7
10.0 - 19.0	30	33.3	35	20.0
20 or more employees	18	38.9	90	15.6
Total	262	100.0	197	100.0

Source: Anglo-German Foundation VAT Study, Question 13.

required. These response rates are consistent with the much greater concern about VAT that exists among small firms in Britain than in West Germany.

Cash Flow Benefits

The collection of VAT by registered traders does confer a cash flow benefit to those firms for whom output taxes exceed input taxes, except possibly where they have to pay their suppliers before they receive payment from their customers. The cash flow benefit or disbenefit is difficult to generalize about since it depends on the pattern of sales (between goods and services that are subject to tax and between those which are exempt with and without credit for input taxes), the phasing of inputs and outputs, the trade credit received and given and the regulations about the timing of VAT returns and payments.

An earlier study (Bannock, 1986) demonstrated that the UK VAT regime is relatively favourable in terms of cash benefits compared with that of West Germany and France and some other EC countries. This contrast was reflected in the response to Question 11, which asked whether VAT was beneficial or harmful (Table 8.13). Thirty-one per cent of UK respondents compared with only 20 per cent of West German respondents thought VAT beneficial to cash flow. At 58 and 61 per cent respectively, however, the percentages of firms which considered VAT harmful to cash flow were high in both countries. These figures were not greatly different if firms employing more than nine persons were excluded. For smaller firms, the percentage of respondents giving 'harmful' rose from 61.4 to 65.3 per cent in West Germany and fell from 57.6 to 55.6 per cent in the UK.

Question 11 had low response rates in both countries and especially in West Germany indicating, perhaps, doubt or a lack of comprehension of the issues. The proportion of UK respondents answering that VAT was harmful to cash flow may be partly explained by the under-representation of cash businesses and

Table 8.13: Number of respondents indicating that VAT has a beneficial or harmful effect upon cash flow

	United Kingdom	Per Cent	West Germany	Per Cent
Beneficial	81	30.9	39	19.8
Harmful	151	57.6	121	61.4
No response	30	11.5	37	18.8
Total	262	100.0	197	100.0

Source: Anglo-German Foundation VAT Study, Question 11.

over-representation of manufacturing, but also perhaps by the widespread delays in credit customer payment which have been reported in the recent period of high interest rates in Britain. Because of extensive zero-rating in Britain (about 30 per cent of traders are zero-rated), it is probable that a higher proportion of firms qualify for regular repayment of tax than in West Germany. It also seems probable that the widespread lack of appreciation of the cash flow benefits of VAT in the UK noticed in Sandford's 1978 study continues to exist there.

It is not quite as difficult to explain why such a large proportion of West German respondents found VAT harmful to cash flow. As we saw earlier (p.185), UK traders (other than net repayment traders who regularly claim back VAT and have the option to make monthly returns) mostly make quarterly returns which allows net repayment traders to hang on to their tax revenues longer. In West Germany, quarterly tax returns are allowed only where tax remittable is normally less than DM 6,000 (£2,000) per annum or £500 per quarter, although this does exempt large numbers of small firms from monthly returns. Also important is the fact that in West Germany only 10 days are allowed after the end of the period for submission of the return, whereas in Britain the delay is 30 days on which, until recently, some latitude was allowed. It also seems that the delay between filing the return and receipt of repayment from the tax authorities is shorter in Britain (less than 30 days) than in West Germany where a delay of two months or more is common, according to our respondents.

The UK probably now gives less liberal treatment to certain items of business costs such as motor car and other expenses than does West Germany, though expenditure may or may not have been counted as an adverse cash flow effect by respondents. Despite the fact that more West German respondents than British find VAT harmful to their cash flow, as we have seen, this tax overall is regarded much less favourably by small businesses in Britain than in West Germany. We consider possible explanations for their contrasting attitudes to VAT later (p.211–214).

RESPONDENTS' COMMENTS

Questionnaire Comments

As mentioned, Question 14 in the postal questionnaire invited comments on the difficulties experienced with VAT or suggestions on how it could be simplified. One hundred and forty-six UK respondents or 55.7 per cent of all respondents made comments; 46 West German respondents or 23.4 per cent made comments.

For both surveys, many of the comments made dealt with problems or suggestions outside the scope of the study. For West Germany, the most frequent of relevant mentions concerned cash flow problems. Of the eight comments under this heading, three covered problems arising from slow payment of VAT invoices, but all were too large to be covered by the cash basis scheme (Table 8.14). Two commented on the imbalance between the delay on VAT repayments (two months) and the time allowed for making payment (10 days). One respondent suggested that the cash basis scheme should be extended to firms with a turnover in excess of DM 250,000.

Seven West German respondents commented that VAT was no problem when accounting systems were computerized. Six respondents mentioned various administrative difficulties: in two cases these concerned *initial* problems with non-deductible input calculations, two dealt with export complications and the remaining two arose from mid-year changes in VAT rates.

Two West German respondents wanted to see a single-rate VAT system and two complained of VAT-free competition from the black economy. One firm, as mentioned, wanted the cash basis scheme to be extended and another wanted the average input percentage scheme extended.

The comments from the British respondents were more numerous and much more critical (Table 8.15). Twenty-five respondents commented on various aspects of administrative complexity and the costs to which they gave rise, for example inconsistent treatment of similar items and the need to retain invoices and receipts for six years. Eleven of these traders pointed out that small firms suffer worst from these problems because they face slower payments and because they lack economies of scale in VAT compliance.

Twenty British respondents felt that VAT rates were too high, wanted abolition of the distinction between zero-rating and exempt or wanted to see a lower rate applied to a broader range of goods and services. Of the 17 respondents who wanted radical change in the VAT system, 11 wanted it abolished altogether, others wanted the abolition of VAT between registered traders or the collection of the tax restricted to the manufacturing and wholesale stages only.

Table 8.14: Comments on VAT – West German respondents

	Number of mentions
Adverse cash flow effects	8
Computerization makes VAT no problem	7
Administrative difficulties, including export	6
Extend small firm schemes	2
VAT encourages black economy, against which action needed	2
Tax rates should be harmonized	2
Total	27
Number of respondents	46

Source: Anglo-German Foundation VAT Study, Question 14.

Note: Multiple mentions possible.

Table 8.15: Comments on VAT – UK respondents

	Number of mentions
Criticism of complexity, compliance cost, small firms suffer most	25
Rate(s) too high, too numerous, tax base should be broader	20
Radical change, e.g. abolition, conversion to sales tax, eliminate retail stage	17
Threshold too low	14
Attitude of tax officials aggressive, uncomprehending, penalties too high	13
Should be assessed on cash basis, not invoice basis	12
Regulations, booklets unclear, constant changes in regulations	7
Positive suggestions: better booklets, more use of computers, beneficial effects, EC harmonization	5
Total	117
Number of respondents	146

Source: Anglo-German Foundation VAT Study, Question 14.

Note: Multiple mentions possible.

Fourteen respondents wanted a higher threshold to allow more traders the option of deregistration. Thirteen criticized unnecessarily aggressive, 'unkind' and unhelpful VAT officials and/or commented on their lack of understanding of small business administration and operations or the severity of penalties. A further seven respondents complained about constant changes in VAT regulations and lack of clarity in the official literature on VAT. Twelve wanted to pay output taxes only when their customers had paid their bills, one pointing out that 'bad debt relief was almost impossible to get'. (For smaller firms cash basis VAT accounting was announced in the 1987 Finance Act; see p.186.) Only one respondent commented on the desirability of longer intervals between VAT returns.

Only one respondent (compared with seven in the smaller West German sample) commented on the use of computers in VAT work. Other positive or constructive British comments covered the effects of VAT in stimulating improved accounting and the need for harmonizing VAT rates in the European Community.

Telephone Interviews

In each country the research team also contacted 15 respondents selected at random from those who included their telephone number in the questionnaire. This was a small sample and the results need to be treated with reservations.

In general, the telephone discussions brought up the same points as those made in the questionnaires and emphasized the contrasting experience of respondents in the two countries. For example, about half the West German respondents, even the smaller firms, used computers in their VAT work (though in some cases for the annual returns only) though none of the UK firms did. It was also clear that the use of qualified internal staff (and the use of external accountants for VAT work) was much more widespread in West Germany than in Britain. A much higher proportion of British than West German proprietors completed VAT returns themselves.

From West German respondents there were single references to cash flow problems, obscurities in the regulations and problems of getting refunds through the EC on VAT paid abroad.

A minority of the UK respondents made complaints about officials, though most of these were cases where the firms had difficulties with VAT or were involved in a dispute over the tax treatment of a particular transaction. There was one comment on the zeal with which VAT officials collected tax due, despite cash flow problems, in a case where the Inland Revenue was willing to be more patient. One respondent, who was a VAT adviser, said that most VAT officials were polite, but that lack of business experience and over-zealousness resulted in much loss of time in explaining business procedures. Three UK respondents mentioned cash flow problems arising from the payment of VAT on unpaid invoices.

There were four comments on specific problems in interpreting regulations, two on construction, one on export to a non-EC customer for work done in the UK, and one on partial exemption on separate elements in a single product.

CONCLUSIONS

Differences in Compliance Costs and Attitudes

Our survey has demonstrated clearly that dissatisfaction with the VAT system among smaller firms in Britain is both deeper and more widespread than in West Germany. Our survey method and problems of exchange rate comparisons do not allow us to attach great confidence to our estimates of compliance costs, but these costs are, for many smaller traders, undoubtedly significantly higher in the UK. The differences in attitudes towards the VAT system and the level of criticism encountered in the telephone interviews were greater than the differences in compliance costs and are unquestionably significant. Were the West German sample fully representative of firms benefiting from the special schemes for small enterprises, we presume these contrasts would be more pronounced.

A number of possible explanations for these differences emerge from our study. We deal with them below, not necessarily in order of their importance, together with some tentative views on the implications of our findings for policy.

(1) *Cultural and historical factors*

There is a much longer tradition and experience of broadly based indirect taxation administered by business in West Germany than in Britain. VAT in West Germany replaced a cascade turnover tax in which each successive stage of production and wholesale distribution bore an *ad valorem* tax. This system, which was much criticized for encouraging vertical integration, had its origins well before World War II and its demise in 1968 was greeted with widespread relief, even though retailers were brought into the system for the first time.[4] In fact, in German VAT is still called '*Umsatzsteuer*' (turnover tax).

Although the predecessor of VAT in West Germany was an unpopular tax, the predecessor of VAT in Britain, Purchase Tax, which was applied only to manufactured consumer goods, was, as taxes go, relatively straightforward and accepted. Purchase Tax was introduced in 1940, but in 1966 it was supplemented by the selective Employment Tax (SET) paid in full only by the construction, distribution and service sectors. SET was very unpopular among the employers who paid it and was subject to criticism on economic grounds, but it was administratively simple (the tax was collected through the National Insurance system). In Britain, therefore, the introduction of VAT was accompanied by a much greater increase in the compliance burden than in West Germany.

Another and more important factor which eases the difficulties experienced by West German smaller firms in bearing the compliance burden of VAT is that, compared with Britain, VAT administration is typically carried out by more highly trained people. The necessity for pre-qualification in many trades as a condition for registering a new enterprise with the local chamber of trade helps to ensure that business proprietors have some knowledge of tax procedures. In the *Handwerk* (artisan) sector, for example, elaborate training procedures include instruction in financial accounts and tax administration (Doran, 1984).

Finally, under this heading, we note the apparently more widespread use of computers for VAT work in West Germany than in Britain (see p.210). Our information on this is weak and based entirely on our telephone inquiries. We know of no comparative studies on computerization among small firms in the two countries. A recent survey in Britain (Small Business Research Trust, 1985) indicated that only 20 per cent of firms with five or fewer employees had a computer, but it may be that the use of computers for VAT work is more extensive in West Germany, even though the degree of computer ownership is not very different.

(2) *Special schemes for small firms*

The recent changes to the UK VAT system (see p.186), allowing the use of cash accounting for small firms, will certainly meet one of the most frequent complaints about the system. It is difficult to see, however, how the new British option for annual accounting will do much to ease the compliance burden on the smallest firms who suffer most from it. The burden is a function not so much of the compilation of the quarterly return as of the bookkeeping and supporting document requirements and the complexity of the regulations, which will remain unaffected. Indeed there are dangers in the new system. Traders who leave reconciliation of their books and supporting documents until the end of the year may find that they cannot remember problematic transactions and that it is too late to rectify error, for example in not requesting a proper VAT invoice from a supplier. We doubt if the take-up of this scheme will be very great except among firms which succumb to the temptation to postpone their VAT administration or other, better organized, firms which, if they are expanding, may find the scheme helpful in improving the cash flow benefit of VAT.

The West German system of average input tax calculations is, we consider, a more effective way of reducing the compliance burden in theory, though it is adopted there by only just over 2,000 registered traders. Such a scheme, which is used in France and other member states, could be dovetailed into the new annual accounting system, but it would be difficult to justify this in view of the low take-up in West Germany. We understand, however, that the West German authorities restrict use of the scheme only to those traders who are not, under West German law, obliged to keep detailed books of account. The attractiveness of this scheme requires further consideration before conclusions can be drawn; take up of the similar scheme in France is very much greater.

There is clear merit in the West German rebate of tax liability scheme. This is taken up by about 100,000 firms. In 1984 96,473 firms, or 35 per cent of the total number of registered traders in the eligible turnover bracket, opted for this scheme. Those firms that do not opt for the scheme are thought to be mainly either start-ups benefiting from the under DM 100,000 first-year exclusion (See p.186) or net repayment traders. In 1984 150,767 firms opted for the cash accounting scheme. The effect of the rebate scheme is to compensate some of the smallest firms, to a diminishing extent as they expand, for the disproportionate compliance burden they bear. The scheme is also intended to graduate the effect of the imposition of VAT on the prices of firms around the borderline for registration and improve the incentives for firms to register. Similar schemes or schemes which accept the principle that the smallest firms should be compensated in cash for VAT compliance costs also exist in Austria, France, The Netherlands and Italy.

This principle would not be readily accepted in the UK where the compliance costs of taxation have until recently received little attention. One objection might be that the West German scheme actually only operates below the British VAT threshold, but this is to ignore the compliance burden borne by over 250,000 firms who choose to register voluntarily so that they may reclaim input taxes. Another objection might be that lowering the registration threshold and introducing such a scheme in Britain would be costly in terms of additional government administration since little additional revenue would be gained.

However, it is difficult to justify the inequity of imposing compliance burdens on the smallest firms which bear on them more heavily than on their large competitors. Some form of rebate scheme can also be justified in the interest of mitigating the effects of competition from the black economy on legitimate small businesses and in the harmonization of VAT thresholds in the Community. On grounds of equity of business burdens it appears certain to us that a good case could be made for extending a rebate scheme above existing threshold levels in Britain and, for that matter, extending the principle to other types of taxation.

In fact, a recent EEC draft Directive makes it clear that the European Commission would like to see some narrowing of the range of VAT thresholds in the Community and the restriction of small firm schemes to the cash accounting and average input tax calculation types. The introduction of other small firm schemes may continue if more favourable than those proposed by the Commission (European Commission, 1986).

(3) *Administration*

One difference between the administration of VAT in Britain and West Germany is that in West Germany one tax office is responsible for business income taxes and VAT, whereas in Britain these functions are split between the Inland Revenue and Customs and Excise. We do not know how important this is in affecting compliance costs, but it may have had some contributory effect on differences in attitudes towards VAT in the two countries. Certainly the frequent changes in the UK system, which contrast with great stability in West Germany, have raised compliance costs and unfavourably affect attitudes to the tax in Britain.

The VAT authorities in Britain and West Germany can, we believe, learn from each other's experience. Perhaps UK officials would be pleased to operate a system with fewer exclusions, no voluntary registration and lower thresholds. This would, in our view, be a better system for business and would reduce the need for constant change implicit in the present system. Such a system would also introduce fewer distortions in the economy (Bannock, 1986). Political objections, which would centre on the regressivity of extending the tax base in the UK (for the burden it would impose on those with lower incomes), could be met by other means. However, preferably this would not be done by the adoption of multi-rating on the West German model, which unnecessarily raises business compliance costs and distorts the structure of demand and production. A move to a common, single-rate system would also be desirable in the interests of community harmonization in the longer run.

West German tax officials and businesspeople will also perceive advantages in the British system of phased quarterly returns and certainly in the longer grace period allowed for returns and in the treatment of bad debts. It may well be that the British system is over-generous in the cash benefits it confers to larger enterprises in certain sectors of the economy and, in the interests of equity, that possibly should be taken account of in long term reform.

APPENDIX 8.1: Statistical Appendix

Table A1.1: Number of respondents by turnover size range in West German sample and in the population of registered traders, 1984

Turnover size range	Sample	Per cent	Population 1984	Per cent
(DM '000s)				
20 - 50	1	0.6	273.6	14.7
50 - 100	2	1.1	314.5	16.9
100 - 250	17	9.4	466.0	25.1
250 - 500	19	10.6	303.5	16.3
500 - 1,000	20	11.1	217.2	11.7
1,000 - 2,000	28	15.6	131.5	7.1
2,000 - 5,000	37	20.6	84.1	4.5
5,000 - 10,000	19	10.6	32.1	1.7
10,000 - 25,000	15	8.3	21.1	1.1
25,000 - 50,000	10	5.6	7.3	0.4
Over 50,000	12	6.7	7.1	0.4
Total	180	100.0	1857.9	100.0

Source: Survey and *Finanzen und Steuern*, Fachserie 14, Reihe 8, *Umsatzsteuer*, 1984, Statistisches Bundesamt.

Table A1.2: Number of respondents by sector in West German sample and in the population of registered traders, 1984

Sector	Sample	Per cent	Population 1984	Per cent
Agriculture, forestry, fishing	5	2.5	34.5	1.9
Energy, mining, water	0	0.0	4.6	0.2
Manufacturing	62	31.5	289.2	15.6
Construction	19	9.6	192.6	10.4
Wholesale and merchanting	17	8.6	182.9	9.9
Retail trades	19	9.6	385.9	20.8
Transportation	9	4.6	81.7	4.4
Hotels and restaurants	9	4.6	218.4	11.8
Liberal professions	19	9.6	468.1	25.2
Other business services	38	19.3		
Total	197	100.0	1857.9	100.0

Source: As for Table A1.1.

Table A1.3: Number of respondents by turnover size range in UK sample and in the population of registered traders, 1985

Turnover size range (£ 000s)	Respondents	Per cent	Population 1984	Per cent
1 - 14	22	8.4	139.2	9.7
15 - 49	61	23.3	470.1	32.6
50 - 99	37	14.1	286.9	19.9
100 - 499	101	38.5	364.5	25.3
500 - 1999	34	13.0	87.9	6.1
2000 and over	7	2.7	30.1	2.1
Not known	-	-	62.8	4.4
Total	262	100.0	1441.4	100.0

Source: Survey.

Table A1.4: Number of respondents by sector in UK sample and in the population of registered traders, 1985

	Respondents	Per cent	Population 1984	Per cent
Agriculture, forestry, fishing	4	1.5	180.6	12.5
Construction	13	5.0	211.2	14.7
Production	60	22.9	140.2	9.7
Transport	17	6.5	59.4	4.1
Wholesale trades	14	5.3	114.3	7.9
Retail trades	51	19.5	261.2	18.1
Business services	60	22.9	351.5	24.4
Personal services	23	8.8		
Hotels and restaurants	8	3.1	122.8	8.5
No response	12	4.6	-	-
Total	262	100.0	1441.4	100.0

Source: As for Table A1.3.

Table A1.5 Total compliance costs of VAT in relation to turnover

	United Kingdom							West Germany						
Turnover band (£ 000s)	No. of firms	Average Turnover £'000s	Av. days spent No.	@£64	Average fee paid Out (£)	Total average cost (£)	Cost/ £1,000 Turnover	No. of firms	Average turnover (£ 000s)	Av. days spent No.	@£64	Average fee paid out (£)	Total average cost (£)	Cost/ £1,000 Turnover
0 - 15	7	7.1	2.7	174	NIL	174	24.6	1	12.1	12.0	864	76	940	77.7
15 - 50	54	29.0	8.0	509	37	546	18.8	6	34.3	3.5	252	NIL	252	7.3
50 - 100	35	65.0	12.9	825	42	867	13.3	22	73.2	4.5	324	105	429	5.9
100 - 250	70	139.7	10.0	640	91	731	5.2	19	171.1	6.6	475	108	583	3.4
250 - 500	29	323.0	14.3	914	106	1020	3.2	27	355.2	8.2	590	291	881	2.5
500 - 2,000	31	709.6	14.7	941	85	1026	1.4	56	1066.5	13.5	972	383	1255	1.2
2,000 plus	5	2440.0	26.6	1702	NIL	1702	0.7	56	12380.0	31.3	2251	583	2834	0.2
Total	231	247.8	11.3	722	67	799	3.2	187	4105.0	16.0	1150	355	1505	0.4
No response	28							10						
Extreme peak responses	3							-						
Base	262							197						

Source: Anglo German VAT study and calculations by Graham Bannock and Partners

APPENDIX 8.2: Postal questionnaire used for VAT study

PRIVATE AND CONFIDENTIAL

GRAHAM
BANNOCK
& PARTNERS LTD

53 Clarewood Court, Crawford Street, London W1H 5DF · Telephone: 01-723 1845

ANGLO-GERMAN FOUNDATION - VAT STUDY

Conducted by
Graham Bannock & Partners Ltd.
in Association with the
Small Business Research Trust

1 Please describe in a few words the precise nature of your business (e.g. 'manufacturing electronic security systems', 'personal dry cleaning services')

____

2 How many years has your present business been trading? ☐

3 How many years have you personally been in business? ☐

4 Different types of products and services and domestic and export customers are treated differently for VAT purposes. Please tick each category below for which you made any sales last year:

Category

4.1 Standard rated (15 per cent) ☐

4.2 [Not applicable to UK respondents]

4.3 Exports ☐

4.4 Zero rated (other than exports) ☐

4.5 Exempt from VAT ☐

5 What is the approximate value of your annual total sales? £ ☐

6 How many people are employed in the business? (Include working proprietors and count part-time employees as 0.5)

7 About how many man-days in total <u>within</u> the business were spent entirely on VAT work in the last 12 months? (For example, you or finance director X days, bookkeeper Y days, = Z days). In your estimates do not include bookkeeping which would still be necessary if VAT were abolished. Exclude time spent by outside professionals).

☐ days

8 **Do you normally employ an accountant or other person in private practice to do any VAT work?**

8.1 Yes ☐ *8.2* No ☐

If you answered 'No' please go straight to question 10.

9 **If you answered 'Yes' to question 8, about how much did you spend on VAT work by a professional outside the firm?**

£ ☐

10 **How does VAT, in your opinion, compare with these other taxes in complexity and administration cost to you? Please tick 3 boxes only:**

	VAT worse	VAT same	VAT better
Taxes collected from employees (e.g. National Insurance, PAYE)			
Income Tax and Corporation Tax			
Local Taxes (Rates)			

11 **Does VAT have a beneficial or harmful effect upon your cash flow?**

11.1 Beneficial ☐ *11.2* Harmful ☐

12 [Not applicable to UK respondents]

13 **Which of these two statements most closely describes your attitude to VAT? Please tick one only:**

13.1 VAT is a simple method of collecting tax. ☐
13.2 As it stands, VAT is unreasonably complicated. ☐

14 **Do you have any further comments on the difficulties you experience with VAT (if any) or suggestions about how it could be simplified?**

____

____

____

15 **Would you be willing to answer a few further questions about VAT on the telephone? If yes, please give your name and telephone number below:**

____

THANK YOU FOR HELPING US

PLEASE RETURN QUESTIONNAIRE IN THE PREPAID ENVELOPE PROVIDED

APPENDIX 8.3: Value Added Tax Return

H M Customs and Excise

Value Added Tax Return

For the period

01 04 88 **to** 30 06 88

Due to reach the VAT Central Unit by 31 07 88

These dates must not be altered.

For Official Use

Registration No: 394 7065 20

Period: 06 88

085 394 7065 20 100 06 88 W12975 *
GRAHAM BANNOCK & PARTNERS LIMITED
53 CLAREWOOD COURT
CRAWFORD STREET
LONDON
W1H 5DF 136578/14

Before you fill in this form please read the notes on the other side. You must complete all boxes — writing "none" where necessary.
If you need to show an exact amount of pounds, please write "00" in the pence column. Don't put a dash or leave the column blank. Please write clearly in ink.
You must ensure that the completed form and any VAT payable are received no later than the due date by the Controller, VAT Central Unit, H M Customs and Excise, 21 Victoria Avenue, SOUTHEND-ON-SEA X
SS99 1AY

An envelope is enclosed for your use.

REMINDER

Small business? Turnover less than £250,000?
You may have to complete only one VAT return each year.
For details ask for Notice 732 on Annual Accounting from your Local VAT Office – look under Customs and Excise in the phone book.

For Official Use

FOR OFFICIAL USE

	Box	£	p
VAT DUE in this period on OUTPUTS (sales, etc), certain postal imports and services received from abroad	1		
Underdeclarations of VAT made on previous returns (but not those notified in writing by Customs and Excise)	2		
TOTAL VAT DUE (box 1 + box 2)	3		
VAT DEDUCTIBLE in this period on INPUTS (purchases, etc)	4		
Overdeclarations of VAT made on previous returns (but not those notified in writing by Customs and Excise)	5		
TOTAL VAT DEDUCTIBLE (box 4 + box 5)	6		
NET VAT PAYABLE OR REPAYABLE (Difference between boxes 3 and 6)	7		
Value of Outputs (excluding any VAT)	8		00
Value of Inputs (excluding any VAT)	9		00

Please tick only ONE of these boxes:

box 3 greater than box 6 — payment by credit transfer ☐ — payment enclosed ☐

box 6 greater than box 3 — repayment due ☐

How to pay the VAT due
Cross all cheques and postal orders "A/C Payee only" and make them payable to "H M Customs and Excise". Make credit transfers through account 3078027 at National Girobank or 10-70-50 52055000 for Bank Giros and keep your payment slip. You can order pre-printed booklets of credit transfer slips from your local VAT office. In your own interest do not send notes, coins, or uncrossed postal orders through the post.
Please write your VAT registration number on the back of all cheques and credit transfer slips.

Please tick box(es) if the statement(s) apply:

box 5 includes bad debt relief ☐ — box 8 includes exempt outputs ☐ — box 8 includes exports ☐

Retail schemes If you have used any of the schemes in the period covered by this return please tick the box(es) to show all the schemes used.

A B C D E F G H J

Remember, you could be liable to a financial penalty if your return and all the VAT payable are not received by the due date.
DECLARATION by the signatory to be completed by or on behalf of the person named above.

I, ... declare that the
(full name of signatory in BLOCK LETTERS)
information given above is true and complete.

Signed .... Date.. 19......
*(Proprietor, partner, director, secretary, responsible officer, committee member of club or association, duly authorised person) *Delete as necessary

FOR OFFICIAL USE

VAT 100 F3790 (October 1987)

*Reproduced by kind permission of HM Customs and Excise

NOTES

These notes and the pamphlet, *Filling in your VAT return,* will help you to fill in this form. You may also need to refer to other VAT notices and leaflets. If you are using the cash accounting scheme, remember that the amounts of VAT due and deductible are based on payments received and made, **not** on invoices.

If you need help or advice, or any of the answers overleaf gives a negative figure, please contact your local VAT office quoting your VAT registration number.

Box 1 You must show the VAT due on all goods and services you supplied in this period. This is your *output* tax.

If you use a retail scheme the *How to work* pamphlet for your scheme will help you work out the output tax due.

Remember to include VAT due on:

- goods taken for private use
- gifts and loans of goods
- sales to staff
- sales of business assets
- imported services listed in *The VAT guide,* Appendix G
- postal imports — other than Datapost — with a value of £1300 or less.

Remember to subtract any VAT credited to your customers.

Box 2 If any of your previous returns showed too little VAT payable by you or too much VAT repayable to you, show the amount here — but leave out:

- adjustments notified in writing by Customs and Excise
- VAT declared on a previous return which you have not paid in full.

Box 4 You must show the amount of VAT deductible on any business purchases you have made, including imported goods and services and goods removed from bonded warehouse. This is your *input* tax.

If this is your first return include any VAT you can reclaim on goods and services received before registration (see *The VAT guide,* paragraph 38).

Exclude any VAT on:

- goods and services not supplied for the use of your business
- business entertainment (except of overseas customers)
- motor cars
- second-hand goods which have been sold to you under one of the VAT second-hand schemes.

If you are a builder see VAT Leaflet, *Construction industry,* about non-deductible input tax on fixtures and fittings.

Remember to subtract any VAT credited by your suppliers.

If you have exempt outputs this may affect the amount of input tax you can reclaim (see *The VAT guide,* paragraph 35).

Box 5 If any of your previous returns showed too much VAT payable by you or too little VAT repayable to you show the amount here.

Include:

- any VAT you are claiming back as bad debt relief under the conditions set out in the VAT Leaflet, *Relief from VAT on bad debts*, and tick the box on the front of this form.

Exclude:

- adjustments notified in writing by Customs and Excise
- repayments of VAT claimed on a previous return but not yet received from Customs and Excise
- assessments already paid in this or other periods.

Box 7 If the amount to be entered is under £1 you must still fill in this form and send it to the VAT Central Unit. You need not send any payment, nor will any repayment be made to you.

Boxes 8 and 9 Show your total outputs in box 8. Include zero-rated sales, exports, exempt income such as rents, and other business income. Leave out the VAT. If exports or exempt outputs are included please tick the appropriate box(es) on the front of this form.

Show your total inputs in box 9. Include imports and other business expenses. Leave out the VAT.

For both boxes 8 and 9 you should show net figures after deducting any credits. Do not deduct any cash discounts. If your accounts are net of cash discounts you should add back a reasonable amount for any discounts given or received.

Some income and expenses must be left out of boxes 8 and 9. There are two ways to work these boxes out — Basis A and Basis B. Use the same basis for both boxes. Whichever basis you use always leave out:

- VAT
- wages and salaries
- PAYE and National Insurance contributions
- money put into or taken out of the business
- loans, dividends, grants, gifts of money
- compensation payments or insurance claims
- Stock Exchange dealings.

If you use Basis A also leave out:

Box 8

- sales of cars on which you paid no VAT (see *The VAT guide,* Appendix C, paragraph 8)
- exempt outputs excluded from any partial exemption calculation.

Box 9

- exempt purchases
- MOT fees and vehicle licence duty
- local authority rates
- purchases on which you cannot reclaim input tax (see *The VAT guide,* paragraph 33).

If you decide to use Basis B check if either or both of your outputs or inputs are above £50,000 on average (or £20,000 if you make monthly returns). If they are you must tell Customs and Excise by attaching a letter to the first VAT return that you make using Basis B, quoting "reference 2B/Basis B".

If you later decide to change to Basis A, you must inform Customs and Excise in the same way.

Remember, you must tell your local VAT office about any changes in your business circumstances. You will find details in *The VAT guide,* Section XI.

DU 2113/2/86 (R)

Printed in the U.K. for H.M.S.O. 9/87 Dd 8055731 C 75000 38806 G 1373

APPENDIX 8.4:

Steuernummer FA-Nr.	Bezirk	Unterscheid.-Nr.	Schlüsseltext	Zeitraum
			21 56 11	siehe unten

1987

30 Eingangsstempel oder -datum

Finanzamt

Unternehmen – Art und Anschrift – Telefon

Umsatzsteuer-Voranmeldung 1987

Voranmeldungszeitraum

bei monatlicher Abgabe bitte ankreuzen

87 01	Jan.		87 07	Juli	
87 02	Feb.		87 08	Aug.	
87 03	März		87 09	Sept.	
87 04	April		87 10	Okt.	
87 05	Mai		87 11	Nov.	
87 06	Juni		87 12	Dez.	

bei vierteljährlicher Abgabe bitte ankreuzen

87 41	I. Kalender-vierteljahr	
87 42	II. Kalender-vierteljahr	
87 43	III. Kalender-vierteljahr	
87 44	IV. Kalender-vierteljahr	

Wenn **berichtigte** Anmeldung, bitte eine „1" eintragen 10

I. Berechnung der Umsatzsteuer-Vorauszahlung

Zeile		Kz	volle DM	Kz	Steuer DM	Pf
	Steuerfreie Umsätze (einschl. Eigenverbrauch) 1) 2)					
1	**mit** Vorsteuerabzug (z.B. Umsätze nach § 4 Nr. 1 bis 6 UStG)	43				
2	**ohne** Vorsteuerabzug Umsätze nach § 4 Nr. ______ UStG	48				
	Steuerpflichtige Umsätze (einschl. Eigenverbrauch) ohne Umsatzsteuer 1) 2) zum Steuersatz von					
3	14 v.H.	85				
4	7 v.H.	86				
5	13 v.H. (für Umsätze in der Zeit vom 1. 7. 1979 bis zum 30. 6. 1983)	45				
6	6,5 v.H. (für Umsätze in der Zeit vom 1. 7. 1979 bis zum 30. 6. 1983)	46				
7	6 v.H. (für Umsätze in das Währungsgebiet der Mark der DDR)	54				
8	3 v.H. (für Umsätze in das Währungsgebiet der Mark der DDR)	55				
9	Umsätze, für die eine Steuer nach § 24 Abs.1 UStG zu entrichten ist (Sägewerkserzeugnisse, Getränke und alkoholische Flüssigkeiten sowie Umsätze aus der Tierzucht und Tierhaltung bei Überschreiten der Obergrenze von 330 Vieheinheiten) 1) 2) 3)	76		80		
10	Umsätze, die anderen Steuersätzen unterliegen 1) 2)	35		36		
11	Summe der steuerfreien und steuerpflichtigen Umsätze					
12	Steuer infolge Wechsels der Besteuerungsart/-form, sowie Nachsteuer auf versteuerte Anzahlungen 2) . . .			65		
13	Umsatzsteuer					
	Vorsteuer- und Kürzungsbeträge					
14	Vorsteuerbeträge (Umsatzsteuer und Einfuhrumsatzsteuer), die nicht vom Abzug ausgeschlossen sind 4), ausgenommen Vorsteuerbeträge, die nach § 24 UStG pauschaliert sind			66		
15	Kürzungsbeträge für Bezüge aus dem Währungsgebiet der Mark der DDR			67		
16	Zwischensumme 2)					
17	Kürzungsbeträge nach § 24a UStG für land- und forstwirtschaftliche Betriebe, die ihre Umsätze nach den allgemeinen Vorschriften versteuern (§ 24 Abs. 4 UStG)			81		
18	Kürzungsbetrag nach § 13 Berlinförderungsgesetz (BerlinFG) **für Berliner Unternehmer**			73		
19	**Zwischensumme** 2) . . . . zu übertragen					

1) Entgelterhöhungen und -minderungen (z. B. Skonti und Boni) sind zu berücksichtigen (§ 17 Abs. 1 und 2 UStG).
2) Negative Beträge sind rot einzutragen oder mit einem Minuszeichen zu versehen.
3) Steuer abzüglich Vorsteuerpauschale (§ 24 Abs. 1 UStG) und ggf. abzüglich Kürzungsbetrag (§ 24 a Abs. 1 UStG).
4) Außerdem sind zu berücksichtigen:
a) Berichtigung des Vorsteuerabzugs bei Änderung der Bemessungsgrundlage (§ 17 Abs. 1 und 2 UStG),
b) herabgesetzte, erlassene oder erstattete Einfuhrumsatzsteuer (§ 17 Abs. 3 UStG) und
c) Berichtigung des Vorsteuerabzugs bei Wirtschaftsgütern, deren Verwendung sich nachträglich geändert hat (§ 15 a UStG).

USt 1 A – Umsatzsteuer-Voranmeldung 1987

Nr. 754/1 – (10. 86) OFD D0 – St 14

Umweltschutzpapier – umweltschonend zu 100% aus Altpapier gefertigt.

– 2 –

	Kz	DM	Pf
Übertrag			
Steuerabzugsbetrag nach § 19 Abs. 3 UStG:			
___ v.H. des Betrags aus Zeile 20, wenn dieser nicht negativ ist	32		

	Kz	Bemessungsgrundlage volle DM	Pf	Kz	DM	Pf
Kürzungen nach den §§ 1, 1 a und 2 BerlinFG						
§ 1 Abs. 1 bis 4 BerlinFG (einschließlich der Kürzungen bei erhöhter Berliner Wertschöpfung)	21			22		
§ 1 Abs. 5 BerlinFG – Überlassung von Filmen – . . . 6 v.H.	23					
§ 1 Abs. 6 BerlinFG – sonstige Leistungen – . . . . 10 v.H.	33					
§ 1 a BerlinFG – Innenumsätze –	37			87		
§ 2 BerlinFG – für westdeutsche Unternehmer – . . . 4,2 v.H.	89					

	Kz	DM	Pf
Zwischensumme [1].			
In Rechnungen unberechtigt ausgewiesene Steuerbeträge (§ 14 Abs. 2 und 3 UStG) sowie **Steuerbeträge**, die nach § 17 Abs. 1 Satz 2 UStG geschuldet werden	69		
Steuer für den Selbstverbrauch (sog. Investitionssteuer) nach § 30 UStG 1973 [1] [2])	77		
Abzug (Anrechnung) der festgesetzten **Sondervorauszahlung** für Dauerfristverlängerung · (Nur ausfüllen in der letzten Voranmeldung des Besteuerungszeitraums, **in der Regel Dezember**) . . .	39		
Umsatzsteuer-Vorauszahlung . . . . (Bitte in jedem Fall ausfüllen) **Überschuß** – rot eintragen oder mit Minuszeichen versehen –	83		

(kann auf 10 Pf zu Ihren Gunsten gerundet werden)

Im Falle eines Überschusses wird der Betrag auf das dem Finanzamt benannte Konto überwiesen, soweit nicht eine Verrechnung mit Steuerschulden vorzunehmen ist. Falls Sie eine Verrechnung des Überschusses wünschen, bitte eine „1" eintragen . . . . 29 ___
Die Verrechnungswünsche sind auf besonderem Blatt anzugeben.

Wenn der vorstehende Betrag entgegen der erteilten Einzugsermächtigung ausnahmsweise nicht im Wege der Lastschrift eingezogen werden soll, bitte eine „1" eintragen . . . . 26 ___

II. Anmeldung der Umsatzsteuer im Abzugsverfahren

Gesamtbetrag der Umsatzsteuer, die im Abzugsverfahren (§§ 51 bis 56 UStDV) bei Leistungen nicht im Erhebungsgebiet ansässiger Unternehmer einzubehalten und abzuführen ist 75

(kann auf 10 Pf zu Ihren Gunsten gerundet werden)

Ich versichere, die Angaben in dieser Steueranmeldung wahrheitsgemäß nach bestem Wissen und Gewissen gemacht zu haben.

Bei der Anfertigung dieser Steueranmeldung hat mitgewirkt:
(Name, Anschrift, Telefon)

Datum, Unterschrift

Vom Finanzamt auszufüllen

Kz	Wert	Kz	Wert	Kz	Wert
12		19		88	
11		20			

Datum, Namenszeichen, Unterschrift

Hinweis nach den Vorschriften der Datenschutzgesetze:
Die mit der Steueranmeldung angeforderten Daten werden aufgrund der §§ 149 ff. der Abgabenordnung und des § 18 des Umsatzsteuergesetzes erhoben.

Bearbeitungshinweis

1. Die aufgeführten Daten sind mit Hilfe des geprüften und genehmigten Programms sowie ggf. unter Berücksichtigung der gespeicherten Daten maschinell zu verarbeiten.
2. Die weitere Bearbeitung richtet sich nach den Ergebnissen der maschinellen Verarbeitung.

Kontrollzahl und/oder Datenerfassungsvermerk

1) Negative Beträge sind rot einzutragen oder mit einem Minuszeichen zu versehen.
2) Steuer- und Kürzungsbeträge aufgrund geänderter Bemessungsgrundlagen sind zu berücksichtigen.

APPENDIX 8.5:

1986

Finanzamt ____________________

Steuernummer FA-Nr.	Bezirk	Unterscheid.-Nr.	Schlüsseltext	Besteuerungszeitraum		Sachbereich
		.	315086	86	99	11

Grün umrandete Felder nur vom Finanzamt auszufüllen

Eingangsstempel oder -datum

Datum Blatt

☐ Geändert ☐ Vorbehalt der Nachprüfung aufgehoben

Umsatzsteuererklärung

Wenn berichtigte Steuererklärung, bitte eine „1" eintragen 110 ☐

Die vollständig ausgefüllte und unterschriebene Erklärung muß spätestens am 31. Mai 1987 bei dem Finanzamt eingegangen sein.

Zeile

A. Allgemeine Angaben

121

Unternehmer (Firma), Telefon

1 ____________________

Art des Unternehmens

2 ____________________

Straße, Hausnummer

3 ____________________

Postleitzahl, Ort

4 ____________________

Zeile	Dauer der Unternehmereigenschaft, falls nicht vom 1. Januar bis zum 31. Dezember 1986		vom Tag	vom Monat	bis zum Tag	bis zum Monat		Tag	Monat	Tag	Monat
5	1. Zeitraum	200					200				
6	2. Zeitraum	201					201				

Die Zeilen 7 und 8 sind nur auszufüllen, wenn der Umsatz 1985 (zuzüglich Steuer) nicht mehr als 20 000 DM betragen hat und auf die Anwendung des § 19 Abs. 1 UStG nicht verzichtet worden ist.

Zeile			Betrag volle DM	Nur vom Finanzamt auszufüllen
7	**Umsatz im Kalenderjahr 1985**	(Berechnung nach § 19 Abs. 1 und 4 UStG)	238	238
8	**Umsatz im Kalenderjahr 1986** Außerdem ist in Zeile 64 eine „0" einzutragen, falls nicht in den Zeilen 26 ff. eine Eintragung vorzunehmen ist.		239	239

B. Berechnung der Umsatzsteuer

Zeile			Bemessungsgrundlage volle DM	Steuer DM	Pf	
	1. **Steuerfreie Umsätze** (einschl. Eigenverbrauch) [1] [2]					
9	**mit** Vorsteuerabzug nach ______ [3]		237			237
	ohne Vorsteuerabzug					
10	a) **nicht** zum Gesamtumsatz (§ 19 Abs. 4 UStG) gehörend nach § 4 Nr. ______ UStG [3]		241			241
11	b) zum Gesamtumsatz (§ 19 Abs. 4 UStG) gehörend nach § 4 Nr. ______ UStG [3]		240			240
	2. **Steuerpflichtige Umsätze** [1] [2]					
12	Lieferungen und sonstige Leistungen . . .	zu 14 v.H.	270			270
13	Eigenverbrauch a) Entnahme von Gegenständen	zu 14 v.H.	271			271
14	b) Entnahme von sonstigen Leistungen . . .	zu 14 v.H.	272			272
15	c) Aufwendungen i. S. des § 4 Abs. 5 Nr. 1 – 7 u. Abs. 7 EStG .	zu 14 v.H.	273			273
16	Unentgeltliche Leistungen von Gesellschaften an ihre Gesellschafter usw.	zu 14 v.H.	274			274
17	Lieferungen und sonstige Leistungen . . .	zu 7 v.H.	275			275
18	Eigenverbrauch a) Entnahme von Gegenständen	zu 7 v.H.	276			276
19	b) Entnahme von sonstigen Leistungen . . .	zu 7 v.H.	277			277
20	c) Aufwendungen i. S. des § 4 Abs. 5 Nr. 1 – 7 u. Abs. 7 EStG .	zu 7 v.H.	278			278
21	Unentgeltliche Leistungen von Gesellschaften an ihre Gesellschafter usw.	zu 7 v.H.	279			279
22		zu übertragen				

1) **Entgelterhöhungen und Entgeltminderungen sowie beim Wechsel der Besteuerungsart in früheren Besteuerungszeiträumen noch nicht versteuerte Anzahlungen / Außenstände sind zu berücksichtigen.**

2) **Negative Beträge sind rot einzutragen oder mit einem Minuszeichen zu versehen.**

3) **Kommt mehr als eine Befreiungsvorschrift in Betracht, so ist Abschnitt A der Anlage auszufüllen.**

USt 2 A Umsatzsteuererklärung 1986 (N)

754/9 – (11.86) OFD Dü – St 14 (gilt nur zur Abgabe bei Finanzämtern in Nordrhein-Westfalen)

Umweltschutzpapier – umweltschonend zu 100 % aus Altpapier gefertigt

- 2 -

	Bemessungsgrundlage volle DM	Steuer DM	Pf	Nur vom Finanzamt auszufüllen
Übertrag				
Steuerpflichtige Umsätze in der Zeit vom 1. Juli 1979 bis zum 30. Juni 1983 [1] [2] — zu 13 v. H.	170			170
— zu 6,5 v. H.	190			190
Umsätze, die **anderen Steuersätzen** unterliegen, und Umsätze **land- und forstwirtschaftlicher Betriebe,** für die eine Steuer nach § 24 UStG zu entrichten ist (zu übernehmen aus Abschnitt B Zeile 33 der Anlage) [3]				
Nachsteuer auf versteuerte Anzahlungen u. ä. wegen Steuersatzänderung		319		319
Summe der steuerfreien und steuerpflichtigen Umsätze				
Umsatzsteuer (zu übertragen in Zeile 40)				
Umsätze, die aufgrund eines Verzichts auf Steuerbefreiung (§ 9 UStG) als steuerpflichtig behandelt worden sind				
Zur Berechnung des Gesamtumsatzes:				
a) Umsätze im Rahmen eines land- und forstwirtschaftlichen Betriebes, soweit in den Zeilen 9 bis 26 nicht aufgeführt (ggf. geschätzt)	361			361
b) Im Gesamtumsatz enthaltene Umsätze von Wirtschaftsgütern des Anlagevermögens aus Anlaß der Einstellung der unternehmerischen Tätigkeit während des Kalenderjahrs	202			202
C. Abziehbare Vorsteuerbeträge [4] [5] (ohne die Berichtigung nach § 15 a UStG)				
Vorsteuerbeträge (Umsatzsteuer und Einfuhrumsatzsteuer), die nicht vom Abzug ausgeschlossen sind, ausgenommen die nach Durchschnittsätzen berechneten Vorsteuerbeträge		320		320
Vorsteuerbeträge, die nach den allgemeinen Durchschnittsätzen berechnet sind (§ 23 UStG)		333		333
Kürzungsbeträge für Bezüge aus dem Währungsgebiet der Mark der DDR, die nicht vom Abzug ausgeschlossen sind				
zum Kürzungssatz von 11 v. H.	326			326
zum Kürzungssatz von 5,5 v. H.	327			327
zum Kürzungssatz von 5 v. H.	323			323
zum Kürzungssatz von 2,5 v. H.	325			325
Summe (zu übertragen in Zeile 41)				
D. Berechnung der zu entrichtenden Umsatzsteuer				
Umsatzsteuer (aus Zeile 29)				
Abziehbare Vorsteuerbeträge (aus Zeile 39)				
Vorsteuerbeträge [6], die aufgrund des § 15 a UStG nachträglich abziehbar sind [7]		357		357
Kürzungsbetrag nach § 13 BerlinFG [8] (Nur für Berliner Unternehmer) 4 v. H.		389		389
Umsätze aus einer freiberuflichen Tätigkeit oder einer Tätigkeit als Handelsvertreter oder Makler:				
Besteht der Gesamtumsatz ausschließlich aus diesen Umsätzen?	373 (ja = 1 / nein = 2)			373
Wenn nein (= 2): Entgelte für steuerpflichtige Umsätze aus der vorbezeichneten Tätigkeit	374			374
zu übertragen				

Entgelterhöhungen und Entgeltminderungen sowie beim Wechsel der Besteuerungsart in früheren Besteuerungszeiträumen noch nicht versteuerte Außenstände sind zu berücksichtigen.
Negative Beträge sind rot einzutragen oder mit einem Minuszeichen zu versehen.
Abschnitt B der Anlage ist auch in den Fällen des Wechsels der Besteuerungsart/-form auszufüllen.
Vorsteuer- und Kürzungsbeträge, die auf Entgelterhöhungen und -minderungen entfallen, sowie herabgesetzte, erlassene oder erstattete Einfuhrumsatzsteuer sind zu berücksichtigen.
Ausgenommen Vorsteuerbeträge, die nach § 24 UStG pauschaliert sind.
Einschließlich der Kürzungsbeträge für Bezüge aus dem Währungsgebiet der Mark der DDR.
Zurückzuzahlende Vorsteuerbeträge sind in Zeile 58 einzutragen.
Bei Einstellung der unternehmerischen Tätigkeit während des Kalenderjahres ist ggf. auch Zeile 32 auszufüllen.

– 3 –

Zeile		Bemessungsgrundlage volle DM	Steuer DM	Pf	Nur vom Finanzamt auszufüllen
47	Übertrag				
48	Kürzungsbeträge nach § 24 a UStG [1]) . . . . 5 v. H.	399			399
49	Zwischensumme[2])				
	Berechnung des Steuerabzugsbetrages (§ 19 Abs. 3 UStG)				
50	Gesamtumsatz nach § 19 Abs. 4 UStG [3])				
51	Entsprechende Umsätze, die außerhalb des Erhebungsgebiets ausgeführt worden sind	365			365
52	Maßgeblicher Umsatz				
53	**Steuerabzugsbetrag:** _______ v. H. [4]) von . . . _______ DM _______ Pf (Betrag aus Zeile 49, wenn dieser nicht negativ ist)		368		368
54	Zwischensumme[2])				
	Umsatzsteuerkürzung nach dem Berlinförderungsgesetz – ausgenommen § 13 BerlinFG –				
55	a) Kürzungsbetrag nach § 2 BerlinFG für westdeutsche Unternehmer [5]) . . . . . . 4,2 v. H.	381			381
56	b) Weitere Kürzungsbeträge nach dem BerlinFG (zu übernehmen aus Abschnitt C Zeile 45 der Anlage)				
57	Zwischensumme[2])				
58	Vorsteuerbeträge [6]), die aufgrund des § 15 a UStG zurückzuzahlen sind [7])		359		359
59	Erhöhung von Steuerabzugsbeträgen früherer Jahre infolge Rückzahlung von Vorsteuerbeträgen nach § 15 a UStG [8]) .		393		393
60	In Rechnungen unberechtigt ausgewiesene Steuerbeträge (§ 14 Abs. 2 und 3 UStG)		318		318
61	Steuerbeträge, die nach § 17 Abs. 1 Satz 2 UStG geschuldet werden		331		331
62	Besteuerung des Selbstverbrauchs (§ 30 UStG 1973) [2]) [9]) .	402	403		402
					103
63	Steuer-, Vorsteuer- und Kürzungsbeträge, die auf frühere Besteuerungszeiträume entfallen (nur für Unternehmer, die § 19 Abs. 1 UStG anwenden – siehe Zeilen 7 und 8) [2]) [10])		391		391
64	**Umsatzsteuer** . . . . (kann auf 10 Pf zu Ihren Gunsten gerundet werden)		316		Betrag zum Soll gestellt
	Überschuß – rot eintragen oder mit Minuszeichen versehen –				
65	Vorauszahlungssoll 1986 (einschließlich Sondervorauszahlung) [2])				
66	Noch an die Finanzkasse zu entrichten (Abschlußzahlung)				
67	Erstattungsanspruch				Datum, Namenszeichen

Die Abschlußzahlung ist binnen einem Monat nach der Abgabe der Steuererklärung zu entrichten (§ 18 Abs. 4 UStG).

Ein Erstattungsbetrag ist auf mein dem Finanzamt benanntes Konto zu überweisen, soweit nicht eine Verrechnung mit Steuerschulden vorzunehmen ist.

Ich versichere, die Angaben in dieser Steuererklärung und in der beigefügten Anlage wahrheitsgemäß nach bestem Wissen und Gewissen gemacht zu haben.

Datum

Bei der Anfertigung dieser Erklärung hat mitgewirkt:
(Name, Anschrift, Telefon)

Eigenhändige Unterschrift des Unternehmers

Hinweis nach den Vorschriften der Datenschutzgesetze:
Die mit der Steuererklärung angeforderten Daten werden aufgrund der §§ 149 ff. der Abgabenordnung und des § 18 des Umsatzsteuergesetzes erhoben.

Ein Umsatzsteuerbescheid ergeht nur, wenn von Ihrer Berechnung der Umsatzsteuer abgewichen wird.

1) Nur für land- und forstwirtschaftliche Betriebe, die ihre Umsätze nach den allgemeinen Vorschriften versteuern (§ 24 Abs. 4 UStG). Ab 1. Juli 1985 entfällt der Kürzungsbetrag für die Umsätze von Vieh, wenn die Obergrenze von 330 Vieheinheiten im vorangegangenen Wirtschaftsjahr überschritten wurde.
2) Negative Beträge sind rot einzutragen oder mit einem Minuszeichen zu versehen.
3) Bei Einstellung der unternehmerischen Tätigkeit während des Kalenderjahres ist ggf. auch Zeile 32 auszufüllen.
4) Der anzuwendende v. H.-Satz kann der Tabelle in Abschnitt 248 UStR entnommen werden.
5) Zurückzuzahlende Kürzungsbeträge sind zu berücksichtigen (§§ 11 und 12 BerlinFG).
6) Einschließlich der Kürzungsbeträge für Bezüge aus dem Währungsgebiet der Mark der DDR.
7) Nachträglich abziehbare Vorsteuerbeträge sind in Zeile 42 einzutragen.
8) Auf Abschnitt 250 Abs. 2 UStR wird hingewiesen.
9) Steuer- und Kürzungsbeträge aufgrund geänderter Bemessungsgrundlagen sind zu berücksichtigen.
10) Hierzu gehören Fälle der nachträglichen Entgelterhöhungen und Entgeltminderungen sowie beim Wechsel der Besteuerungsform in früheren Besteuerungszeiträumen bereits versteuerte Anzahlungen oder noch nicht versteuerte Außenstände.

- 4 -

Nur vom Finanzamt auszufüllen

Art der Steuerfestsetzung/Kennzeichnung des Bescheids	100				

	in v. H.	in DM
Verspätungszuschlag wegen verspäteter Abgabe oder Nichtabgabe der Umsatzsteuererklärung	140	141

Variable Angaben	Kz	Wert	Kz	Wert	Kz	Wert	Kz	Wert

99	12

Erläuterungstexte	Kz	Wert	Kz	Wert	Kz	Wert	Kz	Wert	Kz	Wert	Kz	Wert

Nur vom Finanzamt auszufüllen

Zutreffendes ankreuzen ☒ oder ausfüllen

1. ☐ Steueranmeldung – Steuerfestsetzung unter Vorbehalt der Nachprüfung (§ 168 Satz 1 AO).
   ☐ Steueranmeldung – Antrag auf Steuerfestsetzung (§ 168 Satz 2 AO). Zustimmung wird erteilt.
   ☐ Von der Steueranmeldung abweichende Steuerfestsetzung.
2. Vordruck USt 2 M über die Festsetzung eines Verspätungszuschlags in Höhe von ____________ DM ausfüllen. Der Verspätungszuschlag wird hiermit festgesetzt. — Erledigt ________ Namenszeichen/Datum
3. Vermerk zur Überwachungsliste V. — Vermerkt ________ Namenszeichen/Datum
4. Der Finanzkasse zur Erteilung der Sollanweisung
   a) Jahresumsatzsteuer (Betrag aus Zeile 64 der Erklärung) — ____________ DM
   b) Verspätungszuschlag wegen verspäteter Abgabe der Umsatzsteuererklärung (Betrag aus Nr. 2) — ____________ DM
   Erledigt ________ Namenszeichen/Datum
5. Der Kassenaufsicht zur Prüfung. — Geprüft ________ Namenszeichen/Datum
6. Nach Eingang des Abrechnungsteils Bescheid mit dem Absendetag versehen und an diesem Tag zur Post geben. — Zur Post am ________ Namenszeichen/Datum
7. Z. d. A.

(Sachgebietsleiter)	(Datum)	(Sachbearbeiter/Bearbeiter)

NOTES

1 In fact, the total taxed turnover at the 14 per cent rate in Germany is six times bigger than that taxed at 7 per cent. The limited applicability of the lower rate limits the numbers of firms in Germany which have to operate more than one rate.

2 This figure excludes traders who make annual returns only and are not recorded at a national level. Precise figures are not available, but we estimate that the total number of registered traders is 1 million higher than the figure given, giving a total of 2.9 million traders subject to VAT.

3 A study by Schmölders (1970) suggests that attitudes towards taxation in general are actually *less* favourable and compliance costs higher in Germany than in Britain though at that time VAT had yet to be introduced in the UK. Certainly our contrasting findings on VAT cannot be explained by a greater tolerance of compliance burdens in Germany than in Britain. We show below that VAT scores worse compared with other taxes in the UK than it does in Germany and there is ample evidence of concern about other aspects of the compliance burden in Germany (see Kayser and Friede 1984).

4 The Neumark Committee which recommended a consumption type VAT for the EC in 1962 actually did not recommend that the tax should be applied at the retail stage.

REFERENCES

Bannock, G. (1986), *VAT and Small Business: European Experience and Implications for North America*, CFIB and NFIB, Washington DC.

Bannock, G. (1976), *The Smaller Business in Britain and Germany*, Anglo-German Foundation, Wilton House Publications.

Carsberg, B.V. *et al.*, (1985), *Small Company Financial Reporting*, Prentice-Hall International, Englewood Cliffs, NJ.

Davis, E.H. and Kay, J.A., *Extending the VAT Base: Problems and Probabilities*, Institute of Fiscal Studies.

Doran, A. (1984), *Craft Enterprises in Britain and Germany*, Anglo-German Foundation.

European Commission (1986), Proposal for a Council Directive amending Directive 77/388/EEC on the harmonisation of the laws of member states relating to turnover taxes in respect of the common value added tax scheme applicable to small and medium-sized businesses (COM(86)444).

H M Customs and Excise (1984), *75th Report of the Commissioner of H M Customs and Excise for the Year Ended 31st March, 1984*, HMSO, London.

Kayser, G. and Friede, C. (1984), *Wirkungsanalyse der Sozialgesetzgebung*, Institut für Mittelstandsforschung, Bonn.

Peacock, A. and Forte, F. (eds) (1981), *The Political Economy of Taxation*, Basil Blackwell, Oxford.

Research Associates (1985), *In Burdens on Business: Report of a Scrutiny of Administrative and Legislative Requirements*, HMSO, London.

Sandford, C. *et al.* (1981), *Costs and Benefits of VAT*, Heinemann, London.

Small Business Research Trust (1985), *Quarterly Survey of Small Business in Britain*, Vol.1, no.3.

Small Business Research Trust (1986), *Quarterly Survey of Small Business in Britain*, Vol.2, no 1.

Schmölders, G. (1970), *Survey research in public finance – a behavioural approach to fiscal theory, Public Finance.*

Part III

Regulation

Chapter 9

SOCIAL LEGISLATION AND ITS IMPACT ON EMPLOYMENT IN SMEs*

INTRODUCTION

Increasing concern has been expressed recently about the effects of employment and other aspects of social legislation in exacerbating the crisis in unemployment in the European Community. In recognizing the important role of small and medium enterprises (SMEs) in contributing to employment creation, the Commission of the European Communities has specifically included in its Draft Action Programme for the SME Task Force, among other things, the review of the regulatory environment for SMEs (Commission of the European Communities, 1986). The objectives of this report are:

1 To review the scope of social legislation affecting SMEs in the Community.
2 To review the evidence on the employment impact of this legislation.
3 To assess the broad implications of the foregoing in the context of the economic role of SMEs.

This is not an easy field to work in. Only limited information is readily available on the general scope of employment legislation across the Community, most of it assembled by the Commission itself. A study on the specific Community legislative obligations of SMEs (the Belmont Study) is in hand but is not expected to be completed until early in 1987 (Belmont, 1987). No comprehensive international studies of the impact of national legislation have yet been carried out and such a study would have to confront a number of inherent difficulties. It is, however, hoped that this preliminary review of existing information will be of some help.

THE SCOPE OF LEGISLATION AFFECTING EMPLOYMENT

Introduction

In this section we review the scope of national legislation affecting employment,

---

* A study carried out for the Commission of the European Communities (CEC) DGIII and completed in November 1986. The CEC kindly gave permission for the report to be reproduced here but bears no responsibility for the views expressed.

the special treatment of small firms in respect to this legislation and the progress made in harmonizing employment conditions at Community level. The discussion is restricted to general 'social' legislation directly affecting the hiring of employees, the termination of employment and labour costs. This by no means exhausts the implications of legislation for employment and the costs of employment. For example, legislation on training, including apprenticeships, and many aspects of collective agreements and roles of trades unions may affect employment decisions. We exclude these on the grounds that they are not, in general, of great importance for the smallest firms (which virtually everywhere receive special treatment in these respects). Other legislation, not discussed in this section, for example requiring firms to collect taxes from their employees, may also, in the context of the overall burden of legislation, affect employment decisions. We return to this issue later (p.243).

The history of social legislation affecting employment in business goes back long before the Industrial Revolution. For example, there was legislation governing the payment of wages in ready money in the UK dating as far back as 1464. The scope of legislation began to increase rapidly in the nineteenth century with the growth of employment in factories with, for example, the Health and Morals of Apprentices Act 1802, in the UK and the Imperial Compulsory Liability Act in 1871 in Germany (Peacock, 1984).

Although some social legislation goes back a long way in time, the major elements of it are post-World War II in origin and the volume of this legislation increased particularly rapidly in the 1960s and 1970s. For example, elaborate and comprehensive social security systems are primarily a post-war development and legislation relevant to individual and collective dismissals, although having its origins earlier, in its present form dates mainly from the late 1960s and 1970s, for example in Italy 1966, France 1973 and West Germany, 1978.

The result is a mass of legislation which until very recently had not been even catalogued in the European Community. The Directorate for Social Affairs (DGV) has provided us with a listing of the principal legislation by subject which for 10 member states covers 36 pages.[1] This is, however, simply a listing; to explain in any detail the coverage of these laws, even in summary form, would be an enormous task. Moreover, the legislation has not been static; over time it has been extended and revised frequently. Kayser and Friede (1984) list 59 pieces of social legislation in West Germany between 1969 and 1984.

Employment Protection

Laws limiting the freedom of employers to dismiss employees without reason, notice or compensation are central to social legislation affecting employment and exist in all member states.

Normally, employers are required to give written notice of termination of employment, but pay at the current rate may be given in lieu of notice. Minimum periods of notice are laid down and are usually related to length of continuous service with the employer so that higher compensation is payable to long-serving employees. No up to date assessment of minimum periods of notice was available at the time of preparation of this report, but a 1983 study directed by the author showed that the minimum varied widely from one week to three months for non-manual workers (Economist Intelligence Unit, 1983, see Tables A.1 and A.2). In Italy, Belgium, Greece, West Germany and elsewhere, the periods of notice vary not only with length of service but also between blue- and white-collar workers (wage and salary earners) and, in at least one case, the level of earnings. In some countries there is no minimum notice for employees who have been with the firm for less than a certain period, which is, for example, two months in Greece and six months in France.

In many member states other conditions have to be complied with in dismissing employees. For example, in Belgium during the period of notice employees must be allowed time off to seek alternative employment. The procedures may also be different for collective dismissals, for example consultation with works councils is required in all countries where these bodies are a legal requirement or, in other cases, workers' representatives; these dismissals must normally be notified to the authorities. Italy lays down rules for the selection of employees for redundancy. For collective dismissals, procedures involve delays for consultation or a period of reflection (France, Belgium, Greece, Ireland). In West Germany, permission to dismiss a disabled employee is required from the employment office. Several member states have indemnity funds to which employers contribute to assist with redundancy compensation (Ireland, UK) or to assure compensation in cases of bankruptcy (Belgium, Greece). The Netherlands has a scheme to maintain employment in firms facing temporary economic difficulties and many other member states provide earnings supplement funds for workers on short-time.

As far as we can establish, all member states provide statutory rights against unfair dismissal. These require employers, in most cases, to provide dismissed employees with a written statement of the reason for dismissal and provide for rights of appeal to special tribunals or the courts. A distinction is made between redundancy (where reduction in the workforce is imperative for economic reasons, such as lack of work, financial distress) and dismissals arising from the performance and behaviour of the employee. In the latter case procedures are laid down (for example, except for serious misconduct, warnings must be given that dismissal will result if behaviour does not change).

Most member states make provision for maternity leave for women with the right of reinstatement. In contrast, legislation in several countries actively promotes the termination of employment through retirement. For example, West Germany and the UK have schemes to provide financial inducements to early retirement providing that the resulting vacancies are filled by the unemployed.

Special employment protection is provided for certain categories of employees in some member states. In West Germany, for example, such protection is given to works councillors, pregnant women, disabled workers and women taking maternity leave. In Spain and the UK, special protection is provided to employee representatives.

Conditions of Employment

All member states have legislation affecting working hours. For example, The Netherlands sets limits to maximum working hours; France and Belgium have legislation on shift work. Special rules relate to youths and to night work for women, though there is a tendency for special rules on the hours and other conditions for women to be lifted in line with the policy on equal treatment. Italy regulates overtime and indeed prohibits it in certain sectors (with derogations). The general trend, as in the promotion of early retirement, is an attempt to reduce working hours, earlier humanitarian objectives in promoting health and safety through shorter working hours now being reinforced by a desire to spread work among greater numbers of employees.

All member states declare between 8 and 15 days as public holidays, though not all also have statutory minima for annual paid holidays for employees (The Netherlands and Ireland are exceptions). In most countries, holiday entitlements are led by collective bargaining. In West Germany, for example, 96 per cent of employees have a claim under collective agreements to basic leave of at least four weeks and almost 50 per cent to paid annual leave of six weeks or more (Commission of the European Communities, 1985). Several *Länder* in West Germany have legal provisions for training leave under which all employees are entitled to five days' training leave per year.

Rights to maternity leave have recently been extended in some member states (for example, Greece) to cover other leave associated with the needs of children (such as sickness) and in at least one case (Italy) for the right to apply to working fathers as well as mothers. Several countries plan parental leave legislation along these lines. In Denmark, the last 10 weeks (out of 24) of maternity leave may be shared between the parents.

The position on the organization of working time, that is to say, legislation affecting part-time workers, and temporary contract workers is complex. An earlier trend to extend employment protection and other rights to these classes of employees and to limit by taxation, social security treatment and other means, the growth of these forms of employment has been overtaken in some countries by moves to actively promote them by a relaxation of legislation. For example, the UK, Italy and West Germany have recently relaxed laws — or intend to do so — improving the protection for part-time and temporary workers. In Britain it is proposed to raise to 12 the number of hours worked each week above which employees qualify for the main employment rights while those working between 12 and 20 hours a week (currently between 8 and 16) will qualify after five years' service (Department of Employment, 1986). France and Luxembourg, in contrast, have recently improved the protection in case of dismissal and improved status for part-time workers and temporary workers, whether employed directly or supplied by an employment agency (Commission of the European Communities, 1985). Italy also established basic rules for part-time contracts in 1984.

These conflicting trends arise from a desire to improve employee protection and to stimulate part-time employment as a means of spreading work on the one hand, and the need to remove disincentives for employers to take on part-time or temporary workers on the other. In general, the trend towards extending employment protection to part-time and temporary workers has been little affected. For example, the Employment Promotion Act 1985 in West Germany merely extends the maximum length of time for which a temporary worker can be hired out to one and the same employer (without being counted for employment rights purposes as a permanent employee) from three to six months and then only until 31 December 1989.

Socially Disadvantaged Persons

All member states have legislation prohibiting discrimination in employment on grounds of sex, for example, to ensure equal treatment and equal pay for men and women. Several countries have special laws to promote the employment of blind or otherwise handicapped persons (Italy, Luxembourg, UK, Ireland (public sector)). France, West Germany and The Netherlands have quota schemes for handicapped persons under which employers unable to fill the quota are allowed to pay a fine or contribute to a contribution levy. In West Germany, for example, the quota is 6 per cent (the highest in the Community) and the fine DM 100 per month. Registered handicapped persons are entitled by law to an additional six days' annual leave, the cost of which is borne by the employer.

Health and Safety

The most extensive and complex legislation affecting employment is that concerned with health and safety. The complexity partly results from the need to keep the legislation up to date with changing technologies as the titles of legislation currently in force give witness: Windlass Regulation (Germany), Boiler Explosion Acts 1882–90 (Ireland), Nuclear Energy Act 1963 (The Netherlands). Another cause of complexity is the necessity for monitoring and control systems, for example factory inspectorates, supplemented in many countries (Denmark, Greece, UK, Ireland, Belgium and France) by obligatory health and safety committees involving the workforce. Health and safety regulations cover such matters as sanitation, medical surveillance, office and workshop layout and design, as well as fire prevention, the control of explosive, inflammable and toxic substances and escape and rescue procedures.

Labour Costs

In addition to the legislation reviewed so far (for example on holidays), laws directly affect labour costs in several other important respects in all member states. Governments in some states attempt to control wage increases (incomes policies) in some cases by indexation (Belgium, Denmark, Greece, Italy, Ireland and Luxembourg) though the effect of this may be to oblige small employers to increase wages faster than they would do if market forces were allowed to operate freely. Minimum wages are also completely regulated by law in France,

Ireland, Luxembourg and The Netherlands and partially in the UK through wages councils. There are no legal minima in West Germany or Greece.

Employers' social security contributions are the largest element of all in legislatively imposed costs on employment. Some data on the relative incidence of these are presented later (p.258).

Employee Participation

Representation and consultation and the supply of information to employees within enterprises are governed to a greater or lesser extent in all member states by legislation. In Belgium, West Germany, Denmark, France, Luxembourg and The Netherlands, representative bodies such as works councils are required in all larger firms by law. In Greece, Ireland, the UK and effectively in Italy also, employee representation is left mainly to trades unions although this does not mean that it is unaffected by special legal provisions. For example, in the UK there are laws affecting strike ballots, rules for elections, the provision of information and consultation on health and safety.

Exceptions for Smaller Firms

There have been attempts to lighten the administrative burdens on small firms arising from the legislation reviewed above and in many cases their particular problems were taken account of in the original legislation. For example, in complying with the necessity for authorization for the dismissal of employees from regional government in France, a simplified procedure is adopted for firms with ten or fewer employees. In the UK, industrial tribunals are required, in hearing cases of unfair dismissal, to take the limited financial and administrative resources of small firms into account. Also in the UK, firms with fewer than five employees are not required to produce written policy statements on health and safety. Outright exemption for small firms from employment legislation is, however, limited mainly to requirements for consultation, quotas for the handicapped and, in a few countries, a few aspects of employment protection.

The most widespread exceptions for small firms are, of course, for 'collegiate' representative bodies within the firm. This accords with common sense: there would be no point in requiring firms with just a few employees to set up a works council. Thus the establishment of a works council or similar body is not compulsory for firms with fewer than 5 employees in West Germany, 50 in Denmark and France, 100 in Belgium (though there must be appointed workers' representatives if there are more than 20) and 150 in Luxembourg. Health and safety committees are not compulsory for firms with fewer than 10 employees in Denmark, 50 in Belgium and 100 in Greece.

Similar exceptions are in force for quotas for the employment of handicapped persons. In West Germany the quota applies only to firms with 16 or more employees – the lowest number that would allow the 6 per cent quota to be filled with one full-time handicapped person.

There appear, as far as we can establish, to be very few exceptions for employment protection legislation. In West Germany, the rules about periods of notice and other aspects of employment protection do not apply to firms with five or fewer employees, while in the UK the qualifying period for the right to appeal against unfair dismissal to a tribunal is two years for firms with fewer than 20 employees. Reinstatement after maternity is not mandatory in the UK for firms employing 5 or fewer employees (it is proposed to raise this threshold to 10 employees). In Italy, some of the individual employment protection legislation does not apply to firms with fewer than 35 employees while firms with fewer than 16 employees (industry and agriculture, 6 employees) are not required to reinstate with back pay employees who are deemed unfairly dismissed. In Spain, enterprises with fewer than 25 employees pay substantially lower compensation than larger firms in cases of unfair dismissal, part of the difference being made up by the State.

Although we have not been able to examine the appropriate legislation in all member states, our impression is that there are few — if any — exceptions made for small firms in other fields of employment legislation, for example in equal opportunity laws, health and safety, conditions of work or the level of social security contributions.

Harmonization of Legislation at Community Level

It is clear that the general approach to the legislation reviewed has much in common throughout the EC. The general principles underlying employment protection, conditions of work, equal opportunity, social security and health and safety, though not worker participation and minimum wages, are probably quite similar throughout the Community and becoming closer with the passage of time. It is equally clear, however, that in detail there are very considerable differences between member states. There have been a few Community directives in the areas reviewed here, for example on collective redundancies and health and safety. In addition, there are a number of proposed directives under consideration, for example on worker information and consultation, part-time and temporary work, parental leave and the handicapped. Much less progress has been made towards harmonization in this area than in some other aspects of EC legislation. Given the changing appreciation of the employment situation and differences of view within the Community, it does not seem likely that rapid progress can be expected. We express a tentative view on what the long-term objectives might be, and the principles that should govern harmonization, in a later section (p.254–5).

THE IMPACT OF EMPLOYMENT LEGISLATION ON ALL FIRMS

Costs

Economic theory and common sense suggest that anything which increases the costs of employment will, everything else remaining the same, reduce the demand for labour.

The first difficulty in assessing the impact of employment legislation on employment is that the total costs of this legislation which are borne by the private sector, are not known. Social security contributions are the largest element. In 1983, employers' social security contributions as a percentage of average earnings of manual workers in manufacturing ranged from 9.8 per cent in Ireland to 21 per cent in West Germany and 46 per cent in Italy (see Table A.3, p.258).

There are two types of costs arising from legislation. The first is the direct cost, for example the cost of 'fines' paid for release from handicapped personnel quotas, the additional costs of hiring temporary staff to replace those on statutory leave entitlement, redundancy compensation (if any) paid over and above that which would be paid in the absence of a legal minimum, and the capital and other costs involved in meeting health and safety regulations over and above those which would have been incurred in the absence of regulation.

The second type of cost imposed by the legislation under discussion is the administration cost. The accounting for social security contributions, the preparation of employee information and employment contracts, the time required to keep up to date with, and understand, regulations, are examples of the administrative costs of legislation borne by employers.

It is also clear that some of these costs, and particularly those of the second type, will be fixed, at least within limits. Others will be variable in nature so that some will affect average employment costs and some marginal costs, for example, the costs of taking on an additional employee.

There is also a third type of cost arising from legislation: the cost incurred by employers of rearranging their affairs so as to minimize the costs imposed by legislation, for example in the use of part-time instead of full-time employees, of contracting out work or investing in capital equipment to substitute for labour.

Finally, the incidence of costs will not be the same for all firms. Redundancy costs will only be borne by firms shedding labour, maternity costs will arise in some small firms and not in others, the costs of safety regulations will be greater in some sectors of industry than in others. As we show later (p.243 et seq), costs will not be neutral according to the size of firm since there are economics of scale in administration and there are differences in the proportions of labour (and types of labour) and capital employed in firms of different sizcs.

A second difficulty in assessing the impact of legislation on employment is that not only are the total costs imposed not known at any given point in time, but we have no measure of how these costs have changed over time.

For all these reasons, much previous research in this field has focused on the impact of social security contributions which can be measured. The principal trends can be summarized as follows:

1 Social security contributions have increased generally in the EC since 1965, both as a percentage of GDP and as a percentage of total taxation; in 1984 employers' and employees' contributions amounted to 12.1 per cent of GDP in the EC compared with 8.4 per cent in the United States and 8.1 per cent in Japan:
2 Since 1980 there is clear evidence of a slowdown in the rate of growth of these contributions:

3 On average, since 1965, the employees' share of these contributions has increased faster than the employers' share:
4 Statutory social security contributions are by far the largest element in non-wage labour costs in most member states:
5 Total non-wage labour costs, which include some but not all other elements of employment legislation costs, for example holiday pay, training and severance payments, as well as voluntary costs, have increased as a percentage of total labour costs in all EC countries since 1965 though this increase is slowing down.

Econometric Studies

Economists who have carried out studies in this field virtually all agree that increases in social security contributions and other non-wage labour costs have had a negative impact on the demand for labour (Organisation for Economic Co-operation and Development, 1986b). Differences in views about the extent of these effects arise partly from the difficulty of assessing their incidence: are they ultimately borne by the employee, the employer, or are they passed on to the end consumer? One econometric analysis attributes between 11 and 23 per cent of unemployment in the UK between 1956 and 1983 (depending on the period selected) to social security contributions and other payroll taxes (Layard and Nickell, 1985).

Econometric analysis can do little to capture the effects of other aspects of employment legislation in the absence of data on costs. Even where limited cost or other quantitative data are available, the complexities of the relationships between legislation and employer behaviour make meaningful econometric analysis exceptionally difficult. Nickell (1982), for example, not surprisingly, has found that the relationship between unemployment and the numbers of industrial tribunal cases in the UK was not highly significant. The numerous studies carried out suggest that job security policies have not increased employment, however, except in the short run and at the expense of reducing total worker hours in protected employment. As explained, little is known about the extent to which these policies raise labour costs, but to the extent that they do raise labour costs, a negative impact on employment is inevitable (Hamermesh, 1985). Moreover, as far as we are aware, none of these studies takes specific account of administrative compliance costs.

Changes in the Pattern of Employment

If legislation were pushing up the relative cost of full-time versus part-time and temporary employment (as it probably has) and increasing the relative cost of direct employment versus the cost of buying in goods and services (as it certainly has), we should expect employers to alter the pattern of their employment accordingly. In fact, there is growing evidence that there has been a shift towards part-time and temporary employment and in contracting out in the Community and also in other OECD countries.

According to the OECD (1986b), the proportion of part-time employment to total employment in France rose from 9.1 to 10.9 per cent between 1982 and 1985 and in the UK from 19.2 to 21.2 per cent over the same period, though it fell in the United States. Figures were not available for other EC countries.

There are also indications that the use of temporary workers is also increasing (indeed, concern about this trend underlies the proposed Directive on Temporary Work from the Council of the EC Commission of April 1982). According to the OECD (1986b), 'In France, there was an increase in temporary work during the latter half of the 1970s. Following changes in legislation, this trend was reversed between 1980 and 1983. But more recent evidence points to a resumption of the growth of fixed term contracts ...' (The changes in legislation referred to are the tightening of regulation on temporary work mentioned earlier (p.234).) In the UK, a survey by the Institute of Manpower Studies (IMS) (1986) found that 'three quarters of employers in most industrial sectors make use of temporary workers, and that this use is highest among larger and faster growing organisations. 7.6 per cent of the workforce in the IMS sample were temporary workers. This proportion had grown since 1980 and was on a continuing upwards trend.' Temporary workers included agency staff, employees under fixed-term contract and the self-employed (see also Department of Employment, 1984).

There has also been a growth in the percentage of self employment to total civilian employment in the non-agricultural sector in many countries. In 23 OECD countries this percentage increased only from 9.5 to 9.9 between 1973 and 1984 (unweighted average), although in the EC states the average rose from 10.5 to 11.4 per cent over the same period, and in the UK from 6.5 per cent in 1969 to 9.6 per cent in 1984. There was a decline, however, in the percentage of self employed in France and West Germany (see Table A.4, p.259).

Several explanations have been put forward for these trends. The OECD points out that part of the increase in the use of temporary and part-time workers may by cyclical and associated with the general recovery in output and employment that took place between the early and mid-1980s — employers tend to lay off temporary workers first in a downswing and then rehire them first in the upswing. Another factor may be the shift towards services where part-time workers have always been more prevalent. Finally, however, 'Faced with greater uncertainty about product demand and growing labour costs, including fringe benefits, of employing permanent workers, employers may be resorting more to temporary work as a way of matching their labour input more closely to seasonal and cyclical fluctuations in demand' (Organisation for Economic Co-operation and Development, 1986b). There are also factors on the supply side, notably the increased size of the pool of unemployed and changing attitudes to self-employment, which have stimulated the use of temporary workers. It would be wrong, therefore, to attribute the growth of these alternatives to full-time employment solely, or even mainly, to the long-term impact of employment legislation. However, it is very clear that this legislation, by increasing the costs of employment and severance costs, will have increased pressures on employers to find alternative ways of securing labour flexibility.

A recent international survey carried out for the Financial Times (1986) provides evidence of the growth of contracting out of work previously done by employees within the firm (Table 9.1). An unweighted average of almost 32 per cent of respondents in France, West Germany and Britain claimed that during the past three years they had contracted out on a regular basis work that had previously been done within the firm.

Table 9.1: Recent and future trends in contracting out

	Number of employees in firm				
	1-50	51-200	201-1000	1001+	Total
	Percentage of respondents mentioning				
A. Contracting out of previously in-house work: Yes					
USA	18	17	17	32	21
Japan	37	26	33	52	36
France	18	35	32	60	34
West Germany	25	24	23	33	26
Great Britain	20	29	37	49	35
B. Intentions of contracting out in the future: More (less)					
USA	14(6)	6(7)	14(0)	26(2)	14(4)
Japan	47(3)	43(9)	31(7)	61(5)	45(6)
France	18(2)	9(4)	18(2)	27(7)	17(3)
West Germany	11(0)	10(2)	10(3)	13(4)	11(2)
Great Britain	15(16)	27(7)	21(2)	42(5)	26(7)

Question A: In the past three years, has your firm contracted out, on a regular basis, to other companies, tasks which were previously done by employees within your firm? Yes/No.

Question B: And do you think that, within the next five years, your firm will contract out, on a regular basis, to other companies, tasks which are currently done by employees within your firm more, less or about the same as now?

Source: *Financial Times* (1986).

Moreover, an average of 18 per cent of respondents in these three member states expected to contract out more work in the next five years, compared with only 4 per cent who expected to contract out less. It is striking that the percentage of firms contracting out and expecting to contract out is much higher for firms employing over 1,000 employees than for smaller firms, who are probably the principal beneficiaries of contracting out.

Comparisons with Non-EC Countries

Since we have no quantitative measure of the weight of employment legislation in different countries, it is not possible to see whether or not there is any direct relationship between that legislation and the rate of unemployment or changes in employment. Certainly there appears to be no relationship between the unemployment rate and the level of employers' social security contributions within the EC.

What has frequently been commented on, however, is the contrast between the flexibility of the labour market in the United States and Europe and the greater buoyancy of employment in North America and Japan compared with Europe. The increase in total civilian employment in the first quarter of 1986 on a seasonally adjusted basis, compared with the trough at the end of 1982, was as follows in the three major regions of the OECD (1986b) was as follows (the figures in parentheses are the increase as a percentage of total employment):

North America	10.8 million	(9.8 per cent)
Japan	1.7 million	(3.0 per cent)
UK, France, West Germany and Italy	1.1 million	(1.2 per cent)
of which UK:	0.9 million	

Not only are unemployment rates in Japan and the United States lower than in the EC, but the proportion of the unemployed who have been out of work for more than 12 months is lower by a factor of 3 or 4.

It is difficult to believe that these striking differences are not, at least in part, connected with the higher incidence of taxation (including social security contributions) and the lesser degree of intervention in labour markets in North America and Japan.

There can be no doubt that employment legislation is less onerous for employers in the United States and in several other OECD countries than in the EC. One very important difference between the United States and the EC is in employment protection. In the United States, the employment relationship is governed by the common law 'hire at will' doctrine, which allows employers to dismiss employees at any time and for any reason. This freedom is limited in practice by collective bargaining in unionized industries, but the level of unionization is much lower than in Europe and there is no statutory counterpart to the laws affecting worker participation.

Despite the so-called life employment system in Japan, employment in some large firms has fallen sharply, while that in small and medium sized firms has increased. As comes out clearly from Table 9.1, contracting out (and also the use of part-time and temporary workers) are used as effective buffers to economic change and fluctuations. Hours of work are more flexible in Japan than in

Europe (or indeed the United States) while statutory regulations for employment security are less rigid (OECD working papers).

SMEs AND SOCIAL LEGISLATION

The General Burden of Government

The first point to be made about social legislation is that it should be seen, as it is seen by SMEs, not in isolation but as a part of the overall burden of government. This burden includes taxation and the collection of taxes, paperwork and other elements in addition to the social legislation more or less directly affecting employment.

Surveys among small business proprietors show that they are very conscious of the burdens of government as a whole. A recent international survey (SKIM, 1984) showed that small firms ranked 'government regulations and paperwork' and 'taxes' together as more important (in terms of numbers of mentions) than any other single problem in three EC countries and in North America (see Table 7.16, p.140). Only in Japan, according to this survey, was the basic problem of realizing sales not overshadowed by the burden of government. While no-one can be expected to like taxation, it is also striking that in all five countries other than Japan, the percentage of mentions of government regulations and paperwork was much higher than for taxes and particularly so for West Germany and The Netherlands. Many other studies and surveys could be quoted to make similar points, e.g. Bannock (1984) and Blenkers (1980).

It is not generally appreciated how heavy the burden of compliance costs of government legislation are for business. (We refer here to the administrative burden alone, not the other direct and indirect costs arising from legislation which are very much greater (see p.264). Various studies of compliance costs are, however, available. Professor Cedric Sandford, whose research on VAT is discussed below, estimates that the total compliance costs for taxation of all types, including personal taxation, in the UK are within the range of 1.5–2 per cent of GDP. The total compliance costs of government legislation, however, is very much greater. For West Germany, the total cost of paperwork imposed on firms alone appears, according to various studies quoted in Dicke and Hartung (1986), to be around 2–4 per cent of GNP. The most recent study, quoted by Tauber (1984), put the figure at 3.7 per cent of GNP, of which tax laws alone accounted for 2.3 per cent. Although not fully comparable, these various studies show a clear upward trend since the first study in 1957.

The Regressive Nature of the Burden

The burden of legislation falls on all firms but is proportionately greater for SMEs. As we saw earlier (p.236), this is recognized in the lighter provisions or exemptions applying to SMEs for some legislation. The reason for the regressive nature of compliance burdens is principally that the administrative resources of small firms are very limited and there are economies of scale in dealing with legislative requirements. Unlike the large firm, the average small business with, say, five employees will be directly managed by its proprietor, perhaps with the assistance of a bookkeeper (often the proprietor's spouse) and, in some higher value added sectors, a secretary. Much of the requirements of legislation will have to be met by the proprietors themselves, therefore, since the work cannot be delegated. One survey of UK firms employing fewer than 100 employees found that between 94 and 96 per cent of business proprietors actually completed the work on VAT and social security themselves (Mendham, 1984).

In a large firm, the volume of work will allow the employment of specialist staff and appropriate computer facilities will be available. Only about 30 per cent or less of small businesses employing fewer than 100 employees have a computer (Small Business Research Trust, 1985). In a large firm specialist advice on matters of taxation, labour and other laws is available in-house; in a small firm, it will probably have to be bought in.

It would not, in fact, be humanly possible for an SME proprietor to keep themselves completely informed on the full range of government requirements that are relevant or potentially relevant to their business while devoting most of their time to that business. This is why all surveys of SMEs reveal lack of awareness of government requirements and why those professionals concerned with advising businesses are being obliged to become increasingly specialized.

Although not widely understood, the extremely regressive nature of compliance burdens has been well established in a number of studies in several countries. A UK study found that the compliance costs for VAT were 40 times higher as a proportion of turnover for firms with a turnover of less than £10,000 than for firms with a turnover of over £1 million (Sandford *et al.*, 1981). A Dutch study valuing time spent on VAT administration, fees to accountants and other associated costs, showed a similar reduction with size of firm (Snijder, 1981). Similar results have been found in studies in the United States for other aspects of regulation and taxation.

West German and Swiss studies of the administrative burden of government legislation as a whole show a similar pattern of a rising burden the smaller the firm. In Switzerland, these costs were 4.5 times greater per person employed in firms with fewer than 20 employees compared with firms with 50–199 employees (Table 9.2). As long ago as 1957, Schmölders calculated that these costs were 2.5 times greater per employee in the Handwerk sector than in West German industry as a whole (in Dicke and Hartung, 1986).

Although we have not had access to any studies which calculate the compliance burden of all employment-related legislation specifically, there can be no doubt that these would, in the nature of things, show the same regressive relationships by size of firm. The same relationship also appears in the incidence of some of the direct costs arising from legislation as well as in the administrative or compliance costs.

One West German study, for example, found that although, as is well known, average total labour costs are significantly lower in SMEs than in large firms (because wages are generally lower), legally required additional labour costs accounted for a higher proportion of total labour costs. These government-imposed costs, such as social security contributions, accounted for 20.8 per cent of total labour costs for firms employing 10–49 persons, 20.3 per cent for firms with 100–199 employees, 19.6 per cent for those with 500–999 employees and 19 per cent for those with 1,000 or more employees. This is because large firms employ a higher proportion of individuals with earnings above the cut-off limit for contributions (Giebel, 1985).

Table 9.2: Cost of administrative burden of government regulations in Switzerland

	No. of employees in firm			
	1-19	20-49	50-199	Total
Cost per firm (Swiss Fr)	9600	19700	35800	23400
Cost per employee (Swiss Fr)	1800	600	400	860

Source: Hunkeler (1984).

Another study in West Germany found that for all firms, for every DM 100 net payment to employees (i.e. net of tax), the employer's total expenditure was DM 273, statutory expenditures alone amounted to 120 per cent of the net direct payment in 1982 (Albach *et al.*, 1985). However, because of the effect of higher contractual and voluntary payments, the ratio of employers' expenditure to net employee payments rose from 2.28 for firms with under 750 employees to 2.74 for firms with 1,250 or more employees. In other words, statutory expenditures were a higher proportion of remuneration paid to employees for small than for large firms.

It is well known that SMEs are less capital intensive on average than large firms (i.e. have less capital employed per employee) (Bolton Committee, 1971) even though it may be changing. This means that many government measures which raise labour costs (or lower capital costs) may have a greater proportional impact on their cost structures than on larger firms.

The Relative Importance of Legislative Burdens

Internationally comparable data on the relative importance of different elements in the burden of government are very limited. A recent survey of small firms carried out for the UK government ranked employment protection as the most frequently mentioned burden after VAT, though other aspects of employment related legislation including sick pay, health and safety and employee taxation administration, were also among the top 10 concerns (see Table 7.17, p.141).

In West Germany, a recent survey carried out by the Institut für Mittelstandsforschung for *Impulse Magazine* ranked the tax burden and social costs as the most frequently mentioned obstacle to expansion. A survey among SMEs, specifically on social legislative burdens, ranked sick pay, handicapped persons (quotas) and employment protection as the three heaviest burdens in social legislation, followed by safety regulations and maternity (Table 9.3).

There is ample evidence for several countries that small business proprietors believe that social legislation, and especially employment-related legislation, has led to lower employment than would otherwise be the case.

Effects Upon Employment

In West Germany, among total mentions of various consequences of social legislation selected from a list, not taking on new employees accounted for 28 per cent, reducing employment for 14 per cent, not expanding for 12 per cent and labour saving investment for 11 per cent (Kayser and Friede, 1984). Both the Research Associates Survey and other surveys carried out by SME representative bodies in the UK found that employers asserted that employment legislation had reduced employment.

Table 9.3: Ranking of government social legislation burdens on business, West Germany

Rank		Burden rating (0 = none, 7 = heavy)
1	Sick pay	3.0
2	Disabled/handicapped	2.3
3	Employment protection - workers	2.2
4	Safety regulations	1.6
5	Maternity	1.5
6	Employee information	1.3
7	Youth employment conditions	1.3
8	Military leave	1.3
9	Working conditions	1.1
10	Employment protection - staff	1.0
11	Redundancy payments	1.0
12	Employers pension costs	0.9
13	Employee information - large firms	0.5

Source: Kayser and Friede (1984)

There are, of course, considerable difficulties in establishing the employment consequences of legislation. Employers may not be able to separate out fully and give true weight to all of the many factors that affect their employment decisions. Loaded questions of the type: 'Has employment protection legislation discouraged you from taking on new employees?' invariably receive a large or significantly affirmative response. Open ended questions of the type: 'What factors have prevented you from taking on new employees?' give social legislation somewhat less importance in employment decisions.

Another officially sponsored study in Britain found that

> Only 6 per cent of small firms interviewed included employment legislation among their three main difficulties: VAT, paperwork and taxation all received higher mentions. However, 'a quarter of all the small firms replied to a direct, prompted question that they would have employed more people if the employment legislation had not existed ... The provisions which caused least concern were the provisions against discrimination by race or sex, the requirement for maternity pay ...

Health and safety legislation received only one third of the mentions of employment legislation (Clifton and Tatton Brown, 1978).

A recent review of the numerous studies on the effects of employment protection legislation on employment in the UK, in fact, concludes that there is 'a considerable body of independent research which reports little or no support for the major contention that employment and industrial legislation has seriously hampered either the wish or the capability of small enterprise owners to maintain or expand their workforce levels' (Curran, 1986). The same review points out that small firm owners are not well informed about the details of employment legislation and that only a tiny proportion (less than 1 per cent) of employment terminations involve recourse to industrial tribunals for reinstatement or compensation.

These conclusions, in our view, give insufficient weight to the inherent difficulties of research into these matters and to the very real possibility that fears about the consequences of employment legislation increase the perceived risks of taking on new employees and lead some firms to prefer part-time and contract workers. However, there must be considerable doubt about how important a barrier to employment is, employment protection legislation, as distinct from other social legislation which significantly increases the costs of employment.

The *Financial Times* (1986) international survey cited earlier (p.241) throws some further light on these issues. Of the three EC member states included, 54 per cent of respondents in West Germany and 41 per cent in France considered that changes in employment legislation would be important in influencing employment over the next two years (Table 9.4). In Britain this proportion was only 17 per cent. These differences may be explained by the fact that employment protection legislation in Britain has been considerably eased since 1980 whereas in France and West Germany, at the time of the survey, it remained the subject of a lively debate.

The low affirmative response to this question for Japan was to be expected, but the percentage for the United States was the highest of all. Although as we saw earlier (p.242), employment legislation is less burdensome on employers in the United States than in Europe, the situation there is changing. There is a widespread trend at state level in the USA towards mandatory health care insurance and other benefits and restrictions on employers' treatment of employees. There have also been recent proposals for federal legislation in these areas (Small Business Administration, 1986).

What is particularly interesting about Table 9.4 is that there is a clear tendency in all countries for the percentage of respondents selecting employment legislation from a list of factors influencing employment to increase with the size of firm. This tendency does not continue beyond 1,000 employees and is weaker beyond 200 employees, which suggests that exemptions for SMEs may provide a partial explanation.

Table 9.4: Influences on employment over the next two years

		Percentage of respondents mentioning				
	Rank	No. of employees in firm				
		1-50	51-200	201-1000	1001+	Total
Changes to government employment legistlation						
USA	9	47	63	72	57	61
Japan	8	3	16	15	16	14
France	10	50	60	59	43	54
West Germany	10	38	41	48	37	41
Great Britain	13	11	24	19	15	17
Profitability						
USA	1	86	93	84	83	87
Japan	2	63	64	72	59	64
France	1	76	82	77	87	80
West Germany	1	75	79	85	77	79
Great Britain	2	56	67	56	63	61

Question: Which of the factors listed below will be important in influencing future employment in your firm over the next two years?

Source: *Financial Times* (1986).

Equally striking, however, is the fact that in all cases employment legislation comes towards the bottom of the ranking of factors selected. Profitability was clearly considered the prime influence on employment along with the level of demand, costs and competition. But note that labour costs, including non-wage labour costs influenced by legislation, will affect profitability.

Table 9.5 shows the responses to a different question which again required respondents to select from a list of factors that might lead to increased employment. Only two elements of social legislation were included. The abolition of minimum wage legislation generally received a low proportion of mentions. As might be expected in Europe, the proportion was highest for the smallest firms and lower in Britain where there is no general minimum wage level.

Table 9.5: Factors that would encourage increases in employment

		Percent of respondents mentioning				
	Rank	No. of employees in firm				
		1-50	51-200	201-1000	1001+	Total
Abolition of minimum wages legislation						
USA	8	12	19	21	4	14
Japan	7	0	3	2	2	2
France	9	6	4	2	3	4
West Germany	8	11	10	5	10	9
Great Britain	9	5	2	3	5	4
Relaxation of laws on part-time working						
USA	4	18	20	26	13	20
Japan	4	7	21	15	20	17
France	2	44	46	55	40	46
West Germany	3	29	48	43	44	41
Great Britain	8	7	4	5	3	5

Question: Which of the following changes do you think would induce your firm to increase employment over the next two years?

Source: *Financial Times* (1986).

The proportion of mentions of laws on part-time working, however, was much higher and came in the upper half of the rankings, even in the non-EC states. The proportion was highest in France where these laws have recently been tightened, but was again lower in Britain where they are less onerous. There was a tendency for the proportion of mentions to rise with size of firm up to 1,000 employees.

Conclusion

There are considerable difficulties in carrying out conclusive research into the employment effects of social legislation. Most research effort has been devoted to asking employers about their reactions to this legislation, which are inevitably rather hostile, rather than to actually measuring costs and consequences. There are no rigorous studies of either type covering a large number of EC states, though it is clear that since the burden of legislation varies between countries, the impact will differ. National attitudes to such legislation also appear to differ.

There can be no doubt that any legislation which imposes administrative burdens, as all social legislation does, bears more heavily on SMEs than on larger firms. This must diminish the relative competitiveness of SMEs. The direct cost implications of certain types of social legislation must, in addition, tend to reduce employment in all firms below the levels that would exist in the absence of the legislation through the substitution of capital for labour, part-time for full-time employees, and through its unfavourable effects on the risk-reward ratio.

To judge how important a barrier to employment social legislation actually is, is a different matter. We consider that the available evidence points to considerable differences in the employment impact of the various types of social legislation. Given the inherent difficulties in research in effects of employment protection, it is not surprising that there should be conflicting evidence and some paradoxical results. The strong feelings on employment legislation shown in all surveys in which direct questions are asked, contrast with the lack of concrete evidence on the employment consequences of this legislation and the apparent result from one survey that concern does not seem to be greater in small firms than in medium and larger firms.

Our conclusion on the first class of social legislation, employment protection and redundancy compensation is that, as Layard (1986) points out, these may discourage both sackings and discourage taking on new employees, and the two effects may well cancel out each other. Whether this is so or not, all the evidence suggests that the direct impact of these measures is relatively minor, though the effects of changes in restrictions on the use of part-time and contract workers suggest that they are not negligible. An important qualification to be made is that the negative impact of employment protection may be greater in some countries, for example Belgium, than in the UK where the provisions are less stringent and from where much of our evidence is drawn.

In a second group are laws on race and sex discrimination, health and safety and environmental protection. These laws seem to be generally accepted, even where they raise costs and do not seem in general to be attributed by employers as a serious barrier to employment, except in the case of some health and safety and environmental provisions in particular industries. In any event, strong political consensus through Europe would prevent any significant weakening of these provisions.

In a third group come all those provisions which significantly raise labour costs and range in ascending scale of impact from minimum wages, holidays and conditions of work to employers' social security contributions. These may well have a much bigger impact on employment though it is impossible to quantify this.

Other unquantifiable effects of social legislation, however, need to be distinguished. The impact of any single measure needs to be assessed in the context of the total burden on business enterprise which it imposes. This total burden includes not merely social legislation as we have defined it here, but the whole range of government requirements. These are now very considerable and continue to grow (Table 9.6). Even though many new and very small firms will be unaware of all their obligations, the total weight of them must restrict and retard the establishment and growth of enterprise.

The psychological effects of this burden on the entrepreneurial spirit also need to be taken into account. Fear of getting things wrong or innocently contravening the law, through lack of understanding of often complex legislation, must have a negative impact. Moreover, some laws, such as those in West Germany which, we are told, ban gas-filled struts and require 1.5 m on typists' chairs, or in the UK require fire-proof doors in sink alcoves mistakenly classified as kitchens, are patently absurd, waste the time of businesspeople and government officials alike and bring the law into disrepute.

While it is difficult to point to any single aspect of legislation which seriously curtails employment in SMEs, there can be no doubt that the cumulative burden of all legislation does do so.

IMPLICATIONS FOR POLICY

The Role of SMEs

It is now well established that in the past decade or so, small firms have played a major role in net employment creation and, in many countries, large firms have been shedding jobs faster than SMEs have created them. A recent survey by the OECD Secretariat usefully summarizes some of the research on this subject and confirms that the increasing share of SMEs in total employment in several countries, both within and outside the EC, cannot be wholly explained by a shift to service industries (Organisation for Economic Co-operation and Development, 1985b). There is evidence that this trend can be expected to continue. Table 9.7 shows that among respondents to the *Financial Times* survey, it is SMEs rather than large firms which expect to create jobs in the future.

Table 9.6: Government burdens on business

1. EMPLOYMENT PROTECTION
    - 1.1 Legislation on dismissals, redundancy, maternity leave, employment contracts, working hours, employment of disabled persons, discrimination against race or sex
    - 1.2 Legislation on minimum wages, indexation, forms of remuneration
    - 1.3 Laws affecting collective agreements, participation and information
    - 1.4 Laws on training and apprenticeships

2. THE COLLECTION AND PAYMENT OF TAXES AND GRANTS
    - 2.1 Collection and payment of social security contributions and income taxes for employees. Payments of benefit
    - 2.2 Collection and payment of value added tax, sales taxes and other special taxes such as excise duties
    - 2.3 Payment of national and local income taxes, payroll and property taxes
    - 2.4 Application for grants and rebates

3. HEALTH AND SAFETY
    - 3.1 Working conditions: space, heat, light
    - 3.2 Accident prevention
    - 3.3 Fire prevention
    - 3.4 Pollution
    - 3.5 Compulsory insurance
    - 3.6 Planning restrictions on the construction of new buildings and the usage of existing buildings

4. THE PROVISION OF INFORMATION
    - 4.1 Direct - Data on employees and their remuneration, statistics on a variety of matters, assistance with official inspections and investigations
    - 4.2 Indirect - Comments on proposed and present legislation and policy, principally via trade and employers' associations

5. OTHER LAWS
   Planning and construction, consumer law, privacy laws, customs and exchange control. Company reporting and business registration laws, monopoly and restrictive practices laws

6. INDUSTRY SPECIFIC
   Transport, catering, alcohol, agricultural, placement agencies, home rentals, state monopolies, etc.

Table 9.7: Employers' expectations for future employment

	Percentage of respondents mentioning				
	No. of Employees in firm				
	1-50	51-200	201-1000	1001+	Total
USA					
More	51	54	60	38	51
Same	41	37	34	34	37
Fewer	8	7	5	28	11
Total	100	100	100	100	100
Japan					
More	40	41	35	39	38
Same	53	38	35	39	40
Fewer	0	12	24	21	16
Total	100	100	100	100	100
France					
More	26	35	27	17	28
Same	60	42	45	33	46
Fewer	6	21	27	50	23
Total	100	100	100	100	100
West Germany					
More	35	31	27	38	32
Same	51	60	48	35	49
Fewer	11	9	23	25	17
Total	100	100	100	100	100
Great Britain					
More	49	49	23	22	35
Same	47	44	48	47	47
Fewer	2	7	27	31	17
Total	100	100	100	100	100

Question: Looking forward two years from now, do you expect your organization to be employing more people, the same number or fewer compared to today?

Note: Totals include non-respondents.

Source: *Financial Times* (1986).

The case for promoting SMEs is now widely accepted, though the reassessment of their economic role, which has been undervalued in the past, should not be narrowly focused on their direct contribution to employment. SMEs are equally important in promoting structural change, flexibility and export competitiveness, in short, in dynamic economic adjustment (Bannock, 1981).

Changing Priorities

The enormous increase in the role of the state in economic affairs during the past 100 years or so, and particularly in the period following World War II, has borne more heavily on SMEs than on large firms, and a major reassessment of the impact of the burden of the State on these firms is now necessary. This differential impact does not result simply from the differential incidence of compliance costs but from differences in the impact of taxation, public purchasing and other factors.

This does not mean a return to the *laissez faire* conditions of the nineteenth century; this is neither necessary nor appropriate in contemporary conditions. However, it does mean that all government requirements should be reassessed in the light of the changing balance between the desire to promote social welfare and the needs of the private business sector, which provides most of the necessary resources.

Some Proposed Principles

By way of conclusion, we set out below some principles which we suggest might guide this reassessment:

1 Since complexity discriminates against SMEs, there is a prime need to simplify and codify government requirements of business. Radical simplification will not be achieved, however, without some actual reduction in the number and scope of measures. Since it is the overall burden that seems to count rather than a few isolated measures, this leaves relatively unhindered scope for political decisions on priorities. For example, while employment protection legislation does not appear significantly to protect employment, except at the expense of marginal workers, by the same token it is probably not a serious barrier to employment by SMEs and could be retained at a modest cost if that were a political priority.

2 As far as is practicable, all measures should be designed or redesigned to be neutral in their impact by size of firm. This principle has already been accepted for some legislation through giving exemptions for the smallest firms and, in other cases, by compensatory devices (for example, in West Germany and The Netherlands SMEs are allowed to retain a proportion of the VAT they collect to compensate them partially for the administrative burden).

3 Social legislation needs to be harmonized throughout the Community in the interests of promoting equality of costs and competition in the internal market. This harmonization provides an opportunity for the simplification and lightening of burdens on SMEs. If this is to be achieved, then some levelling down of requirements will be necessary. In the past, the EC has sometimes been a force for increasing the legislative burden through levelling up.

4 Impact statements for new and harmonized legislation should include separately an assessment of the direct cost implications and the compliance or administrative costs for firms, and not just direct costs alone. This is important because the latter may, in some cases, be much higher than the former. Impacts should be assessed both before legislation is introduced and afterwards.

5 As far as possible, social costs which are not sector specific should be borne by society as a whole through general taxation rather than by business in ways which distort business decisions and consumer choice. It is appropriate that business should pass on to consumers the costs of preventing environmental pollution in the production of certain products. It is not clear, however, why business should bear the administrative costs of collecting taxes, for example, or maternity costs or the non-employment of handicapped persons. This is particularly the case where these costs fall more heavily on SMEs, and therefore distort the size structure of the business population and lead to a less than optimum level of output and employment.

STATISTICAL APPENDIX

Table A.1: Employment legislation: non-manual workers – redundancy and periods of notice, 1983

	Length of Service	Period of Notice[a] (months)
Belgium		
Employees earning BFr 250,000 or less	Under 5 years	3
	5 - 10 years	6
	10 - 15 years	9
	15 - 20 years	12
	20 - 25 years	15
	25 - 30 years	18
Employees earning over BFr 250,000	Minimum as above Actual period to be agreed at time of notice or determined by arbitration	
Denmark	Under 6 months	1
	6 months - 3 years	3
	3 - 6 years	4
	6 - 9 years	5
	9 years and over	6
France	6 months - 2 years	1
	2 years and over	2
	plus 1/10 of a month's earnings for each year of service	
West Germany[b]	Minimum	1½
	8 years after age 25	4
	10 years after age 25	5
	12 years after age 25	6
Greece	2 months - 1 year	1
	1 - 4 years	2
	4 - 6 years	3
	6 - 8 years	4
	8 - 10 years	5
	plus for every full year after the 10th year	1
	Maximum	24
Irish Republic	13 weeks - 2 years	1 week
	2 - 5 years	2 weeks
	5 - 10 years	4 weeks
	10 - 15 years	6 weeks
	15 years and over	8 weeks
Italy	Periods of notice vary according to earnings level.	
Luxembourg	Under 5 years	2
	5 - 10 years	4
	Over 10 years	6
The Netherlands	Minimum	1
	plus	
	For each year	1 week (maximum 13)
	For each year over age 45	1 week (maximum 13)
UK	1 month - 2 years	1 week
	2 - 12 years	1 week for each year
	12 years and over	12 weeks minimum

a) Period of notice or earnings equivalent to be given by the employer
b) Rules apply only to enterprises employing more than six persons

Source: National legislation

Table A.2: Redundancy: comparative position of manual and non-manual workers with selected career characteristics,* 1983

	Period of notice or equivalent earnings in lieu of notice				
	Manual worker (days)			Non-manual worker (months)	
Characteristics of individual					
- Age	30 years	50 years		30 years	30 years
- Length of service	6 years	21 years		6 years	6 years
Belgium	28	56	earnings under BFr 250,000	6	15
			Earnings under BFr 250,000	8	30
Denmark	49	49		5	6
France	73†	115†		2 1/2†	4†
West Germany	14	56		1 1/2	6
Greece	30	60		4	17
Irish Republic	28	56		1	2
Italy	31.‡	55.‡		1 1/2‡	3‡
Luxembourg	56	84		4	6
The Netherlands	49	91		2 1/2	3 1/4
UK	42	84		1 1/2	3

† Includes the time equivalent of 1/10 of a month's earnings per year of service.
‡ EIU estimate.

*Refer to following comments on practices in Community countries.
Includes the time equivalent ofo 1/10 of a month's earnings per year of service EIU estimate
Source: EIU assessments based on national legislation.

Table A.3: Social security: employers' contribution as percentage of average earnings of manual workers in manufacturing, mid–1983

Country	Employers' contribution (% of average earnings)
Belgium	30.09
Denmark	15.00
France	19.34
West Germany	21.00
Greece	21.75
Irish Republic	9.80
Italy	45.93
Luxembourg	12.20
The Netherlands	23.90
UK	11.45

Source: EIU calculations based on national security regimes, EIU (1983).

Table A4: Proportion of self-employment to civilian employment in the non-agricultural sector

	Percentages				
	1969	1973	1979	1981	1984
Australia	9.3	9.5	12.4	12.1	12.4
Austria[a]	13.1	11.7	8.9	8.6	7.9
Belgium	11.9[b]	11.0	11.2	11.5	12.3
Canada	-	5.8[c]	6.7	6.4	7.4
Denmark	-	9.7[c]	9.2	8.3	8.4[d]
Finland	-	-	-	-	6.9
France	-	9.7	8.7	8.7	9.1[d]
West Germany	8.3	7.6	7.7	7.6	8.2
Greece	-	-	-	27.8	27.3
Iceland[a]	10.2	8.3	7.0	7.0	7.3[d]
Ireland	9.6[e]	10.1	10.4	9.6	11.4
Italy	-	17.8	18.7	19.6	20.6[d]
Japan	14.6	14.1	14.0	13.6	13.0
The Netherlands	-	3.7[c]	4.1	5.6	4.9[d]
New Zealand	7.5[e]	9.1[f]	-	8.4	-
Norway	7.6[g]	7.6	6.4	6.6	6.3
Portugal	-	11.5[h]	12.1	11.6	-
Spain	16.1[b]	16.3	15.9	16.3	17.9
Sweden	5.6[b]	4.8	4.5	4.6	4.6
Switzerland	7.6[b]	-	7.5[i]	-	-
Turkey	25.0[b]	25.0[c]	20.8[i]	-	-
United Kingdom[j]	6.5	7.3	6.6	7.9	9.6
United States	7.0	6.7	7.1	7.3	7.6
Unweighted average[k]	-	9.5	9.4	9.5	9.9
Coefficient of variation (%)[k]	-	40	42	42	44

Notes

[a] Data include unpaid family workers

[b] 1970. [c] 1975. [d] 1983. [e] 1971. [f] 1976. [g] 1972. [h] 1974. [i] 1980.

[j] Data may include some unpaid family workers.

[k] Summary statistics are calculated excluding Finland, Greece, New Zealand, Portugal, Switzerland and Turkey.

Sources: Organisation for Economic Co-operation and Development (1986b). Australia, Austria, Belgium, Canada, West Germany, Iceland, Ireland, Japan, Portugal, Spain, Sweden, The United Kingdom and The United States: OECD Labour Force Statistics; Denmark, France and Italy: Eurostat, Labour Force Sample Survey; Finland: Data supplied by Central Statistical Office, based on the Labour Force Survey; Greece: Data supplied by Service National de Statistiques; The Netherlands: Central Bureau of Statistics Labour Force Survey; Norway: Data supplied by the Central Bureau of Statistics; Switzerland: Data supplied by Office Fédéral de la Statistique based on the Population Censuses of 1970 and 1980; New Zealand and Turkey: International Labour Organisation, *Yearbook of Labour Statistics*.

NOTE

[1] Working Party on Labour Market Flexibility, *Final Report*, 20 September 1985. We have drawn heavily upon this document in this report and also upon working documents on job security provided to us by the Directorate for Social Affairs, Manpower and Education of the OECD.

REFERENCES

Albach, H. *et al.*, (1985), *Kosten der Arbeit*, Poeschel, Stuttgart.

Bannock, G. (1981), *The Economics of Small Firms*, Basil Blackwell, Oxford.

Bannock, G. (1984), *Surveys of Forum Members*, The Forum of Private Business.

Belmont (1987), *EC Legislative Obligations in Respect of Small and Medium Sized Enterprises, Final Report*, Brussels.

Blenkers, F. Klein (1980), *Beiträge zur Mittelstandsforschung*, Verlag Otto Schwartz

Bolton Committee (1971), *Small Firms, Report of the Committee of Inquiry on Small Firms*, HMSO, London.

Clifton, R. and Tatton Brown, C. (1978), *Impact of Legislation on Small Firms*, Department of Employment Research Paper No.6.

Commission of the European Communities (1985), *Report on Social Developments*, Year 1984.

Commission of the European Communities (1986), *Draft Resolution of the Council Concerning the Action Programme for SME*, COM(86) 445 final, Brussels, 7 August.

Curran, J. (1986), *Bolton Fifteen Years On: A Review and Analysis of Small Business Research in Britain 1971–86*, Small Business Research Trust.

Department of Employment (1984), *Employers' Use of Homework, Outwork and Freelancers*, (Catherine Hakim), *Employment Gazette*, April.

Department of Employment (1986), *Building Businesses ... Not Barriers*, HMSO, London.

Dicke H. and Hartung, H. (1986), *Entwicklung von Verfahren zu Ermittlung Externer Kosten von Rechtsvorschriften*, Institut für Weltwirtschaft an der Universität Kiel.

Economist Intelligence Unit (1983), *The European Climate for Small Businesses*, A 10-Country Study.

Financial Times (1986), *International Research into Attitudes to Employment*, Social Surveys (Gallup Poll) Ltd, June (unpublished tabulations).

Giebel, U. (1985), *Sozialleistungen und Unternehmens Grossenstruktur, Untersuchung zur Wirtschaftspolitik*, Institut für Wirtschaftspolitik, Universität zu Koln.

Hamermesh, D.S. (1985), *Job Security Policy and Labour Demand: Theory and Evidence*, Michigan State University for OECD (Mimeo).

Hunkeler, U. (1984), Doctoral Thesis, Schweizerisches Institut für Gewerbliche Wirtschaft and der Hochschule St Gallen für Wirtschafts- und Sozialwissenshaften.

Institute of Manpower Studies (1986), *Temporary Work in Britain*, (Nigel Meager), *Employment Gazette*, January.

Kayser, G. and Friede, C. (1984), *Wirkungsanalyse der Sozialgesetzgebung*, Institut für Mittelstandsforschung, Bonn.

Layard, R. (1986), *How to Beat Unemployment*, Oxford University Press.

Layard, R. and Nickell, S. (1985), *The causes of British unemployment*, *National Institute Economic Review*, February.

Mendham, S. (1984), *Exploiting and Overcoming Government Regulations — An Entrepreneur's Viewpoint*, Forum of Private Business.

Nickell, S. (1982), *The determinants of equilibrium unemployment in Britain*, *Economic Journal*, September.

Organisation for Economic Co-operation and Development (1985a), *Revenue Statistics of OECD Member Countries*, OECD.

Organisation for Economic Co-operation and Development (1985b), *OECD Employment Outlook*, OECD.

Organisation for Economic Co-operation and Development (1986a), *Revenue Statistics of OECD Member Countries*, OECD.
Organisation for Economic Co-operation and Development (1986b), *OECD Employment Outlook*, OECD.
Peacock, A. (ed) (1984), *The Regulation Game*, Basil Blackwell, Oxford.
Sandford, C. *et al.*, (1981), *Costs and Benefits of VAT*, Heinemann, London.
Skim Industrial Market Research (1984), *International Small Business Survey*, Rotterdam.
Small Business Administration (1986), *Issue Handbook*, The White House Conference on Small Business, Washington DC.
Small Business Research Trust (1985), *Quarterly Survey of Small Business in Britain*, Vol.1, no.3.
Small Business Research Trust (1986), *Quarterly Survey of Small Business in Britain*, Vol.2, no.3.
Snijder, M.A. (1981), *De Invloed van de Fiscus op Het Midden – en-Kleinbedrijf*, Fed – Oeventer, Amsterdam.
Tauber, G. (1984), *Folgekosten der Besteuerung*, Spardorf.

Chapter 10

REMOVING GOVERNMENT BURDENS ON SMALLER ENTERPRISES*

INTRODUCTION

The post-World War II period saw a substantial increase in government revenues as a percentage of the gross domestic product in all OECD countries, and with it a rapid extension in both public expenditure on welfare and in the role of the State in economic affairs. The decade or so of slow growth and greater inflationary pressures which began in the early 1970s has led to some curtailment in the growth of public expenditure and has been accompanied by a reassessment of the burdens placed by government on business. This has occurred at a time when the creation of jobs in the private sector has become an overriding objective of economic policy.

Although government burdens are borne by all economic units, including state-owned enterprises, and may be partly or wholly passed on to consumers, they bear most heavily on small and medium enterprises (SMEs) and particularly on new enterprises, which are the major source of employment growth in many countries. The paper therefore focuses on lifting the burdens on SMEs. The next section briefly reviews the latest thinking on the economic role of SMEs. Subsequent sections discuss the nature of government burdens, why they matter and the inherent difficulties in containing them. The final two sections review international experience in attempting to reduce government burdens. Bureaucratic burdens are not the only obstacles to the development of SMEs that lie within the government sphere of influence but positive initiatives, such as measures to improve the functioning of capital markets, lie outside the scope of this paper.

---

* A paper commissioned by the Ministry of State, Turkey and the Technical Co-operation Service of the Organisation for Economic Co-operation and Development (OECD) to provide a framework for discussions at a symposium on *Lifting the Burden* held under their auspices in Istanbul, 11 – 12 January 1988. We gratefully acknowledge permission from the sponsors to reproduce the text here. Neither the Ministry of State nor the OECD is responsible for the views expressed.

THE ROLE OF SMEs

Up to the mid-1960s or later, the share of SMEs in output and employment had been falling over the long term in most advanced OECD countries (Japan was a notable exception). This was generally seen as an inevitable consequence of the importance of economies of scale in modern production technique and in research and development, influenced by other factors such as the growth in international trade (Bannock, 1981).

However, the rise in unemployment in the 1970s has led to a re-appraisal of the role of SMEs. Research carried out in the United States and the United Kingdom, published in 1979, and later in other countries, demonstrated that SMEs had recently played a disproportionately large role in employment creation (Organisation for Economic Co-operation and Development, 1985). Other research had earlier demonstrated the persistence of SMEs in all sectors, of the economy, including advanced technology sectors and the major contributions of SMEs to invention and innovation, highlighting the efficiency with which SMEs made use of scarce resources of skilled manpower and capital. More recently, attention has also been increasingly drawn in some countries to the role of SMEs in facilitating shifts in economic resources from declining to expanding sectors and in their functions in on-the-job training, the regeneration of decayed inner city areas and the promotion of competition among other things. As a result of this reappraisal, virtually all OECD member countries are now pursuing policies to promote SMEs despite, in some quarters, reservations about the quality of jobs created in the small firm sector. In some countries these measures are relatively recent, though in others (West Germany, Japan and the United States, for example) there is a much longer history of small business promotion.

This reappraisal has been global in scope and has taken place in many countries including China and the developing world, as well as in the OECD member countries. Disenchanted with the results of the promotion of large scale investment projects which were heavily dependent on foreign capital, enterprise and technology for example, in the late 1960s many developing countries began to turn their attention to small scale industry (SSI) as offering more potential for truly indigenous development. In the mid-1970s the World Bank began to shift the balance of its development efforts towards SSI which provided more jobs per unit of investment than larger ones and the World Bank and other international agencies such as the United Nations Development Programme and the International Labour Organization became more heavily involved in the provision of technical assistance, particularly in the field of technology appropriate to SSI (World Bank, 1978).

In fact, in all OECD member countries, SMEs account for the vast majority of all enterprises (well over 95 per cent), but their share of employment differs considerably. For example, enterprises employing fewer than 500 persons account for about 67 per cent of employment in manufacturing in Japan, but only 33 per cent in the United Kingdom (Organisation for Economic Co-operation and Development, 1985).

Comprehensive statistics on SMEs are not available for Turkey, but we know that some 21 per cent of civilian employment in the non-agricultural sector is self employed, compared with 28 per cent for Greece, 19 per cent for Italy and 6–8 per cent in the UK, United States and West Germany (Organisation for Economic Co-operation and Development, 1985). There are some 1.7 million VAT registered traders in Turkey compared with 1.5 million in the UK and 1.9 million in West Germany, although the turnover threshold at which VAT registration is compulsory is TL 5 million in Turkey ($5,800), £20,500 in the UK ($31,800) and DM 20,000 in West Germany ($10,600).

THE NATURE OF GOVERNMENT BURDENS

Table 9.6 (p.252) listed the principle taxation, regulatory and other burdens imposed by government on business in the OECD member countries. These burdens are of two types: those which apply to all or most businesses (categories 1–5) and industry-specific burdens or restrictions, which apply in addition to businesses in particular sectors (category 6). Government burdens are far from identical under each of these headings between countries; for example, there is less intervention in labour markets in North America and Japan than in the European Community, but virtually all countries impose legislative burdens of some kind under all the headings in the table.

The burdens of government impose two broad types of costs on business. First, there is the *direct cost*, for example the cost of employers' social security contributions or other taxes paid over to the government or the cost of installing equipment to control emissions at a factory. Under this heading we may also place the cost of delays incurred as a result of legislation, for example the cost of expensive machinery or premises which cannot be used productively until necessary permissions are obtained. We might also include the profit lost through restrictions on freedom of action, for example to enter a market or complete an acquisition and losses of competitive advantage through, for example, enforced disclosure of information in company accounts filed for public inspection. Important as they are, we are not concerned in this paper with these direct costs.

Second, over and above these direct costs there will be *compliance costs* involved in meeting legislative requirements. These will consist of the cost of the time needed to understand the law, in dealing with the necessary paperwork, visits to government offices and in training and paying staff where necessary to carry out this work. In many cases there will also be paid out costs to legal advisers or accountants as, for example, in the preparation of audited accounts for company law and tax law purposes, and possibly costs of storing information or modifying computer programs or administrative procedures to meet government requirements.

Although relatively little work has so far been carried out in assessing the weight of these burdens (see p.262) and their relative importance, some indications are available in addition to the representations made in all countries by trade and other business associations. Surveys among small business proprietors show that they are very conscious of the burdens of government as a whole. A recent international survey showed that small firms ranked 'government regulations and paperwork' and 'taxes' together as more important (in terms of numbers of mentions) than any other single problem in the United States, Canada, the UK, West Germany and The Netherlands (see Table 7.16, p.140). Of the six advanced OECD countries covered in the survey, only in Japan was the basic problem of realizing sales not overshadowed by the burden of government. The survey also showed that the percentage of mentions of government regulations and paperwork was much higher than for taxes (again with the exception of Japan).

In discussion, many business people are reluctant to rank the burdens of government in order of weight or even to express views about which of the burdens are unreasonable. It is accepted that there are good intentions behind most government requirements, what is regarded as unreasonable is the total burden, which is also seen to be aggravated by unnecessary complexity, obscurity and slowness of response on the part of the public administration.

The relative importance of government burdens clearly varies from country to country and from firm to firm. Some industries, for example, are more closely regulated than others, while individual firms will encounter different aspects of legislation at various points in their life-cycle. Table 7.17 (p.141) and Table 9.3 (p.246) present the results of two surveys in the UK and West Germany.

In the UK, an officially commissioned survey of small firms found VAT at the head of the list in terms of numbers of mentions, though local authority planning regulations received the highest score in a ranking of seriousness. Clearly, planning regulations are a major problem, particularly when the fact that most firms will only need planning permission when they are moving, setting up or modifying premises is taken into account in interpreting the rankings (see Table 7.17, p.141).

A similar survey of all sizes of firm in West Germany was restricted to the burden of social legislation (see Table 9.3, p.246). Sick pay and requirements for the employment of disabled or handicapped persons (for which mandatory quotas which can be bought off for a 'fine' apply for all but the smallest firms) came at the top of the list, and, as in the UK, employment protection legislation was also ranked highly.

On the basis of this and other information we estimate that in EC member states, taxation including social security, planning regulations and legislation are generally regarded as giving rise to the heaviest burdens on business, though the ranking might well be different in particular sectors of the economy.

Appendix 10.1 displays the findings of a study carried out in the UK on the procedures that have to be complied with by an entrepreneur setting up a new business. The appendix summarizes the key features of the process and shows how many public bodies are involved.

WHY BURDENS MATTER

It is not easy for officials in public administration to appreciate the weight of the burden their activities place on business or the urgent necessity to reduce it. This is partly because few of these officials have personal experience in business administration and particularly few in small business. The proportion of all public administration staff actually in contact with business people in the course of their daily work is inevitably low, and those who do have such contact are of relatively junior status (for example counter staff).

Another difficulty is that officials are fully aware only of the procedures for which they are responsible and not those of their colleagues. Business people, by contrast, are dealing with all of them and are obliged to inform themselves about all requirements of government (ignorance of the law is no excuse) in addition to their prime task of running their business. Officials are trained and indeed obliged to enforce the law, and see compliance with the law as an absolute requirement whatever the cost or consequences.

Most business people in SMEs know that the laws affecting business are so wide ranging and complex that it is quite impossible for any single individual to be familiar with all of them or to run a business without transgressing some minor law or regulation, if only through ignorance. Surveys of SMEs in several countries have shown a low degree of familiarity with many aspects of legislation affecting business. Finally, while business people face sanctions if they do not meet government requirements and officials face sanctions if they knowingly allow transgressions, the imposition of unnecessary burdens on business imposes no obvious cost or sanction on the officials involved.

Not least of the reasons why the weight of the burden on business is not widely appreciated within government is that it has not anywhere been properly measured and is, in fact, a social cost of large but unknown magnitude. Nor has the rate at which this burden has increased over the past 40 years or so been measured.

Some indications are, however, available. Professor Cedric Sandford of the University of Bath has tentatively estimated that the total compliance costs (excluding what we have called direct costs and the government's own collection costs) of taxation of all types, including personal taxation, in the UK, are within the range of 1.5–2 per cent of GDP. The total compliance costs of legislation are, however, very much greater than this. For West Germany, the total cost of business compliance has been estimated, according to various studies quoted in a recent review, to be around 2–4 per cent of GNP (Dicke and Hartung, 1986). The most recent study quoted in this review put the figure at 3.7 per cent of GNP, of which taxation compliance alone accounted for 2.3 per cent (over 60 per cent of the total). Although not fully comparable, these various studies show a clear upward trend since the first study in 1957.

If compliance costs of all kinds for business are indeed of the order of 3–4 per cent of GNP in advanced OECD countries then this represents a very substantial use of resources. It should be remembered that these costs do not include the government's own costs, nor do they include what we have called direct costs to employers which, it could be argued, are offset by net social benefits (contributions to pensions, welfare, etc.) The government's own administrative costs of business taxation and regulations are, of course, very substantial indeed. It would be interesting to calculate them (for VAT it has been shown that the government's costs are about one-fifth of the costs to business) but that lies outside the scope of this paper.

It is an arresting thought, however, that the compliance costs of business taxation and regulation (excluding the direct costs) might be of the same order of magnitude as expenditure on defence in several major OECD countries or as much as double the total value added in the primary sector (agriculture, forestry and fishing) in, for example, the UK or West German economies.

Perhaps more important than the overall scale of government burdens is the fact that they bear most heavily on the smallest businesses. The regressive nature of compliance burdens results from the limited administrative resources in small firms and the scope for economies of scale in dealing with government requirements. In small firms employing five or fewer persons (the majority) the business will normally be directly managed by the proprietor, perhaps with some administrative assistance from a spouse. Since they cannot be delegated, much of the requirements of legislation will involve the proprietor's own time, which is the most valuable resource in the business.

In a large firm, the volume of work will allow the employment of specialist staff and, where appropriate, computer facilities. Specialist advice on legal or tax matters will be available in-house; in a small firm it will probably have to be bought in. SMEs operating in more competitive markets may also be less able than large firms to pass on compliance costs to their customers. Studies of compliance costs for taxation or other aspects of the burden of government have been carried out in a number of countries, including West Germany, The Netherlands, Switzerland and the United States. All these studies illustrate a steeply regressive burden according to size of firm.

In a very recent survey in Britain and West Germany, a sample of small firms in each country was asked to give the number of man-days spent entirely on VAT work and the amount spent per annum on outside professional help for the same purpose. After valuing the cost of the time spent and adding it to the expenditure on outside help and expressing that average total as a percentage of turnover for firms in different size classes, it can be seen in Figure 8.1 (p. 184) that in both countries costs fall steeply by size of firm. In fact, costs as a percentage of turnover were 2.5 per cent of turnover in the UK (West Germany 7.8 per cent) for the smallest size band and only 0.07 per cent (0.02 per cent) for the small firms at the top of the size range. Costs as a proportion of turnover were 36 times higher for the smallest compared with the largest firms in the UK sample and very much higher than that in West Germany. (The survey was restricted to SMEs.)

Value added tax imposes a particularly disproportionate compliance burden on very small firms; for government requirements as a whole the compliance burden may be less regressive. A study in Switzerland indicated that these total costs were 4.5 times greater per person employed in firms with fewer than 20 employees compared with firms with 50 – 199 employees (Hunkeler, 1984).

No attempt anywhere has yet been made to estimate the overall impact of government burdens on employment and economic performance, though this impact is clearly negative and, given the scale of the resources involved, it must be considerable. Moreover, not all of the dimensions of the differential burden on SMEs are captured by the studies discussed above. Government burdens, for example, impose psychic costs on small business proprietors which have not been measured. Fear of unwittingly contravening regulations may cause anxiety for some business people and perceptions of the burden of regulation may deter people from starting up new businesses or expanding existing ones. It is to be expected that the direct costs of regulation will also be regressive. For example, larger firms, able to afford the best professional advice, may be able to avoid some of the direct costs; this is likely to be particularly true of the tax burden.

The diversion of real resources from productive use in business to compliance with unnecessarily complex and onerous government regulations must have an adverse impact on economic performance. A small business proprietor has limited funds and limited time and if a proportion of these is devoted to the direct and compliance cost of government requirements, then this will be at the expense of the growth and efficiency of the business.

The democratic process by which governments are increasingly called on to take measures to improve the welfare and security of their citizens, and which leads to increased legislative complexity and burdens on business, is well known. Although legislation affecting business goes back a long way in time in the advanced countries (there was legislation governing the payment of wages in ready money in Britain in 1464), the scope of legislation began to increase rapidly in the nineteenth century with the growth of employment in factories. The major elements of social legislation, however, are post World War II in origin and the volume of this legislation increased particularly rapidly in the 1960s and 1970s, for example in the field of environmental planning, social security and employment legislation.

APPROACHES TO THE PROBLEM: INTERNATIONAL EXPERIENCE

Most, if not all, OECD member countries are now making an attempt to reverse the growth of burdens on business. This is not an entirely new initiative; efforts in this direction in the United States date back to the 1950s but there has been a new political impetus since around 1980. In many countries new machinery has been established to give focus to the efforts of governments.

In late 1983, for example, the German Federal Government set up an independent committee to review legislative burdens. The UK established an Enterprise and Deregulation Unit (EDU) in 1986 following an in-depth review of the problem. The Commission of the European Communities also set up a central SME Task Force in 1986, one of the most important functions of which is to control regulatory burdens. One of the lessons of experience in this field, however, is that a top-down approach is insufficient and unless central government departments and lower levels of government are involved, little will be achieved. This is why, in Britain, the central EDU is complemented by deregulation units in each government department.

Whatever the machinery used, a number of more or less distinct, but complementary, approaches to the problem have been taken.

(1) *Arresting the Growth of New Burdens*

This has been the first priority and probably rightly so, since it is easier and less costly to stop new regulations than it is to modify or eliminate existing ones. Stability is important in minimizing the compliance costs of regulation since each time there are changes, costs of learning and adaptation in business (and in public administration) are incurred. Probably the most effective technique for controlling new burdens is to require the preparation of impact statements by initiating departments which set out the effects on business of the measures proposed. The work on these statements should be done early on in the policy formation process before commitments to new measures begin to harden. The impact statement approach is used in the United States, in Britain and in the EC SME Task Force.

(2) *Simplification within Existing Legislation*

A great deal of scope undoubtedly exists everywhere for the simplification of procedures involved in implementing past legislation. This may involve collaboration between departments in the establishment of single-window bureaux to which business people may address themselves so as to save the time of contacting several different departments in different locations. This has been done, for example, in France and in the United States at state or local level for environmental and construction permits, and might well be an effective solution to the problems in this area experienced in Turkey. Another way in which interdepartmental co-ordination may help is in the elimination of unnecessary demands for information from business. Much of the information required in statistical and other returns to some departments, for example, is already in the possession of other departments. The use of computer systems may alleviate this problem in time, although there are everywhere countervailing concerns about personal and business privacy. Efforts to simplify the language used in government instructional material and forms also fall under this heading.

(3) *Reduction in Regulation*

Some legislation is outmoded, unnecessary or overlapping, and economies can be achieved by the repeal and consolidation of existing law. In some cases complex regulations may be lifted and replaced by general requirements backed up by codes of conduct, which eliminate the need for complex legislation. All this can often be done without radical reform, which is time consuming and frequently politically contentious.

More radical reform can, of course, also be embarked on with more spectacular results. The economic deregulation of telecommunications in the

United States is an example of reform for which economic benefits both through enhanced competition and trade as well as through the removal of bureaucratic controls have been claimed. The abolition of exchange controls and controls on bank lending are examples from the UK.

(4) *Specific Treatment for SMEs*

Another approach, which implicity recognizes the regressive nature of government burdens on small firms, is to remove or lighten the burden on firms below a certain size. In many cases this is a recognition of the irrelevancy of some legislation to small firms. For example, the establishment of a works council or similar body is not compulsory for firms with fewer than 5 employees in West Germany, 50 in Denmark and France, 100 in Belgium and 150 in Luxembourg. In other instances, special administrative procedures may be made optional for small firms. For example in Turkey, as in France, Italy, Belgium and other countries, very small firms may opt to pay over VAT liabilities to the authorities on the basis of an agreed percentage of turnover without the necessity for maintaining the elaborate records and documentation required of larger businesses.

Another approach is the designation of enterprise zones in depressed, generally inner-urban, areas in which special tax concessions and reliefs from certain administrative requirements are granted to newly established firms. Some 23 such zones in which firms are exempt from local taxes and a number of planning restraints have been designated in Britain since 1981. In 1982 Belgium, and in 1986 the United States, introduced similar zones.

The French government has set up some 500 management centres (*Céntres de Géstion* and associated bodies) which provide management consultancy and accounting services, including assistance with tax compliance. Some 600,000 enterprises have signed up with these centres and most receive valuable tax concessions in return for doing so.

(5) *Changing Attitudes*

Organizational cultures cannot be altered quickly, but it is increasingly recognized that a really significant lightening of government burdens on business will not be achieved until public administrations as a whole become more sympathetic to the needs of the business sector and indeed to those of the public at large (Organisation for Economic Co-operation and Development, 1987). Training systems are already being adapted towards this end in many countries. Consideration is also being given to the adaptation of incentives and reward systems to stimulate more responsiveness towards the needs of the public.

ARE MORE RADICAL APPROACHES PRACTICABLE?

Given the magnitude of the task it is not surprising that progress in lightening burdens on business has been slow. Most administrators in this area recognize, privately, that the most that has been achieved is a slowing down in the rate of increase. The dilemma is that while the needs of the wealth-creating sector are now increasingly recognized, pressures from the general public and interest groups to retain and extend the protection of the State over employment rights, consumer protection, social security benefits, privacy and the environment, for example, remain strong.

There is indeed a conflict between the needs of business and regulatory pressures. This might be eased if the public were made aware of the fact that the costs of regulation are ultimately borne by the consumer either through higher prices or slower growth or both. Nonetheless much can be done to reduce the burdens on business without giving up the objectives of regulation simply by making regulatory procedures less burdensome.

One idea is to make use of professional intermediaries who could, after new legislation, be given the power and the responsibility for 'signing off' compliance with government procedures for their clients. Professional intermediaries between the public administration and the public exist in all countries, from 'red-tape cutters' who will queue at government offices to apply for passports or permits, to qualified surveyors and accountants. The very existence of these intermediaries is, of course, evidence that economic forces are moving, through specialization, to reduce the high costs of compliance.

The attitude of public officials to these intermediaries should be, and is, ambiguous, since through their expertise the intermediaries make life easier. At the same time they isolate the administration from the client and create a new powerful vested interest in continuing complexity, thus postponing solutions to the real problem.

In the long run, there may be no alternative but to pursue the approaches already described in the previous section. However, more might be achieved if the following principles were adopted:

(1) *Strengthen Countervailing Forces*

In the United States, radical action has been taken to reduce the freedom of the public administration arbitrarily to increase burdens. Under the Regulatory Flexibility Act and the Paperwork Reduction Acts of 1980, the administration is required to consider the impact of new regulations on business (and specifically on SMEs), to publish intentions and to leave time for comment. These requirements are monitored by the Small Business Administration (SBA) and the Office of Management and Budget, which has powers to reject existing paperwork requirements which are excessive and to place limitations on each agency's total paperwork burdens. Individuals cannot be punished for failing to comply with new regulations which have not conformed to these procedures.

Under the Equal Access to Justice Act, 1980, citizens are entitled to compensation if the government imposes a rule which is overturned in court. These measures incorporate, but go much further than, the impact statement procedures mentioned earlier (p.269). Sunset legislation, under which new laws expire automatically unless re-enacted, is another powerful means of restraining the legislative burden. Much discussed in the United States, Sunset legislation has, however, received only limited implementation.

Another aspect to the strengthening of countervailing forces is a policy of supporting business representative bodies and involving them and the business population more closely in the actual design of administrative procedures. Although consultation is carried out in all countries it is often inadequate because it stops short of administrative detail and, in some countries, because business bodies are insufficiently representative or have divided interests.

Independent research can also play an important part in creating more understanding of the problems of SMEs, both within and outside the public administration, which will itself increase pressures for change. Several countries (West Germany, the UK and Switzerland, for example) have Small Business Research Institutes and both the SBA and the European Community's SME Task Force carry out or commission research.

(2) *Compliance Cost Budgeting*

The compliance costs of both existing and new legislation should be measured and the burdens should be regarded as a form of business taxation complemented by the equivalent public expenditure and budgeted accordingly. Indeed there is a strong case, particularly given the regressive nature of the burden, for public reimbursement of compliance costs at a basic level so as to go some way towards equalizing the burden. There is a precedent for this in the administration of the VAT systems in West Germany and The Netherlands. The disciplines and pressure that this would exert for the control of compliance costs would be powerful and effective. The underlying principle should be that only sector-specific compliance costs, for example for pollution control, should be borne disproportionately by the businesses concerned.

Compliance cost budgeting should complement the impact analyses mentioned earlier (p.269) and should be used in conjunction with a more rigorous and fundamental approach to the whole process of regulatory reform. Cento Veljanovski, in a very interesting recent paper, argues that the purpose of regulatory reform should be seen as not to lift the burden from business 'but to ensure that there is efficient regulation and that the benefits derived from regulation must outweigh the costs' (Veljanovski, 1987). (This is a different point from the one we are making, which is about where the costs should fall and how they should be measured and controlled.) Veljanovski advocates the use of cost-benefit analysis, which takes 'the unregulated market as the baseline and not the existing regulatory framework' under the presumption that 'market like regulatory devices are to be preferred to command and control techniques'. This reform would, therefore, be seen as a process in the interests of consumer and industry competitiveness, a viewpoint which could be used to help both to educate the public and to transform attitudes in the public administration.

(3) *Transfer of Responsibilities*

In lightening the burden on SMEs, a decentralized approach should be adopted as far as possible. Not only is centralized policy making with decentralized administration a good general principle of management, but SMEs are essentially localized in their sphere of activity. Communication and understanding are likely to be more effective at a local level. Policy in this area may take either or both of two forms. First, responsibiltiy for dealing with SMEs may be pushed downwards to lower levels of government, and second, governments may be able to transfer some functions to the private sector or to its representative bodies, such as chambers of commerce and industry, as is done in West Germany and some other countries.

(4) *Isolate the key constraints*

It seems probable that much of the political energy and will in tackling the burdens problem in other countries have been dissipated in practice, by seeking to reduce burdens on too wide a front. Since some aspects of the burden are disproportionately important, concentration on a limited number should lead to more dramatic results. In the advanced countries, probably at least half of the paperwork burden on SMEs is accounted for by taxation.

REFERENCES

Bannock, G. (1981), *The Economics of Small Firms: Return from the Wilderness*, Basil Blackwell, Oxford.

Dicke, H. and Hartung, H. (1986), *Entwicklung Von Verfahren Zu Ermittlung Externer Kosten von Rechtsvorschriften*, Institut fur Weltwirtschaft an der Universität Kiel.

Hunkeler, U. (1984), Doctoral Thesis, Schweizerisches Institut für Gewebliche Wirschaft und der Hochschule St Gallen fur Wirschafts- und Sozialwissenschaften.

Organisation for Economic Co-operation and Development (1985), *Employment in Large and Small Firms in OECD Employment Outlook*, September, OECD.

Organisation for Economic Co-operation and Development (1987), *Administration as Service. The Public as Client*, OECD.

SKIM Industrial Market Research (1984), *International Small Business Survey*, SKIM, Rotterdam.

World Bank (1978), *Employment and Development of Small Enterprises*, International Bank for Reconstruction and Development, February.

Veljanovski, C. (1987), Reasoned Regulation, Paper delivered at an Institute of Economic Affairs Conference, 21 October (mimeo).

APPENDIX 10.1 Setting up in business

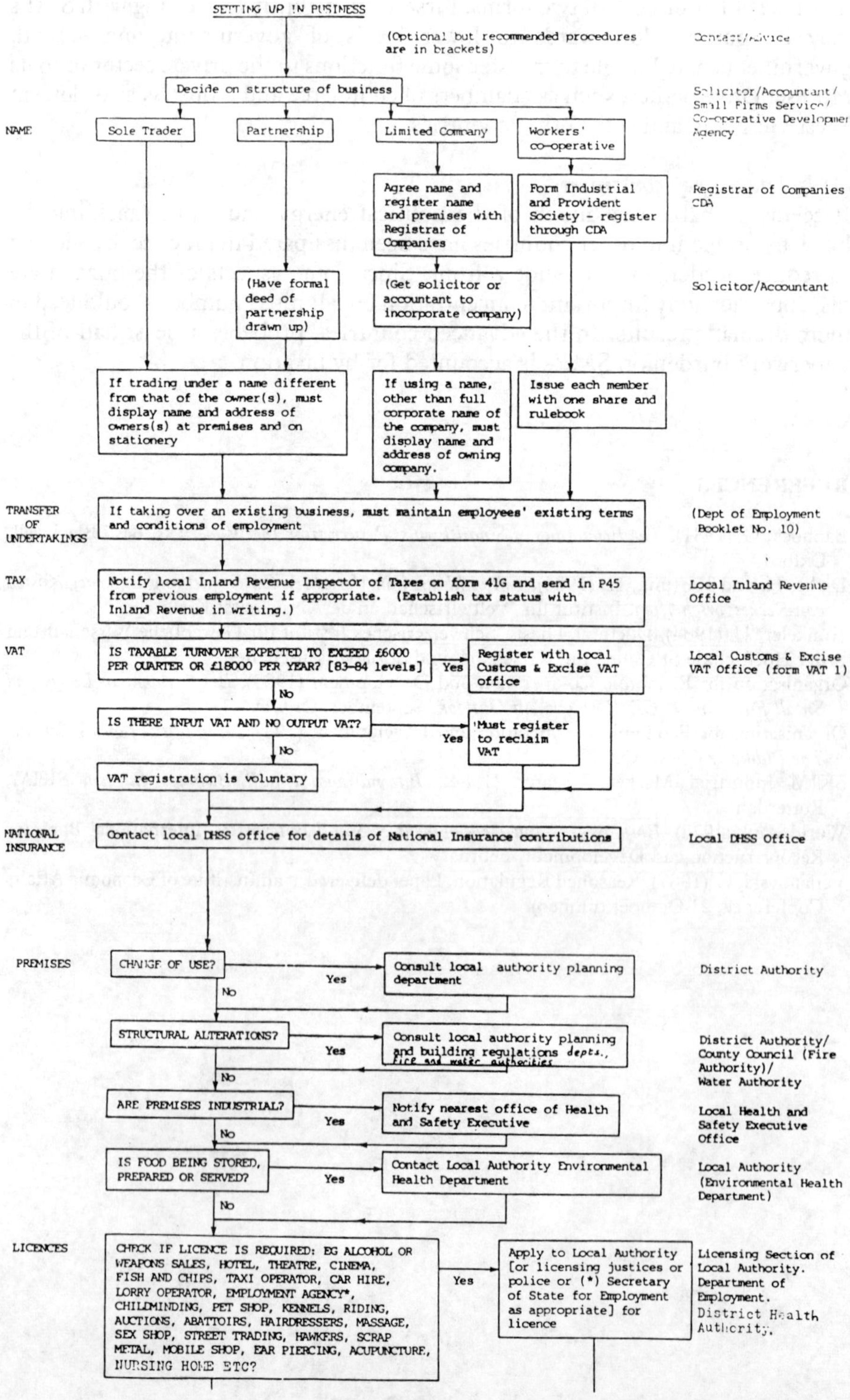

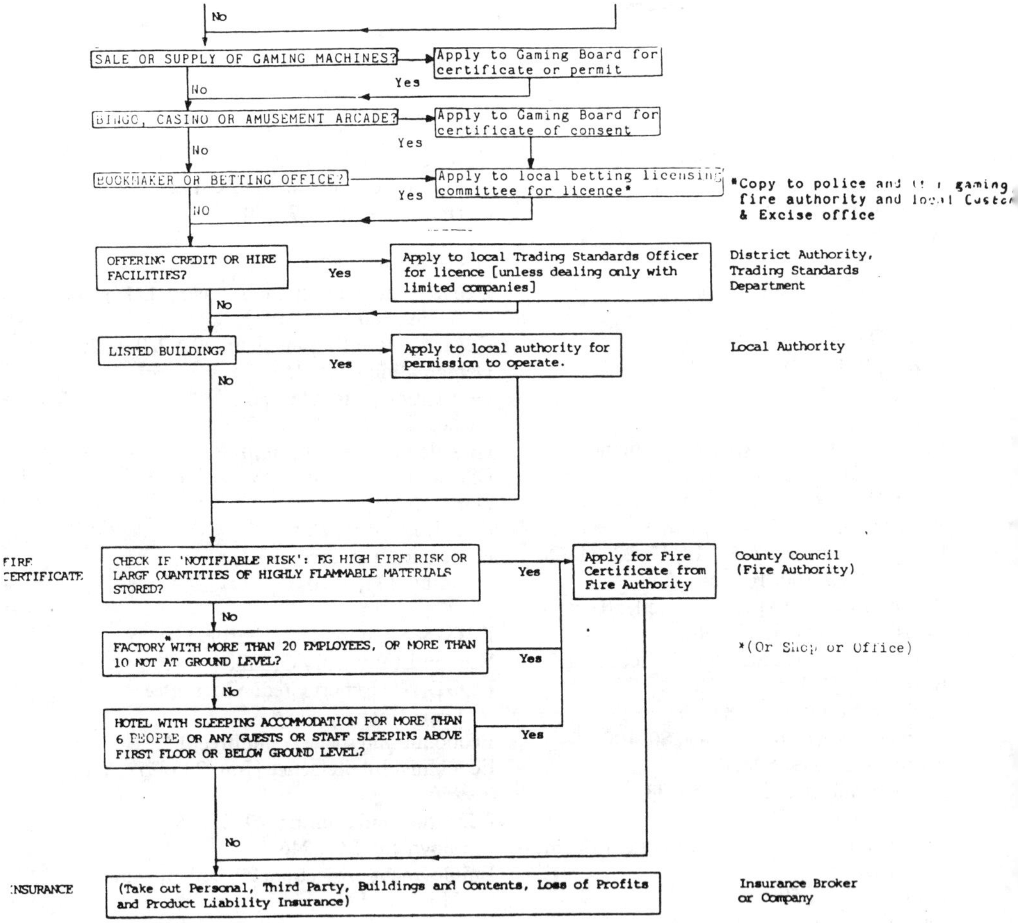

Source: Exploiting and Overcoming Government Regulations: An Entrepreneur's Viewpoint (The Forum of Private Business)

INDEX